How to Catch Fish and where

How to
Catch
Fish and where

THE COMPLETE KiWi BEGiNNER'S GUiDE

Mike RENDLE

HarperCollinsPublishers

HarperCollins*Publishers*

First published 2013

HarperCollins*Publishers (New Zealand) Limited*
PO Box 1, Shortland Street, Auckland, 1140

Copyright © Mike Rendle 2013

HarperCollins*Publishers*

Unit D1, 63 Apollo Drive, Rosedale, Auckland 0632, New Zealand
Level 13, 201 Elizabeth Street, Sydney, NSW 2000, Australia
A 53, Sector 57, Noida, UP, India
1 London Bridge Street, London SE1 9GF, United Kingdom
2 Bloor Street East, 20th floor, Toronto, Ontario M4W 1A8, Canada
195 Brodway, New York, NY 10007, USA

National Library of New Zealand Cataloguing-in-Publication Data

Rendle, Mike.
How to catch fish and where : the complete Kiwi beginner's
guide / Mike Rendle.
ISBN 978-1-77554-013-7
1. Fishing—New Zealand. I. Title.
799.10993—dc 23

ISBN 978 1 77554 013 7

Publisher: Bill Honeybone
Design and typesetting by Scallop Publishing & Photography
(kimatscallop@gmail.com)

Cover and internal images by Mike Rendle
Other images by Kim Standfield (pages 105, 122, 140, 156, 161, 177, 255, 257);
Mark Roberts (pages 25, 68, 73, 74, 82, 83, 92, 95, 102, 106, 107, 109, 111,
116, 194, 267); Tony Dawson (pages 91, 139, 147, 277, 283); Milan Radonich
(*PlaceMakers Big Angry Fish*) (pages 27, 110, 259, 261); Carl Cooper (page 243);
Pure Fishing NZ (pages 26, 28, 35, 38, 39, 40, 42, 43, 47, 51, 52, 54, 55, 56, 57,
59, 76, 77, 78, 79, 81, 252); Dan Govier (page 183); Joe Dennehy (pages 189,
190, 191); Water Safety New Zealand (page 13); Craig Rendle (page 128); Rob Fort
(page 131 left); Aquanaut NZ (page 131 right); Keith Ingram (page 135); plus the
wonderful fish identification images in chapter 18 (and repeated throughout the book)
supplied by Kenichi Miyamoto
Drawings and illustrations by Mike Rendle

All charts sourced from Land Information New Zealand data
Crown Copyright Reserved

Charts are **Not for Navigation**

Printed by RR Donnelley in China, on 128gsm Matt Art
6 5   21 22 23

Dedication ⤢

There are many people who influence your past, but probably only a handful that stay good friends regardless of what you may be doing or where you go. Some are family, some are mentors, some you meet through work and some are, well, just very special.

John and Christine Erkkila are in that last category. I have never met two more generous people. Through their generosity I have been able to explore, fish and photograph some of the most unique locations in the Pacific, including Vanuatu, Chesterfield Reef, Tonga, Hawaii and New Caledonia. They, and their children Alex and James, are wonderful company and have shared their family adventures with me for a decade. I can never repay their hospitality and friendship.

My partner Kim is a match for me with a softbait rod in hand, a match for me when debating politics and wonderful company across a coffee table. She even puts up with me having to do 'a bit more in the office'. How did I get so lucky? **MR**

My thanks

A number of people have made this book possible and I'd like to thank them.

Bill Honeybone from HarperCollins made this project happen. He knows books, and has been responsible for some of the most successful books published in this country. He is a delight to work with.

Kenichi Miyamoto kindly allowed me access to his wonderful fish identification photos. Ken has a fantastic and extensive website covering New Zealand and Pacific fish species, with great photography. It's an excellent resource for finding the name of any species you don't know. You'll find it at **www.fishguide.co.nz.**

Kevin Green and Ben Spooner from Allied Outdoors Ltd always support the projects I am working on, and have supported this project too. Many of the products seen attached to big fish in this book are theirs — because they work!

Mal Dawson is the manager of Pure Fishing in New Zealand and is another with whom I've worked closely over many years.

Pure Fishing is the biggest tackle company in the world and they are at the cutting edge of tackle development, manufacture and distribution. Again, it's no surprise that many of their products can be seen in this book.

Mark Roberts is a good friend and a talented photojournalist. He is an expert when it comes to fishing from the shore. I interviewed him before writing the beach fishing section, as there are few better proponents of the art in this country. I am happy I was able to include many of his superb photographs as well.

Hunts Sports Store, at Milford in Auckland, has been around since 1963, and was started by Stu Hunt. His son Ian is a fishing legend and a genuinely nice guy. I drew on Ian's knowledge and experience when it came to rigs and baits.

Gasoline Alley Services Ltd, they're the orange g.a.s. petrol service stations you see all around the country, also helped with the fishing spots section.

My thanks also to everyone I've fished with to get the photos I needed!

Contents

The author with the biggest
snapper he has caught to date!
It weighed 32 lb and came from
Norfolk Island.

Introduction

Back in the 1960s and 1970s there were many well-thumbed fishing books in our house. Hardly surprising really as fishing was the whole focus of my life and reading books was how we learnt. Those books were our guide and inspiration ...

Dad and I fished together every chance we could, mostly at Raglan where we had a family bach. My brother was an occasional fisherman, but really enthusiastic about spearing flounder; we thought nothing of getting up at 2 a.m. to catch the tide. I learnt to dive, as did Dad and my sister, at a time when Jacques Cousteau was enthralling us on TV every Sunday night. Our fishing books were read and re-read into oblivion …

At the time I had no idea that fishing would so totally dominate my life, although the writing was on the wall, I guess. I left school with the choice of two boat-building apprenticeships; however, the now-infamous Muldoon boat sales tax saw that situation change a few months later. Instead, I became part of the third generation of plumbers in my family (my brother is one too, and one of his boys is now the fourth generation).

This gave me a springboard from which to follow the real love of my life — fishing.

To shorten the story, plumbing evolved into marine electronics, tackle retail, magazine editing, photography and book writing. It also meant fishing throughout the Pacific, including twice to the remote Chesterfield Reef, fishing and diving around New Zealand and even working the deck in Cairns. Through it all I've met amazing people, had amazing adventures and never stopped learning.

Writing a new fishing book for the twenty-first century feels like taking things full circle. This is a book for beginners but, I hope, with enough tips for those with advanced skills. The problem wasn't what to include, but what to leave out. There is so much more I could have written.

My hope is that by reading this book I will inspire you to begin your own fishing journey and to build your own fishing memories. I also hope your copy of *How to Catch Fish and Where* becomes well-thumbed as you use it as your own ready reference.

Mike Rendle

1 ⌒ Safety

Whether you are new to the sport of fishing or whether you have fished all your life, please take a few moments to read this chapter and absorb it. No matter what your level of experience, safety should always be foremost in your thoughts.

Lifejackets

It's natural to think 'boats' when you think about lifejackets, yet they can be just as important to use when fishing from the shore.

Big, bulky kapok lifejackets have been consigned to history. There are now two main styles of support to choose from: the first is thin, high-tech foam built into beautifully comfortable jackets; the second is the inflatable lifejacket. Both are great, both have their place and the choice may come down to intended use.

Lifejackets in New Zealand should comply with the relevant New Zealand or Australian standards. These regulations cover the construction, amount of buoyancy and the most important part, that the jacket will turn an unconscious or prone wearer face up. Be aware that there are also jackets made for water sports, such as kayaking and water skiing, that don't turn the wearer face up. Generally such a jacket will be marked accordingly and will be missing one obvious feature — a collar.

When it comes to inflatable jackets, none of the features mentioned above are visible as the whole package is very low in profile and more compact than a foam jacket, before the air is added. The inflatable relies on a carbon dioxide (CO_2) cartridge to fill the jacket. Extra air can be added via an inflation tube. There are two types of inflatable jacket: manual and automatic. An auto-inflation model relies on a tablet to dissolve, near instantly, to allow the CO_2 cartridge to fill the jacket. The manual version has a pull cord to achieve the filling (this is also fitted to the auto version). Each includes an oral tube, as mentioned, so additional air can be added to the jacket. You got it — it's just the same as all those airline safety briefings you have watched!

All lifejackets need checking regularly to ensure there is no damage. Check buckles and straps in particular. It is worthwhile having inflatable jackets professionally serviced.

Boats and lifejackets

The boat's skipper is responsible for ensuring the safety of all passengers. He or she has a legal requirement to carry a correctly fitting lifejacket for every person aboard. If you are the skipper, that is a hefty obligation that is backed to the fullest extent of the law. Do not take this responsibility lightly.

Which jacket is best?

Inflatables generally fit a wider range of people than foam models, for a given size. That can make it easier to comply with the 'correctly fitting' clause if you carry a variable crew. An inflatable jacket is easy to wear for long periods and doesn't inhibit movement. It is the best option for wearing all day, in hot conditions or where unrestricted movement is paramount.

Personally, however, I like to have a foam jacket if my trip includes a bar crossing. The rationale behind this is that if things go pear-shaped, there is a high likelihood of being thrown from the boat with a chance of head injury. A manual-inflation jacket won't help an unconscious person; and while an auto one will, I'd prefer to know that I was being supported to the greatest extent if I was unconscious. The best option here is a properly fitting foam lifejacket.

The best solution? I carry both styles on my boat ... There are also two rules that are never compromised if you fish with me — one, young children have to wear a correctly fitted foam jacket at all times; and, two, the wearing of lifejackets on all bar crossings is compulsory, no matter how calm the conditions.

Lifejackets ashore

It is of great frustration to the good people at Water Safety New Zealand, the body charged with improving water safety in this country, that so many drownings could be avoided. Many of those drownings involve fishers on rocks and ledges being washed into the sea while wearing heavy clothing. Some of those incidents are due to fishers taking risks close to the water; some are due to being on the rocks in inappropriate conditions. Almost all would have had a different outcome if the victim had been wearing a lifejacket ...

Let's not sugar-coat it — if you fish from the rocks and you are inexperienced or unfamiliar with the area and you don't wear a lifejacket, then you put your life at serious risk.

The Ministry of Transport has estimated the value of a statistical life as $3.35 million, and from this Water Safety

New Zealand reckons that the annual social cost of drownings is a little over $400 million. That's a statistic that makes death by drowning even crazier, considering that it's possible to buy an inflatable jacket for less than $100.

Proper lifejacket fit

Incorrectly fitting lifejackets can kill. Correct fitting is even more critical when it comes to children. Back in my retail days, we would occasionally get a customer who would want a slightly bigger jacket so their child could 'grow into it'. If they still didn't get it after having their error explained, they were shown the door. This is the one occasion where the customer isn't always right.

ABOVE: *The three common lifejacket styles. From left, the foam-filled supporting jacket to NZS 402 designed to turn the wearer face up. In the middle, the sports jacket to NZS 403. Note it has no collar but allows almost unrestricted movement. At right is the inflatable lifejacket. It is very low in profile and has little to impede movement.*

www.watersafety.org.nz

A properly fitting jacket that is properly adjusted will support the wearer, won't be exceptionally tight across the chest yet will prevent the wearer from slipping through. It's something that can't be completely explained in words. Fortunately, the New Zealand marine industry is a mature one with very good operators. The high-profile retailers and chain stores will have staff who are trained and experienced in helping you select the right jacket. Make use of their skills.

It's not just jackets …

Over the years I have written thousands of words on the subject of water safety. Literally — 50,000 and counting. I've taught Coastguard qualifications in the classroom and taught practical safety on the water. I've fished from a dinghy close to shore and kept watch during the night in the middle of the Pacific. A lifetime of learning (an education I hope I'm only halfway through) can't be summed up in one chapter. However, there are some absolute essentials:

• **Check the weather, often and well in advance of the trip.** Watch the patterns. Check the forecast from several sources. In this age of smart phones and 'Nowcasting' on the marine VHF radio service, there is no excuse for not having the information instantly and with a high degree of accuracy.

• **Get better educated.** Coastguard does a fantastic job of both rescue and education. With more of the latter, you hopefully won't need the former. The Day Skipper course

can even be completed from the comfort of your home. The Boatmaster course will give you everything you need to operate safely in our coastal waters.

• **Communication is critical.** *Every* boat needs a VHF radio. Cell phones make a great second source of contact but shouldn't be the sole method. An EPIRB, which communicates your emergency via satellite when activated, is the greatest safety-net ever invented for us boaties. They are even available in a compact size for personal use, small enough to be attached to a lifejacket.

More information

• Local fishing and boating clubs are a great source of information. You'll find enthusiastic people willing to help.

• The Coastguard Boating Education service is the one to contact about courses to further your education and enjoyment. www.boatingeducation.org.nz

• If you need information about learning to swim, then go to the Water Safety New Zealand website.

www.watersafety.org.nz

How to Catch Fish and Where

- **Preparation is still the most important thing you can do to prevent a situation developing.** From motor servicing to equipment inspection, from education to crew training, the more you plan in advance and cover off the 'worst-case scenarios', the safer you will be at sea.

- **Navigation remains an essential skill.** Freely available and cheap GPS and chart-plotters are both a blessing and a curse. There are many boat operators who have no idea where they are once the video screen is turned off. The ability to read a chart and to navigate between spots, to work out your position by 'dead-reckoning' and to understand latitude and longitude is an essential skill. If you can't, then please, please revisit the piece about education.

The coolest thing about this sport is the people. It's a great leveller, and you will find that the vast majority of fishers and boaties will help if you ask. Whether it's local information about a bar crossing, advice on conditions or help with boat handling, this is no place for ego — ask for help!

My thanks to Water Safety NZ for the great work they do and also for their assistance with this chapter.

Freak waves

How often have you read about fishers being washed off rocks, or boats being rolled, by 'freak waves'? I find it disappointing to read such press reports, because poor planning and poor judgement should never be able to be written off.

The fact is that you have more chance of being hit by lightning than of experiencing a freak wave. Have you noticed that most 'freak' waves occur when boats are overloaded or are crossing bars, or the conditions are less than favourable? For those ashore, they always seem to strike when people are fishing in conditions of substantial swell or venturing too close to the edge.

Use good judgement, observe the conditions, get local knowledge and stay home in bad weather. Do all those things, and the chances are you will never be struck by lightning or experience a 'freak wave'.

Standing room only! Another successful Kids Gone Fishin event, this one held on the Raglan wharf.

2 ∽ Take a Kid Fishing

For most Kiwis, their earliest fishing memories will be around Christmas holidays and involve fishing with Mum or Dad, probably on a wharf or from the shore. Many go on to fish from dinghies, then increasingly bigger family boats, before repeating the pattern with their own kids. That's how I did it, how my friends did it and how their kids will likely do it.

My fishing career proper started on Raglan's wharf. My mother took us fishing there at least once every school holidays. We also fished aboard an uncle's dinghy. Later, as his business grew, Dad bought a boat, and then a bach at Raglan. We learnt to spear and net flounder. We learnt to dive. We caught hundreds of snapper and scores of crayfish. We learnt to catch marlin. I got a job as an apprentice boat-builder, later started a marine electronics business, edited a top fishing magazine and got to fish around the Pacific as well as all around New Zealand. Now I'm writing fishing books. In other words, my love of fishing has become my career. And all of that started the day I caught my very first fish off the Maraetai wharf …

Graeme Sinclair is a legend in New Zealand fishing circles. His TV show *Gone Fishin* has spanned more than two decades and no one can match his longevity or popularity. Over that time, Sinclair has had many good sponsors. One,

though, is closest to his heart and that is the work he does with the New Zealand police in conjunction with his *Kids Gone Fishin* events. We aren't talking about a handful of kids off the local wharf, here — a *Kids Gone Fishin* event is huge, with hundreds (at times up to 1000) kids and parents gathering to fish, meet and learn from the man himself. Sinclair long ago recognised the many benefits of teaching kids to fish — as should we all, but where to start?

Safety is the first thing to keep in mind. Kids move quickly, and they have an underdeveloped appreciation of the risks involved. There is absolutely nothing wrong with outfitting young ones with a lifejacket. Fishing is also an opportunity to teach life skills and how to recognise dangers. But don't overdo it — it has to be fun!

While wharves and jetties feature in most early fishing expeditions, they aren't the only likely places. I can still

remember that the biggest 'sprats' (let's get that sorted first — they are actually yellow-eyed mullet) we caught as kids came from a place in Raglan Harbour that dried out at low tide. On a rising tide we could stand on a rock, set the 'baitcatcher' (a plastic fish-trap) and cast small baits into the rising water, and catch 'monster'-sized fish. That spot taught an eight-year-old and his five-year-old brother the skills to read tide flows, rock safety (okay, it was only a metre high but it was an adventure for a couple of kids!) and how to target a species, in this case those monster sprats. Every part of those early lessons would become important in later years.

What gear do I need?

We have much to thank China for — the last two decades have seen an amazing array of affordable, good-quality tackle reach our tackle stores. That includes gear suitable for kids to use off the wharf, from the beach and also from the boat. Then there is softbait fishing — kids love it! The

LEFT: *Hand lines are still a great way to catch fish from a wharf. Not only that but they can be used from beach and boat. And they don't cost a lot!* **TOP:** *The quality has improved and the price has come down for entry-level kids' fishing tackle, such as this two-piece spin set.*

reason is that there is no need to keep the rod still or resist dropping and retrieving. Plus spinning reels are easy to master.

Something to keep in mind is that wharves and jetties attract big fish too! All those bait fish are kept there by the structure, and those bait fish will attract kingfish, kahawai, john dory, snapper and barracouta. While looking after the kids, there is no reason why you can't have a bigger bait set on another rod. Imagine the family memories you might create!

To take the kids out on a wharf for the day, the minimum you are going to need is a hand line. Ideally, it should be on a plastic hand-spool to make it easier for them to use. Expect tangles, expect break-offs and make sure you have some spare line. While success teaches us that the lightest line possible catches more fish, hand lines are always the exception — the line needs to be thick enough to reduce the possibility of cuts and to be easily seen. A good-quality 'soft' nylon (it will have less 'spring' when laid flat) of around 15 kg breaking strain is ideal. About 30 to 50 metres on the hand-spool will be enough.

There are two possible ways to rig the line to keep things simple.

• *Option one* is to tie a small swivel at the end of the line and then tie on a lighter nylon 'trace'. This can be nylon of around 6 kg breaking strain and maybe half a metre long. At the end of the line is tied a small hook. Hook sizes in a tackle shop can be confusing — a size 16 is way smaller than a size 1, which is smaller again than a size 1/0 (more on this subject later), and to make it worse each pattern has its own sizing regimen. Often you can buy a packet of mixed hooks, which can be useful. Look for something that is around 8–10 mm in overall length. Depending on the current and tide, it may be necessary to slide a small ball sinker onto the main line before the swivel is fitted. A line rigged this way is ideal for catching most wharf species and has a higher likelihood of catching the desirable piper, especially when unweighted.

• *Option two* is much the same; but instead of attaching a nylon trace, a flasher rig — also called a sabiki — is attached. You will find a huge range of them in most tackle shops. Sabikis have a number of small traces branching off, each with a 'dressed' hook attached. The dressing can be a fine nylon 'hair' or an opaque product called fish skin. They all work! The ones with small hooks generally have six branches. Three (or even two) is enough, so the sabikis can be cut in half to make two rigs. All that's left to do is to tie on a small ball sinker, this time at the end of the main trace.

Next, add some bait, even to the sabikis. Stale bread crusts still work well, but a flesh bait is even better. Squid is great and very difficult for small fish to pick off the hook. Tuna, trevally and kahawai are all suitable as bait. A good option is to get salted bonito, available in frozen packs (the salt stops it going hard) or better still in plastic re-sealable containers that don't need refrigeration. That way you will have bait for next time and no waste.

Add a bait knife and spare hooks, sinkers and swivels, and you are about ready for a day of family memories! Make sure the kids have extra warm clothing and a change of clothes just in case. You might want some wet-wipes too, if you don't want bait smeared through the car.

If you elect to buy rods and reels for the kids, make sure that they aren't too long; if it's unwieldy or difficult for them to hold they won't, and interest will quickly wane. Look for

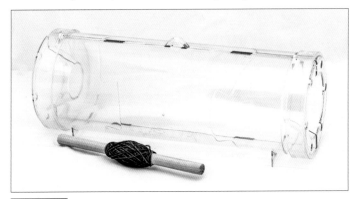

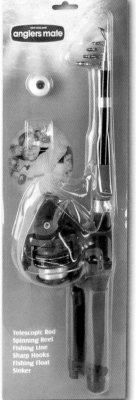

a spinning set with good-quality components. Yes, you can buy a $20 set — but the target price for good entry-level gear is currently $39.

Life skills

Learning to fish is often the first time that kids get to learn the realities of life. For example, realising that fish don't come pre-packed on polystyrene trays from the supermarket or in newspaper from the local takeaway; they have to be caught, killed and prepared. Teaching respect for the catch, safe handling, careful treatment of undersized fish being returned, and how to prepare the big ones for consumption is all part of the deal.

But, again, don't overdo it. Almost every kid will want to dissect their first fish with a knife. It's almost a rite of passage, and an important

LEFT: *The plastic bait trap is still a very popular way to catch yellow-eyed mullet.* **ABOVE:** *This kid's set from Anglers Mate includes a telescopic rod for easy transport.*

learning time. Let them go to it. It's how they learn what makes things work.

Make sure nothing is wasted. If they are going to keep their catch, make sure that they do chop it up and feed it to the cat. This is one of the most important lessons, particularly with an ever-diminishing resource.

Kids love to do research. Make sure they know what species they have caught. Just as importantly, make sure they know the rules and regulations. Undersized snapper are a regular by-catch from wharves. Educate them on the fishing regulations, minimum lengths particularly, and also on how to safely return a fish to the water.

Kids love to have their own tackle; I can still remember being given my own lifejacket, at around age seven; then my first proper rod and reel. Buy the kids their own tackle box. Encourage them to maintain and add to it. And just to show that age is no barrier, last Christmas I gave my two nephews a tackle box each. Less than a year later the oldest, now 18, is working part-time in a tackle store.

Regardless of where or how you go about it, take your kid fishing. You won't regret it!

RIGHT: *There is nothing better than being able to share the thrill of fishing with your own kids! Good friend Stu and his son Andre spent a great day fishing with the author a few years ago.*

Ian Hunt owns one of the best-known and longest established tackle shops in New Zealand. He loves his job and his experience is available to everyone who visits his store. Get to know your local tackle shop proprietor!

3 ∽ Before We Start — the Basics

One of the greatest pleasures you can experience is to walk into a well-stocked tackle shop and wander around. No matter what your level of experience, you will find things you want to buy. And no matter what your level of experience, you will still buy things you don't really need. Tackle shop proprietors rely on that! Plus, they love things with teeth that bite off traces, snags, saltwater damage and new fads. Consumable tackle and poor maintenance is what keeps them afloat (no pun intended).

In coming chapters, I go into detail about the specifics you need to fish across different techniques, species and places. However, the terminology used can be daunting for the uninitiated; so this chapter is intended as an introduction to those new to the sport, to help you make more sense of the terms used and what is to follow. Start here, and enter a world of fun, friendship and fresh fish fillets!

Action — Correctly used to describe the relative rod strength: a light-action rod is designed for light lines, a heavy-action rod for heavy weights and lines. It is sometimes mistakenly used to describe the rod taper (see *Taper*).

Angler — A person using a fishing rod or hand line to catch fish.

Angling — Usually refers to the recreational catching of fish by hand-held hook and line.

Anti-reverse — The mechanism that stops the reel handle from turning backwards.

Attractant — A scent applied to bait, berley or even directly to lures, to add appeal for the fish.

Backing — Any type of line (and it can be any type, depending on the planned use) used to partially fill a reel before the main fishing line is added. Once the domain of fly-fishing, it's now a common technique for softbait fishers and game fishers. Sometimes the main line is attached to the backing; sometimes it isn't.

Backlash — An overrun of a revolving-spool reel where the line gets loose and then tangles up in itself. Generally you are going to be busy for a while sorting that lot out ... see *Bird's nest*.

Bag limit — The maximum number of fish of a particular species, or combined species, which may legally be taken on a given day.

Bail arm — The wire that runs across the face of a spinning reel and engages the line and winds it on the spool.

Bait — Generally this refers to fish flesh, such as pilchards, squid and bonito, used to attract the target fish which then eats it before being (hopefully) hooked. Lures are also referred to as baits.

Baitcaster reel — A small overhead reel designed specifically for casting lures. In New Zealand they get used quite a bit for salmon fishing, but the vast majority are used for straylining lightly weighted baits for snapper and other common species on light tackle. I love my baitcaster reels!

Baitcasting — The action of using baitcasting reels to cast lures. An American term.

Bait fish — Generally, small schooling fish that congregate in large numbers. Finding the bait fish generally means finding the target species.

Baitrunner — Actually a brand name which has become a generic description for a type of spinning reel that has two drags — one to control the pressure on the line when the bait is fished with no weight on it, and the second to fight the fish.

Baitwell — Also called a livewell or live bait tank; a tank designed to keep fish alive for use as live baits.

Bar — A build-up of sand at the entrance to a harbour or bay. The water shallows rapidly, causing waves to break on the bar. A bar is a dangerous area that requires local knowledge to navigate safely.

Barb — The sharp curved piece past the hook's point is the barb. It is designed to stop the hook falling back out of the fish's mouth.

Barbless — A hook without a barb. On many hooks the barb can be flattened with a pair of pliers to achieve the same result.

Berley — Also known as 'chum'. Berley usually consists of ground-up fish, generally frozen, that is used to attract fish to your position from some distance away. It can be tied to the boat or the rocks, or lowered to the sea floor, depending on the species targeted and the water depth. Fishing around working mussel barges is also an example of using berley.

Bird's nest — You don't want one of these! A descriptive name for the mess left after a reel overruns, creating masses of loose, tangled line.

Bite — When a fish attacks a bait, the action is usually transmitted through the rod or hand line. The angler feels a 'bite'.

Bite indicator — Generally, used in freshwater fishing to track the progress of a fly fished in a current, it is also used in some types of saltwater fishing. A float is an example of a bite indicator.

Bottom-fish — Bottom-fish are those generally found on or near the bottom. Snapper and hapuku are regarded as bottom-fish (although they can be caught near the surface), while a marlin wouldn't be considered a bottom-fish (even though they are known to eat flounder!) That's why we love this sport. Generally, someone saying 'I'm going for a bottom-fish' means they are heading out to catch table species such as snapper and cod, rather than sportfishing for game species.

Braid — A generic term to describe the zero-stretch lines that are generally created by braiding together multiple strands. Braid is very thin and very strong. Dacron has been around for decades longer; it is also a braided line but not quite as thin as the current generation of lines.

Break-off — A fish lost when the line breaks, as opposed to one lost when the hook pulls out. Also known as a bust-off.

Catch-and-release — Refers to catching a fish and then releasing it. It is a great way of enjoying the sport while looking after the resource for future generations.

Chum — See *Berley.*

Closed-face reel — A distinctive reel where the line is hidden behind a cover over the spool and exits through a hole in that cover. Once the domain of kids' toy rod-and-reel sets, closed-face reels have had something of a resurgence and high-quality versions can be found.

Cover — A hiding place for fish. Any rock, reef, channel, bank, etc, can be cover. All fish need shelter to survive — remember this when finding a spot to fish.

Crankbait — An American term starting to find its way into our vocabulary. It describes a wide range of hard plastic or wooden lures that dive when retrieved.

Curly-tailed grub — A curved-tail, soft plastic bait often fitted on a jig head. Another American term now in common use due to the growth of softbaits.

Disgorger — A device for removing a hook deeply embedded in the throat of a fish. There are many kinds, from a simple tapered stick (also known as a gob stick) to long plier-type arrangements.

Dorsal fin — The big fin (usually) along the back of the fish.

Double — For many types of fishing the main line is doubled for a short distance, by way of a special knot, then attached to the trace. This gives additional protection and a stronger way to attach the trace.

Downrigger — A device designed to present a bait or lure at a specific depth. The downrigger holds a wire line that is lowered using a heavy weight. The lure or bait is attached to the wire by way of a release clip.

Drag — A device on the reel that tires the fish when hooked. It is adjusted by way of a lever or a star wheel. It is set to allow line to be taken under pressure but not to exceed the breaking strain of the line.

Lever drag

Star drag

Drift-fishing — Fishing without setting an anchor (see *Sea anchor*), which allows more ground to be covered.

Drop-off — Usually a sheer drop or fast change of depth around a channel or reef edge. A drop-off will affect the water flow, often creating cover or fish-holding areas.

Dropper — The branch off a trace or rig.

Dropper rig — A rig where the sinker is on the bottom with usually two or more hooks above. See *Ledger Rig*.

Eyelets — Another name for the line guides or rings on a fishing rod.

FAD — A 'Fish Aggregating Device'. FADs are usually deployed in deep water to attract bait fish which then attract tuna and marlin. They can sometimes be anchored in more than 1000 metres of water.

Feeding times — Certain times of day when fish are most active. Generally based around the position of the moon.

Ferrule — The fitting sometimes used where two parts of a rod join together.

Ferrule

Fillet — The act of removing the flesh from the side of a fish. The completed product is also called a fillet. Cutting through the backbone and cutting the fish into segments is usually called steaking a fish.

Fish hook — The sharp, pointed item used to capture the target species. A fish hook comes in many sizes and patterns, as will be explained later.

Flasher rig — A generic term describing a trace that may have from two to six decorated hooks attached. The hook decoration is generally an artificial, brightly coloured hair-like material designed to create movement. The hooks usually have bait added as well.

Float — A device designed to present a bait at a pre-determined level. Balloons are often used as floats when live baiting for kingfish and other game fish.

Fluorocarbon — A material used to make traces. A fluorocarbon trace is said to have the same refractive index as water, making the trace almost invisible. It is also far more hard-wearing than nylon while also sinking rapidly.

Foul-hook — When a fish is hooked somewhere other than the mouth, it is said to be foul-hooked.

Strike! The explosive moment when a kingfish nails a live bait. Captured by Milan Radonich, host of PlaceMakers Big Angry Fish.

Free-spool — A free-spool reel is also known as an overhead reel *(see page 30)*. In simple terms, it is the common 'boat reel'. To free-spool a reel means to disengage the gears and allow the line to run freely, usually controlled with the thumb.

Gaff — A device with a large hook at the end that is used to secure a fish and aid in lifting it into the boat or onto the shore. A flying gaff is used in game-fishing and differs by having a head that comes off the handle. The hook has a rope attached and allows the crew to secure the fish without the problem of leverage caused by the attached handle.

Game fish — In reality, any hard-fighting species of fish is a game fish. Specifically, a fish is considered to be a game fish if it is listed by the International Game Fish Association (IGFA) and records are kept for it.

Gear — Another word for tackle. Also used to describe the position of a marlin or other game fish when it is seen behind the boat amongst the lures — 'there's a fish in the gear'.

Gimbal — The fitting at the end of many rods (generally boat and game rods) designed to stop it twisting in a suitably equipped rod-holder or fishing belt.

Gimbal

Gimbal belt — Worn around the waist, a gimbal belt is designed to support the butt of the rod, allowing the angler to work it properly. The gimbal fitting on the rod, if present, will usually lock into the pin on the gimbal belt so the rod doesn't twist.

Grub — A softbait term describing a short, plump bait that has a curly tail. The first 20-pound (9 kg) snapper ever caught in New Zealand on a 'Gulp!' softbait was caught on a fluoro-yellow-coloured grub.

Hand line — Fish can still be caught without a rod and reel! A hand line is a generic term for any line, be it stored on a stick or on a plastic hand-spool, used to fish that way.

Hard bottom — As opposed to a soft mud or silt bottom. It may be rock, gravel or hard-packed sand. Hard bottom can be distinguished on a quality fishfinder.

Harness — An item worn around the hips or shoulders and attached via clips to the reel. If properly designed and fitted, it will take the load of the rod and allow the angler to work the rod more efficiently. Generally used for game-fishing.

IGFA — The International Game Fish Association, which is the keeper of records and the rules of the sport. Many contests and practically all game-fishing tournaments are based around the rules set by the IGFA.

Iki stick — A sharp spike designed to kill fish instantly when applied to a point generally above and just behind the eye (this action is known as ikijime).

Jerk bait — Another softbait term. A jerk bait is more fish-shaped and is designed to be given action by moving it sharply or 'jerking' it.

Jerk shad — Also a softbait term. A jerk shad has a thin bait-fish pattern.

Jig — A generic term that usually describes a weighted lure designed to be fished on or near the bottom.

Jig-fishing — The act of using metal lures to catch fish.

Jig head — A jig head is used with softbaits and is usually a hook with a lead head attached.

Keeper — A fish of a size to take home. Usually refers to the legal size limit — anything over that is a 'keeper'. Others use the term to describe the size they prefer to keep, which could be well over the legal size. For example, many fishers don't consider a snapper to be a 'keeper' until it reaches 300 mm, even though the minimum size is less.

Landing net — A bagged net attached to a handle, used to lift a heavy fish aboard or to secure, without damage, a fish that will be released.

Ledger rig — A rig consisting of a sinker tied at the bottom with two or more droppers above the sinker. Each has a hook attached. Designed for bottom fishing. Most flasher rigs are in fact ledger rigs.

Levelwind — Some overhead reels have a device at the front that moves backwards and forwards across the spool to lay the line evenly without assistance.

Limit-out — To catch the daily limit legally allowed for a species of fish.

Line guides — The eyelets or rings on a rod. The line passes through these.

Live bait — A smaller live fish used to catch a bigger one!

Longline — A fishing device consisting of a set line (it's also called a set line) with up to 25 hooks attached (the maximum legally allowed for recreational use). It is anchored at both ends, with a line and float attached to mark its position.

Longline

Lure — Generic term for an item designed to entice fish to strike. Lures come in a million styles, types and colours. Fishing with lures is great fun!

Mono — Short for monofilament. *See below.*

Monofilament — A single-filament line traditionally made from nylon. Manufacturers can engineer various characteristics around stretch and wear to make a mono for every purpose.

Open-faced reel — See *Spinning reel.*

Outrigger — Used to hold a bait or lure out to the side of the boat. Allows extra gear to be run without tangles and for lures to be presented in clear water.

Overhead reel — The traditional 'boat reel', also sometimes called a multiplier. The spool turns to regain line. Can be made in sizes from the smallest baitcasters to the biggest lever drag game reels.

Pan fish or 'pannie' — Variously refers to any fish of a variety that can be eaten, but nowadays more often refers to a snapper/tarakihi/cod or other common species where the fillet is of a size suitable for one or two people. A snapper from 300 mm to 400 mm fits the bill perfectly …

Paravane — A device used to pull a lure below the surface. It may be a moulded plastic device, a curved timber board or a stainless steel plate with a mechanism to trip it when there is a strike.

Pattern — Describes the colour and composition of a lure or fly being used. Also the term for a set of lures being trolled behind a boat.

Pelagic — A species of fish that spends most of its time in surface waters. Marlin are pelagic even though they can dive to great depths.

Pitch baiting — A fishing technique where fish, specifically marlin, are attracted to the boat by trolling hook-less lures. When sighted, a prepared bait is presented directly to the fish. Very effective and very exciting!

Popper — Top-water plug with a concave head, designed to splash and pop when pulled sharply. Imitates a wounded bait fish.

Priest — Slang name given to a bat used to despatch a fish quickly. Generally associated with trout fishing. The priest gives the fish its 'last rites'.

Ratchet — The noisy thing that buzzes when a fish takes line off the reel. Used primarily to indicate this fact audibly. They can also be used (carefully) to prevent overrun when the reel is fished in free-spool.

Reel — Device designed to hold line and release it under pressure. IT IS NOT A WINCH! Many kinds are available for specific uses.

Reel seat — The fitting on a rod that holds the reel. It usually has two collars, one to restrain and one to lock it in place.

Rod — Device used to cast for and fight the fish. Correctly designed, a rod will help tire the fish while reducing the chance of sudden impacts pulling out the hook or lure. It also helps keep the line clear of obstructions.

Rod butt — The lower part of the rod, specifically from the front hand-grip down, although that depends on how the rod has been built.

Sabiki — A flasher rig, generally with around six very small hooks, designed for catching small bait fish.

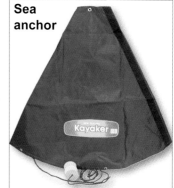

Sea anchor

Sea anchor — A device like a parachute (which it is sometimes called), designed to slow the drift of a boat. For most primarily a fishing tool (essential for fishing with softbaits), but also a safety item.

Set line — See *Longline*.

Shad — An American species of bait fish. We know it well now, as many softbait patterns are based on it and include the name.

Shoal — An area of shallow water, generally indicated by wave movement. A group of fish can also be described as being in a shoal. To be correct a shoal describes a gathering of fish in a family or social group while a school is a group of fish all travelling the same way.

Short strike — When a fish hits at a lure and misses it ... Bugger.

Short stroke — A technique for gaining line and getting a fish off balance (generally used in game-fishing). The rod is pumped in short bursts, and maybe as little as a half-turn of the reel is gained each time. Very effective.

Sight-casting — A technique requiring the fish to be spotted first before casting to them.

Sinker — A device, traditionally made from lead, designed to get a bait to the bottom and hold it there. Comes in many sizes, from small ones designed to drift a bait naturally down-current to monsters of more than 1 kg used when fishing in very deep water.

Size limit — Generally refers to the minimum size that can legally be taken. We now have the first slot size regulations in the country (for Marlborough Sounds blue cod) that set the legal limit between a minimum and a maximum size. Please be aware of your local regulations.

Skip bait — Less often used nowadays, skip baits were the preferred method of catching game fish in past decades. Trolled from an outrigger, a properly rigged bait would splash on the surface to attract the prey.

Slack line — Line held without tension back to the lure or bait. In many styles of fishing, getting slack line is a no-no. When hooked up, particularly when using lures, any slack line can result in the loss of the fish. Thus the old fishing salutation — 'Tight lines!'

Slot — See *Size limit*.

Softbait — A scented lure made from a soft, biodegradable material that fish eat like a bait. Generally made in a fish shape and/or with a tail that imparts movement or vibration. The Gulp! brand dominates the market and single-handedly created this type of fishing.

Soft bottom — Typically a bottom consisting of soft mud, fine sand or ooze.

Soft plastics — The original 'plastic' baits, soft plastics are made from hydrocarbons —meaning that they don't degrade in the same way as softbaits. While they can look the same, it is this point that differentiates softbaits from soft plastics.

Spinning — Fishing with the use of a spinning reel.

Spinning reel — A style of reel where the spool is fixed when line is retrieved. The line is wound on by a 'bail arm' that rotates around the spool. The spool is mounted on the front of the reel. It still turns to release line under the pre-set drag when the fish runs. Spinning reels run the full gamut from cheap reels for kids to incredibly powerful, incredibly expensive models built for jig fishing the biggest predators. Also known as spin reels.

Split ring — Looking just like a key ring, only smaller, a split ring is a device primarily designed to attach hooks to lures yet allow free movement.

Split shot — Very small sinkers, generally a ball shape with a slit down the middle. The trace or line is placed in the slit and the sinkers are squeezed to keep them on.

Spook — To inadvertently scare a fish.

Spool — That part of the reel that holds the line.

Spooled — What it's called when a fish takes the line, races off and completely empties the spool … Exciting but not at all recommended.

Stick bait — Similar to a popper but without the cupped (concave) face. More like a bait fish in profile, but fished the same way as a popper on the surface of the water.

Stinger hook — An additional hook placed in a bait or on a lure, generally near the back, to reduce the incidence of short striking.

Stinger hook

Strayline — A method of fishing where a baited hook is drifted with the tide and current using the least possible amount of weight. Berley is usually used to attract the fish.

Strike — The act of lifting the rod in an attempt to hook a fish. Also what a fish does when it hits a lure trolled behind a boat or a bait that has been set.

Structure — Any item that interrupts the flow of water. It could be a reef, it could be an artificial device like an FAD. Around structure is always a prime place to find fish.

Superlines — The current generation of lines, often referred to as 'braid' because they are made up of many strands of material, have transformed much of our fishing. They are exceptionally thin, meaning that they sink better, have less resistance and need smaller reels. They have near-zero stretch, meaning that every movement is transmitted.

Swivel — A device designed to allow the trace or lure to rotate without twisting the main fishing line. Also useful for creating strong joins between trace and main line.

Tagging — The action of applying a special numbered tag to a fish so that information on growth and movements can be gained if it is recovered.

Taper — Usually slow, medium or fast taper, which describes the elapsed time from when the rod is flexed to when it returns. A fast rod has most of the bend in its tip. A slow rod bends throughout. Each has its place, depending on style of fishing or species targeted.

Terminal tackle — Any item attached to the end of the fishing line, except the lure. Swivels, hooks, sinkers and clips are all terminal tackle.

Thermocline — Bodies of water often have distinct temperature changes through them. A horizontal layer with a sudden change in temperature is called a thermocline. Fish often congregate on the edge of a thermocline.

Top-water lure — A lure designed to be fished on the surface, such as a popper or stick bait. Fishing top-water lures is spectacular!

Trace — The line attached to the end of the main line. A trace is usually heavier to protect from a rough bottom or damage from fish. A trace may be just a segment of line between main and lure, or it may have droppers off it with hooks attached.

Trawling — A method of fishing used by commercial fishers where a net is towed behind a boat. It has no connection to anything recreational fishers do. Using this term to describe pulling lures behind your boat shows a high degree of inexperience — don't fall into the trap!

Treble hook — A hook that looks like three hooks attached to each other. Effective on some lures, although they can be very difficult to remove from a fish. Not recommended if a fish is to be released. Dangerous to fishers, too!

Trolling — Towing a lure or several lures behind a boat. It is not trawling! It's trolling …

Trolling board — Another name for a paravane.

Trolling motor — A secondary motor used to propel the boat at slower speeds and with lower fuel use. Often a small-horsepower outboard mounted on the boat's transom, but can also be an electric motor mounted on the front of a boat.

Ultra-light — Exceptionally light tackle used to target a particular species. The definition depends on the species. A 2 kg line may be considered ultra-light tackle for snapper, while 10 kg would be ultra-light if you were chasing big black marlin.

Water column — A water section taken vertically. Usually discussed in the context of where in the water column the fish may be holding or feeding. Knowing that is critical to getting the bait in front of the fish.

Weedless — A description given to a hook or lure designed to reduce the chances of catching on weed or structure. They generally incorporate a movable structure in front of the hook point to deflect things.

Weigh-in — Typically, the weighing of fish at a tournament.

Work-up — The name given to the feeding frenzy created when birds are chasing bait fish from the air while fish herd the bait from below. Typically there will be diving gannets and usually fish such as kahawai, trevally, tuna or kingfish visible on the surface. Snapper and other species may be feeding on what is left over as it drifts to the bottom.

4 ⌇ Rods and Reels

At its most basic, a rod is an instrument designed to cast (or place) a lure or bait where a fish should be, to absorb the shocks of a fish and to tire the fish so it can be caught.

A reel stores the line, releases it, retrieves it and assists in tiring the fish. It is not a winch. It may be designed — some types more than others — to assist in casting. A reel has a drag which creates a load against the fish, also to help tire it.

Did I mention that it is not a winch?

Unfortunately there is no one rod/reel that does all, although it is possible to compromise to a point. Just like your car may well tow your boat, it won't do it as well as a four-wheel drive — and won't do it at all in some conditions, such as where a four-wheel drive is essential.

That same four-wheel drive won't carry 10 pallets of goods like a truck will, just like your surfcasting rod will never stop a marlin on its first 500-metre run. You don't shoot ducks with a revolver; you don't run a marathon in high heels. Well, you get the idea. The beauty of this, though, is that there is an endless succession of birthday and Christmas presents to buy!

Basic rod and reel combo specifications

• For **boat fishing** using cut baits on the bottom, a typical rod will be from 1.5 to 2.1 metres long, be rated for line from 8 kg to 15 kg (a 10 kg boat rod is a good all-round option), usually be of medium action and be fitted with an overhead reel. It is fished with the reel on top of the rod.

• For **straylining** from boats using unweighted or lightly weighted baits, a rod is typically 1.8 to 2 metres long with a fast action. Overhead reels are again the best option (better control and feel); however, many people fish with a baitrunner/baitfeeder type reel. This is a spinning reel, and because of that the rod will differ by having bigger first guides and the reel will hang below the rod. In a runner/feeder reel there are two drags; one is pre-set to control the pressure the fish feels when it picks up the bait. The main drag is engaged by turning the handle or engaging a lever. Line weights from 4 kg to 15 kg are typical — the lighter the better, as baits will be presented in a more natural manner.

- A 2-metre **strayline set** with a spinning reel can also be used for wharf, live bait and light surf fishing.

- For general **surf fishing**, the benchmark is a 3.6-metre rod fitted with a grunty spin reel and probably a 10 kg to 15 kg mono. A phenomenally large number of such sets are sold in New Zealand every year. A good-quality set can even be purchased for under $100. Specialist rods and reels can cost five to ten times that amount.

- A **softbait fishing** rod is a specially designed tool with a medium action — it may look fragile, but it is in fact a potent device that will handle incredibly big fish. They are fitted with small, powerful spinning reels that can handle high drag pressures. I sometimes strayline with my softbait rod. Kids love fishing with them! They are also ideal for fishing with small metal lures for snapper and cod on the bottom. It's fair to say that our specialist softbait sets have become very versatile.

- **Light spin sets** are not too dissimilar to softbait sets, although the rods are generally lighter in construction. Spin rods in short sizes are ideal for kids fishing off wharves. Longer and better-quality rods in the 1.6- to 2.0-metre range are used for freshwater and saltwater spinning. Nylon, rather than braided line, is the usual choice when spinning with small lures — line stretch becomes your friend. There are specialist spin sets available that may be built in four or six pieces, designed to be carried into remote areas or stored in a vehicle ready for use.

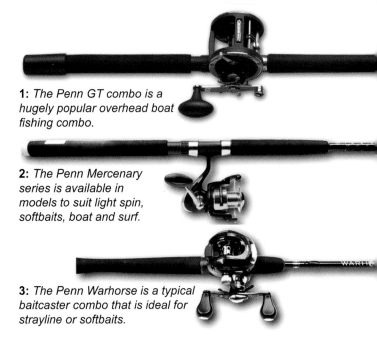

1: *The Penn GT combo is a hugely popular overhead boat fishing combo.*

2: *The Penn Mercenary series is available in models to suit light spin, softbaits, boat and surf.*

3: *The Penn Warhorse is a typical baitcaster combo that is ideal for strayline or softbaits.*

- **Game rods** and reels are matched to the line class; 24 kg and 37 kg sets are the most prevalent in New Zealand. A 24 kg game set is a versatile tool, ideal for live baiting kingfish as well. The length of the rod is mostly determined by the planned use. Shorter 'stand-up' rods are ideal in small boats when fishing with a harness and belt. Longer rods are usually used in bigger boats and from a game chair. Often the extra length is required to keep the line clear of obstructions. A good compromise length will be around 1.7 metres.

- **Jig rods**, designed for fishing with heavy metal jigs for species such as kingfish, are very specialised tools. In some cases the rods and reels used are amongst the most expensive of any type. Generally the rods are short and bend through the whole length. They use the best guides and reel seats. The reels can be spin or overhead; however, they are usually models made specifically for the job with beefed-up drags.

- **Popper and stickbait rods** are generally around 2 metres in length, very strong and with a firm tip to allow action to be imparted to the lure. Spinning reels are used, and they are also built with very powerful drags.

Reels

There are several types of reel in common use, and they have specific purposes. This book doesn't cover freshwater fishing specifically so we won't cover fly reels, closed-face reels or other types specifically designed for trout. Which leaves two basic types of reel and several variations:

1 — Overhead reels

Also called a multiplier or a boat reel, **overhead reels are designed to be mounted on the top of the rod**. The overhead is a broad-ranging design that starts with small models, generally known as 'baitcasters', through to the full-blown 130-pound game reels designed to catch the biggest predators. The common thing with all of them is that they consist of a spool mounted laterally between two side plates. That means the line comes off and returns to the spool the same way. No twist is imparted to the line in an overhead reel.

ABOVE: *This Penn reel is typical of the excellent design seen in today's star drag reels. Note the levelwind.*

Having the spool in that plane also means that the drag surface can be substantial, right up to nearly the diameter of the spool, and can even have a drag surface acting on both sides (that is the case with the biggest and best lever drag reels). More typically, though, the reel will use a 'star drag' mechanism. This consists of a wheel with multiple prongs that is turned clockwise to tighten the drag and anti-clockwise to loosen it. The drag surface will consist of multiple smaller washers stacked against each other, every second one being a metal washer. Properly designed, the drag pressures can be substantial. A star drag reel will have a separate lever to release the gears and put the reel into free-spool.

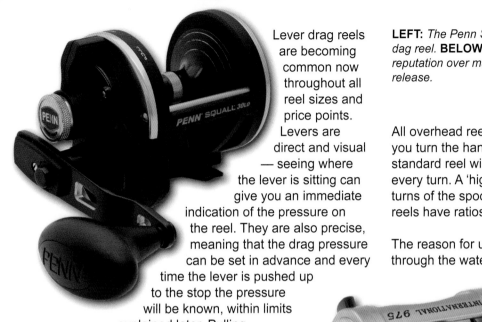

Lever drag reels are becoming common now throughout all reel sizes and price points. Levers are direct and visual — seeing where the lever is sitting can give you an immediate indication of the pressure on the reel. They are also precise, meaning that the drag pressure can be set in advance and every time the lever is pushed up to the stop the pressure will be known, within limits explained later. Pulling the lever fully back puts it into free-spool without the need for gear disengagement.

'Baitcast reel' is a term used to describe very small overheads, designed particularly for casting small lures with accuracy over relatively short distances. Small lures and jigs are called baits in many countries, hence the name.

LEFT: *The Penn Squall is an example of a modern, compact lever dag reel.* **BELOW:** *The Penn International Baitcaster has built a reputation over many years. Note the levelwind and push-button release.*

All overhead reels are geared. This means that every time you turn the handle the spool will revolve several times. A standard reel will likely turn the spool three to four times for every turn. A 'high-speed' reel will probably have five or six turns of the spool for every handle rotation. Some baitcast reels have ratios as high as 8 : 1!

The reason for using a high-speed reel is to move a lure through the water quickly or to regain the line faster. The negative sides to this include being more difficult to retrieve when under load and, arguably, being more susceptible to damage. The solution in many cases is to have a two-speed reel. Common in game reels, this option is finding its way through to the general boat reel market as well. A simple push of a button or turn of a lever will drop the reel from, say, 3.8 : 1 down to 2.0 : 1. The lower ratio makes it much easier to regain small amounts of line when fighting a fish under heavy drag pressure.

One thing to be aware of when selecting a reel to buy is that it's not just the gear ratio that decides how fast a lure will move through the water or how quickly line will be retrieved; the diameter (and hence circumference) of the spool also has a huge effect. The circumference of the spool decides how much line is retrieved on each rotation. If the spool circumference is 100 mm and its gearing is 5 : 1, then 500 mm of line will retrieved at each turn of the handle. If the circumference is 150 mm and the gear ratio is 3.8 : 1, then 570 mm of line is retrieved per handle turn.

The other items that may be fitted to the reel are:

Ratchet — Also known as a line alarm, this is designed to make lots of noise when the line is removed from the reel at speed! It acts as a useful warning, plus there is nothing like the sound of a reel screaming with a big fish attached… A ratchet can also be useful for stopping overruns when the reel is fished in free-spool.

Levelwind — This is a mechanical device on the front of the reel that lays the line backwards and forwards along the spool to prevent it bunching on the spool. They are more common in smaller reels, particularly baitcasters.

Spool tension knob — A rotating screw is fitted to many reels in the centre, typically on the side opposite the handle. This adjustment is primarily designed as an aid to preventing tangles when casting, although there is nothing better than a properly educated thumb for that job. Fishing wisdom says that when the tension knob is correctly adjusted, a lure should drop slowly to the floor from a rod held horizontally.

Magnetic or centrifugal cast control — Overhead reels remain the most efficient line-storage and fighting tool; the challenge has always been to turn them into casting tools, too. Traditionally, the way to do this has been to use a mechanism based around either magnets or centrifugal force to slow the spool. They all work, not always perfectly but reasonably well in the hands of a good operator. There are hybrid systems and even original and unique ideas like the plastic flapper system Abu Garcia built a few years ago.

Thumb bar — Many baitcast reels have a bar at the back that releases the gears, putting it into free-spool. It's a great idea as it means casting is faster — push the bar and your thumb is already in position to control the cast.

Drag pre-set — Lever drag reels have an additional adjustment, usually a rotating knob, which sets the drag range through which the lever will operate.

The things that will dictate the price of the reel include:
- the material used and whether the frame of the reel is one-piece
- whether it is a star drag or a lever drag
- the quality of the drag washers
- how many ball bearings are used and whether they are sealed, waterproof ones.

2 — Spinning reels

Once upon a time long passed, spinning reels or spin reels were cheap items designed for kids on wharves, for spinning for trout or for surf fishing. The changes they have gone through almost parallel the changes cars have gone through over the past few decades. From the use of high-quality materials such as titanium, through incredibly fine tolerances and unbelievably powerful drags, to very, very waterproof construction, these are serious fishing tools. Even the most basic spin reels from major manufacturers are very well constructed.

Spin reels are also known as fixed-spool reels. The reason is that the spool is designed to stay immobile during line retrieval while a device known as a bail arm rotates around the spool, winding the line back on. The line sits against a roller to reduce any potential wear on the line. The negative side of the spin reel is that the line turns through 90 degrees when leaving and returning to the reel. Basic physics says this will impart spin to the line. The trade-off is that spinning reels are simple and foolproof items to cast with. Overruns caused by spool inertia can't happen.

Spin reels generally have their drag adjusted on the front of the reel. It's not the most convenient way to have it if you want to quickly change the pressure; however, technically it's the best way to do the job. A few reels have rear drags. Around 30 years ago, it looked like rear drags would be the next big thing. I had a wonderful Abu Garcia Cardinal rear-drag reel and loved it. Unfortunately, rear drags have yet to take over the world. **Spin reels hang under the rod.**

There is such a huge range of spin reels on the market that it can be hard to figure out what suits your purpose. Let me break it down by style:

RIGHT: *The quality of mid-range spin reels today is amazing. The Penn Slammer is an example of such a reel.*
FAR RIGHT: *The Spinfisher Live Liner is Penn's version of the double drag spin reel.*

Boat fishing — Spin reels, while simple and foolproof to use, aren't the best option for boat fishing. Feel and control will always be better with an overhead reel. There is one exception to this: there is a second type of spin reel that incorporates two separate drags. Depending on brand, they are variously known as baitrunner or baitfeeder reels (or variations on the name). The way they work is by way of a rear drag, which has a lever or handle that allows the spool to be set with a light tension so that a fish can pick up a bait and run with it. By pushing the lever or turning the handle, the main, heavier drag is engaged. Simple and effective.

Softbait fishing — In our market, the sport of softbait fishing has altered the range and quality of small spin reels available. Here in the domain of braided lines, capacity isn't the key thing — drag performance is. So is weight; casting all day with a rod and reel can be tiring, so small and light is great. Reels constructed from magnesium are superb, albeit more expensive. The species targeted — snapper, kingfish, cod, groper — can be big, so drag performance is critical. Look for a spin reel that can handle salt water.

Surf fishing — Big, strong and resistant to the effects of salt water and sand are the features that make a great surf reel. Price is a reasonable indicator of quality, with choices available from budget to fully submersible.

Jig fishing — Very high-performance spin reels, designed to work under high drags with strong braided lines, are the result of some very intensive development over the last

Freshwater fishing — Spin reels for fresh water don't require any special features. Corrosion resistance is less important. The size and the capacity are the main determining factors. The quality of the drag is one of the key indicators of price; the lighter the line used, the better the drag needs to be. Another key feature could be the weight of the reel.

Light saltwater/wharf fishing — Again, no special features are required. Small spin reels can be great for fishing from small boats with light line. The quality of construction and corrosion resistance are the key things to look for.

decade or so. And the best performers aren't cheap — prices in excess of $1000 aren't unusual and the matching rods are not a lot cheaper. The good news is that, while you get what you pay for with top-end reels, the technology has filtered down to lower-priced reels. If your sport of choice is jigging with metal lures for big predators like kingfish, or casting stick baits to them, then there is a spin reel for the job.

The other items that may be fitted to the reel are:

Interchangeable handle — Almost all spin reels have the option to remove the handle and reinsert it on the other side. Strictly speaking, if you are right-handed the handle should be on the left. Don't feel you have to fish by any convention, though — set it for how you are most comfortable. I'm right-handed and have the handle on the right.

Spool grip — Increasingly common now, particularly on reels for softbait fishing, is a rubber insert around the arbor (the hub of the spool), designed to stop the line (specifically braided line) from slipping under pressure.

Anti-reverse — A small lever lives under the spool on many spin reels. It releases the anti-reverse, allowing the spool and handle to wind backwards. Basically useless for the sort of fishing most of us will do!

Line clip — Most reels have a clip on the side of the spool to hold the loose end of the line to stop it unravelling.

The things that will dictate the price of the reel include:

- the construction material used — graphite is cheap and light; aluminium is stronger; magnesium is light, strong and more expensive!
- the spool oscillation system and also whether stainless steel shafts, etc, are used
- the quality of the drag washers — sealed drags are more common now, and a great feature
- how many ball bearings are used and whether they are corrosion-resistant
- whether an anti-reverse bearing is fitted — this stops any movement at all in the handle; that is, it won't turn backwards even slightly.

Use the reel properly ...

When using a spinning reel, don't turn the handle when line is being taken by a fish or when the rod is loaded and you can't take line. By doing so, all you will do is turn the bail arm around the spool and twist the line. Either increase the drag pressure (if it has been set too lightly), pump the rod and retrieve on the down-stroke, or wait until the fish slows and settles.

Fishing rods

Wow, how the art of designing and building rods has changed over the last 50 years! First there was cane and other timbers, such as Zane Grey's famous hickory rods. Next came steel (not very successful) and then, in the 1940s, fibreglass.

For this last we can thank Dr Arthur Howald, a keen fisherman who saw the potential for fibreglass to be a game-changer. He developed a method of creating a fishing rod from glass fibres, then turned over his development to the Shakespeare Company. The first fibreglass rod, called the Wonderod, hit the market in 1947. An interesting point, particularly given the amount of development that has taken place since that first rod, is that Shakespeare Ugly Stik rods, probably the best-known and biggest-selling rods in the world, are still made by the Howald Process.

For a long time, solid glass was the common method of construction; hollow glass was far more expensive. Now, most rods are hollow and can be manufactured from fibreglass or graphite, or combinations of both. The basic process involves a piece of cloth, impregnated with resin and cut to the shape required to produce the desired action. The cloth is then rolled around a mandrel, which is a tapered steel rod of the appropriate length and diameter, wrapped with a plastic film and then baked in an oven. With the mandrel removed, a hollow glass fishing rod is created.

ABOVE: *The author hooked up to a big snapper at the Aldermen Islands. Note the curve of the Berkley Dropshot softbait rod and its parabolic action. Carefully applied, hand pressure can be used to increase drag pressure.*

The blank, as it is called at that stage, may be sanded, painted or coated with epoxy before being cut to its final length and sent to have the guides and other hardware attached.

Rod design and features

Understanding the effects of different materials in fishing rod design is an art that could fill several books and is beyond the scope of this one. There are some basics which are useful to understand, though.

Fibreglass is strong — as in resistant to damage — but the trade-off is that it is relatively heavy. Graphite is incredibly strong, and stiff, but it can be brittle. The way the two are used together is where the art begins. Another trick used is to insert a solid glass tip into the rod blank; Ugly Stik rods are an example of this.

The rod may need to perform several functions: it has to be able to tire the fish in conjunction with the reel drag, it needs to be capable of placing the bait or lure into the strike zone, which could mean casting, and it may also be required to steer the fish around obstructions, such as would be found while fishing off the rocks. The rod also cushions the line against shocks and is designed to assist in lifting the fish by the way it recovers from the loaded position.

It's almost impossible to describe in words exactly how a rod should feel and look, given such a wide range of possibilities, which is why they invented professional tackle stores! I recommend getting to know your local tackle shop proprietor. The following will help explain the characteristics and the components:

Action

Action describes the relative strength or power of the rod, not necessarily the specific line to be used. The terms used are ultra-light, light, medium-light, medium, medium-heavy and heavy. A rod using 15 kg line for game-fishing would rate medium-light, while a trout rod using the same line weight would rate as ultra-heavy.

What is modulus?

It is all about comparing the graphite material used to build different rods and rating its stiffness to weight ratio. Modulus is a confusing topic because there are several graphite manufacturers, there is no exact standard, and there are personal ratings by rod manufacturers.

The most common graphite used in rods has a designation of IM6. It has a rating of around 40 million. This is not a count of fibres, but rather a measure of stiffness to weight. IM7 and IM8 are stronger and lighter for the same thickness; however, they are more brittle — rod building is an art of design and compromise!

ABOVE: *A guide to taper — from the top, fast taper, medium taper, slow taper.*

To confuse things a little, many anglers (and less-knowledgeable shop staff) also refer to 'action' when describing the effects of rod taper. The two should actually be separated and described individually.

Taper

Taper describes the bend of the rod when loaded. The action derived from the rod taper is controlled by how much glass or carbon is wrapped into it. A fast-taper rod will bend through approximately the first 20 percent at the tip, a medium rod through approximately the top half, and a slow-taper rod will bend through most of the rod. Each has its place.

- Most rods for general boat or shore fishing will be medium in taper.
- Rods used to work lures or strayline baits with mono lines will be fast in taper.
- Rods used for softbaits and fishing with metal lures on braided lines will likely be slow or slow-medium.
- Game rods are typically medium to fast taper; however, they need the ability to 'recover' and assist in lifting the fish. With line breaking strains of 24, 37 or 60 kg, it's essential that they produce genuine power to be able to use the full potential of the line.

Often the effect of taper won't be fully appreciated until the rods are in real-world use. There, the combination of taper and the action designed into the rod combine to create a genuine fishing tool.

Where the guides should be ...

Remember that spin reels hang below the rod and so do the guides, while overhead or free-spool reels sit on top, as do the guides. Two rarer kinds of rod are:

- the interline rod, where the line runs through the blank instead of over it
- the spiral wrap, where the guides are increasingly offset, starting on top of the blank and finishing on the bottom.

Length

At the beginning of this chapter I suggested rod lengths for various uses. They are just a guide, though, as many things affect the desired length. This is the point at which you need to get into a shop and try different models. Just remember that the longer and stiffer the rod, the more that leverage is working against you.

Guides

The improvement in guide quality and materials over the years has been impressive. About the worst thing that happens to a guide now, and usually only at the low-quality end of the market, is that they pop out of their frame. Cracked ceramics and grooved brass are almost things of the past.

The world leaders in guide technology are Fuji. It is no wonder that their products are fitted by all the name-brand rod manufacturers. If a rod says it has Fuji fitted, it's a pretty good guide to its quality. There are other good-quality options (particularly Pac Bay for regular guides or AFTCO when it comes to roller game rods), but a rod with Fuji guides will serve you well. Fuji makes a range of styles at various price-points, from the basic Hardloy or aluminium oxide to the premier silicone carbide (SiC) guides.

More information on this subject can be found online or at your tackle shop. You get what you pay for!

Hardware

Fuji also dominates the rod hardware market. There are two main components — the reel seat and the gimbal fitting.

Reel seats fall into two broad categories: standard and trigger grip. For most, the rod blank passes through the reel seat, which is a separate unit, and is glued with epoxy to the blank. The trigger grip is just as described: it has a trigger that hangs below the seat, simplifying single-handed casting with overhead reels.

The exceptions are (1) some newer types of seat that are in two pieces and expose the blank; (2) AFTCO (and other) game-rod butts that are made of aluminium and are in two pieces to allow the rod tip plus the reel/butt combo to be stored separately; and (3) specialty surf seats that are able to slide on the blank to different positions.

The gimbal fitting may consist of nothing more than a tidy cap, or it may be a beach spike if it is on a surf rod. If on a boat or game rod, it will likely be a keyed gimbal where the slots drop into a pin in the rod-holder (or gimbal belt), thus preventing the rod and reel from twisting.

Don't hang up ...

Please don't hang up your hooks, lures or jigs on your guides! They can be damaged by rubbing or by the swinging of heavy lures. Hooking into the frame is a lesser evil, although still to be avoided if possible. Many modern rods now sport a small loop bound to the rod just above the handle. It's designed to retain your hook or lure when not in use!

Grips

For light spin, trout and softbait fishers, it's all about weight. Cork has been the first choice for decades, but affordable, good-quality cork is getting harder to source. It's still the best option, being easy to work and great to hold.

'Rubber' grips are usually made from EVA or Hypalon. EVA is harder, slicker and lighter and is often found in places where cork once dominated. Hypalon is much heavier, more spongy in feel (an advantage to many) but harder to clean. Both materials have their place.

The length and placement of the grips is important. Keep fighting the fish in mind when you test a rod in a store, and note where your hands naturally reach for.

Broken rods ...

The bane of tackle shops and manufacturers everywhere is the broken rod. I'd guess that 90 per cent of the broken rods replaced by the manufacturer aren't the fault of the rod. As I write this, I have a rod I broke last week sitting beside me. Is it faulty? Possibly, but probably not. It broke in my hands as a fish struck a lure I was working. Because it has broken on a heavy part of the rod, close to a join, it may be faulty. However, it could well be that the rod has rubbed at that point or been pressured, allowing the wall of the blank to collapse. I'll let the manufacturer view it and accept their decision either way.

Most rod breakages happen for these reasons:

- High sticking, otherwise known as point loading. This happens when the rod tip is lifted vertically, which puts the load on one part of the rod rather than spreading it across the blank. It then goes bang as the design load is exceeded. Not the manufacturer's fault.
- Travel damage — putting rods in side pockets of boats with other rods or gear is a recipe for blank damage and later disaster.
- Exceeding the rod rating. It has a line and or lure rating for a reason!
- Car doors — 'nuff said!
- Travelling with the rod in the rod-holder with a heavy weight attached, such as a sinker wound up to the tip.

No rod should be treated that way!

5 ⌒ All About Lines

The two basic components required to go fishing are a line and a hook. Line, and the technology around it, has become a very confusing topic, though. It's time to demystify it!

Nylon versus superlines

Those of us who started fishing more than a few decades ago will undoubtedly remember the braided green hand lines wrapped on a stick! You can still buy them — they are easy on the hands (especially for kids) and they still catch a lot of fish. However, the world has moved on and with rods and reels more affordable than ever, it's more likely that most new fishers will start with a rod rather than a hand line.

There are two types of line you will generally run into: nylon and what is generically called 'braid'. Braided lines have received huge amounts of press over recent years. They have their place, are better than nylon for certain uses, and worse for others.

Let's cover both types and describe the advantages and limitations of each individually.

Nylon lines

If you took a vote on which company has made the greatest contribution to the advancement of fishing tackle, the winner is a no-brainer. The giant that is DuPont, the inventor of nylon (brought to market in 1939), has done more than anyone to change the game.

Early nylons were harsh, springy things, totally unrelated to the product we use today. Mind you, DuPont was concentrating on making nylon stockings for demanding female customers, and then on supporting the war effort, so fishing took a back seat. Even though the early products were comparatively low-tech, the future was clear and the market started to develop. It would be two decades, however, before nylon truly became the future. DuPont introduced Stren — a thinner, more practical nylon for fishing — in 1958 and the market was forever changed. As recently as 2006, Stren was still the number one nylon brand in the world. An impressive achievement! Stren is now owned by the huge Pure Fishing Corporation, so its future is assured.

Nylon is often referred to as monofilament, or mono for short. This relates to the fact that it is created from a single filament, as opposed to the multiple filaments used in braided lines. Nylon lines have also appeared as co-filaments, where there is an internal core and an outer core. The most expensive and highest-performing nylons are generally co-polymers, where the raw products are blended to create a higher grade of finished product. All nylon lines have specific properties engineered into them. A few years ago I visited the Platypus nylon factory in Australia. Reckon I got a look at how the manufacturing process takes place? Not a chance! All the manufacturers are very protective of their methods and finished products. I did learn a lot about the basic method and design process, though.

If any product is a compromise, it is nylon fishing line. There is a very good reason why so many types are available, even within an individual brand — different types of fishing require different characteristics. Let's take a look at those characteristics now.

Stretch — Nylon stretches. That's a positive and a negative. The advantage of the stretch is that it allows pressure to stay on the hook, reducing the problems caused by a slack line. Too much stretch, however, and you could be fighting that rather than the fish itself. Stretch is good where impact strikes happen, such as when trolling lures for game fish; the stretch also helps keep the lure in place. Low stretch is good where it is necessary to strike a fish, to get a direct contact sooner.

Diameter — While thin is generally good because it has less friction and resistance in the water, plus it means more line will fit on the reel or a smaller reel can be used, the opposite view says that a thicker line is more resistant to damage. The general rule is to use the thinnest line that has the other characteristics you need. I personally like a very thin line when straylining for snapper, and prefer a slightly thicker line when trolling for game fish. If you are using mono while bottom fishing in deep water, a thin line will mean the line stays more vertical with less weight on it.

Limpness — Stiffer lines, generally, are stronger lines for a given diameter. Limpness is a characteristic that can be very important for casting and for straylining, where the bait has to be able to move naturally — springy coils of nylon just don't look natural. Lines for trolling and bottom fishing will generally be stiffer. Line memory is also a factor. Modern manufacturing methods reduce the problems of line retaining its shape after being on the spool for some time. Most tangles are caused by stiff line loops (either from the stiffness engineered in during manufacture, or loops caused by memory), jumping off the spool and tangling with other loose line.

Abrasion resistance — A balance between the hardness of the line, its diameter and any special surface coatings will determine the abrasion resistance of the line. If this is the key factor for your style of fishing, then buy a line made for the job and specifying that characteristic — an example is Stren's DuraTuf line.

Colour — Nylon is available in literally any colour. Tradition suggests that clear, light blue and sea green are the three colours we are most likely to use in general fishing. Dark colours also find favour in dirty water. Game-fishing is a field where colour is often important — many lure-trollers prefer colours such as orange, gold, chartreuse or bright blue so they can clearly track the point where the line enters the water.

Breaking strain — Oh boy, here we go, let's open a can of worms! You need to be crystal clear that what it says on the label isn't necessarily what you are going to get. The only way to be absolutely sure is to pre-test the line on a proper machine, which has been calibrated, and after soaking the line for the prescribed time according to the regulations. The chances of you doing that are, naturally, remote. However, if fishing records is your aim, it's probably prudent to actually do so. No manufacturer guarantees the breaking point of their line, although all manufacturers of game lines work to stay close to, but below, the rating. Some, like Platypus, will pre-test their lines and hand-write the result on the spool. Most use very, very hi-tech extrusion machines (and in-house testing) to keep the line within a certain range. For general lines, it's likely that the breaking strain printed on the spool is around about the actual breaking strain or a bit lower than where it will actually break. There have been cases of manufacturers making exceptionally 'strong' lines by massively underrating what is on the spool. Game lines are more likely to be true to label.

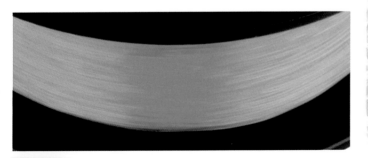

Things to know about nylon ...

- Nylon floats.
- Nylon breaks down in sunlight — store carefully and replace regularly.
- Nylon weakens when wet — in fact, testing for line class records is done after soaking the line for a specified period.
- Nylon can break even when there is no pressure on your reel — if a large fish is able to get enough line in the water, it can break the line when the pressure applied to the surface of the line exceeds the breaking strain. This is usually a trick employed by big game fish (blue marlin are the masters), but is equally likely when fishing with light lines for snapper, kingfish, hapuku and other big or fast-moving fish.

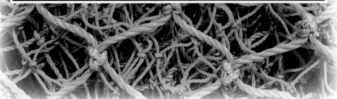

Braided lines

Of all the products that have been introduced over the last few years, none has confused as much as braided lines. Often called superlines, this new category has transformed many of our fishing styles.

What are they?

The early braids were known as Dyneema or Spectra. In fact, those are the brand names of the two major producers who manufacture polyethylene line, which is the raw product in braided lines. Dyneema and Spectra lines are called PE lines for short, and you will often see rods rated with a PE number — more on that later. It's also sometimes called GSP (particularly in Australia) which is short for Gel Spun Polyethylene, or just Gel Spun for short. Rather than a product name, this actually describes the manufacturing process.

Early braids were scary things that created monumental tangles and reputedly cut off anchor lines. Fortunately, technology has seen things improve out of sight and those problems are in the past.

Fishing braids are created by braiding the PE threads into a line. Currently, the best lines use Micro-Dyneema and are very tightly woven, giving lines of exceptionally fine diameter. Many lines are then fused to give a smooth, strong line with almost no stretch.

The differences between braids

The things that separate the different braids come down to the following:

•   The braid is either fused or unfused. Heavier lines tend to be braided only. Lines such as FireLine are fused. A fused line is generally smoother and a little stiffer, which is easier to handle. The tighter the braid, the better the quality.

•   Better and more expensive braids will have more threads: four is typical, eight is top-end. More threads create a rounder braid, although the current methods of manufacture also help with that (for example, FireLine has an axial core within it).

- Denier (the thickness of the individual fibres) is a quality indicator. Thinner fibres are better but more expensive. The way the threads cross, and how often, also add to the quality.

The pros and cons

On the plus side:

- PE lines are exceptionally thin and have almost no stretch. First and foremost, that makes them particularly suited to fishing in deep water. The days of heavy mono at depth are long gone.

- Braid is also suited to fishing where direct contact is essential. Softbait fishing is nearly impossible to do well without the use of braid. I can't believe we ever fished with metal lures on mono — the hook-up rate using braid is through the roof!

There are some negatives, though:

- Knots are more difficult to tie in braid. Specialist knots generally need to be used for heavy work.

- Braid has little resistance to wear — a trace is essential (see page 60 for the section on fluorocarbon).

- Ratings on the spool aren't necessarily what they say. There has been a tendency to describe lines by comparing

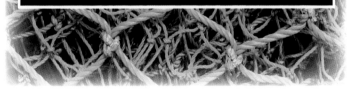

Understanding PE numbers ...

Many rods, but particularly those designed for heavy vertical metal jigging, are rated with a PE number. Most believe that the number relates to a breaking strain, but in fact it actually signifies a suitable line diameter for the particular rod.

My suggestion is that you test the rod properly before purchasing it to work out what breaking strain it can be comfortably fished with. However, by way of a guide and breaking all the official rules, an indicative PE guide would be to take the number and multiply by 10:

PE3 = 30 pounds
PE4 = 40 pounds
PE5 = 50 pounds
PE6 = 60 pounds
PE8 = 80 pounds

them with their diameter-equivalent in nylon, rather than their breaking strain. With the original FireLine product, a 6-pound line would break somewhere near 20 pounds; the line has a similar diameter to 6-pound nylon. It would be a big surprise if you found a braid that tested accurately at its rating; however, most manufacturers seem to be describing by breaking strain now. There is more on this subject in the softbait chapter.

Cost is still an issue with braid, but you have to take into account the bigger picture — good braid will outlast mono several times over. The reduced diameter also means that smaller, less expensive reels can be used. Add lighter sinkers and less lost gear, and braid becomes very good value for the right purposes.

When to use braid

•   With all deep-water fishing, be it for tarakihi in 60 metres or groper/ hapuku in 300 metres, braid is the only way to go. A high-quality, braided, unfused line, such as Berkley Whiplash, is perfect for that job.

•   Fishing with softbaits — braid is essential for good hook sets and total feel. Typically, we have used 6-pound or 8-pound FireLine which breaks at 20–25 pounds.

•   Heavy metal jigging for kingfish, bass and hapuku; typically, line weights from 40 pounds to 80 pounds are used.

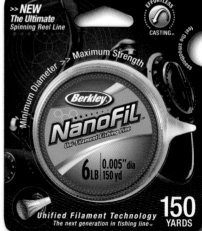

RIGHT: *Not a braid, not a mono and not a fluorocarbon, Berkley describe NanoFil as a completely new line with huge benefits.*

• Metal jigging for species such as snapper. In shallower water, we will use our softbait rods for the job. In mid-depths, an overhead reel and matching rod is ideal. Lines that break at 20 pounds to 30 pounds are ideal.

• Surf fishing, where the thin diameter helps stop the rig moving with current and wave action. The braid needs to be kept away from any obstructions as it will be easily damaged, so it's not ideal everywhere.

Fluorocarbon

This is magical stuff with incredible properties that will transform your fishing!

Fluorocarbon has several endearing qualities. Firstly, it has an incredible ability to handle wear and tear. We have regularly run an experiment that involves dragging nylon and fluorocarbon, with a large weight attached, over

Dacron, still an important line ...

When it was introduced in the early 1940s, Dacron became almost a space-age replacement for the old linen lines early game fishers were using, the ones that had to be dried every day. Dacron has little stretch, is easily spliced and added to, and lasts well on the reel. It's not ideal where stretch is an advantage, such as when trolling lures for game fish, but it does just about everything else well.

Dacron was our original deep-water braid. It's much thicker than current braids, but has almost no stretch meaning that it out performed mono.

In recent years, Dacron has had a resurgence in use. Game fishers have found that putting Dacron on their game reels then 'top shooting' with a couple of hundred metres of pre-test mono is a great way to go. They can get as many as five fills from a 1000 metre roll of mono, and the Dacron will last for many years. Trout fishers continue to use Dacron as a backing, while those who manufacture 'wind-on' leaders use Dacron to create the attachment point for the main line.

Don't expect Dacron to disappear any time soon!

a sharp knife edge. Fluoro blitzes nylon by a substantial margin!

Fluorocarbon's second claim to fame is that it has nearly the same refractive index as water, rendering it nearly invisible in water. Add to that its density, which means it sinks — nylon and braid float — and you have the perfect trace material.

To be honest, I seldom if ever use anything else as a trace now. For softbait fishing it's essential. There is an extra cost to buy it; however, a single 1-metre-long trace will potentially last for months. It's actually economical to buy and use.

Bulk spools and what I use ...

A good way to keep the cost of re-spooling reels down is to get your local shop to re-spool for you from their bulk spools. It's generally cheaper and much easier.

After several decades of intense, sometimes professional fishing, plus a decade in retail and more than that as a fishing magazine editor, I certainly have my own ideas on what nylon I favour.

My absolute favourite, all-round line for general use and straylining is Berkley Big Game. The 6 kg line is an exceptional one for straylining snapper. It's thin and limp, yet very resilient. I once won a contest on it after the snapper tried to shred the line against shallow rocks. The line held together. I've also had great success with Berkley Big Game on marlin and tuna.

My overall favourite game line though is Platypus Pre-test. It's totally reliable. Several years ago I played a black marlin for nine and a quarter hours on 15 kg Platypus Pre-test, and the fish towed us 22 miles out to sea ...

6 ⌒ Hooks, Sinkers, Swivels and Clips

The hook is one of the most basic components needed to catch a fish. It's a simple thing, yet hundreds of thousands of words have been written about it over the years. A discussion on hooks could, indeed, fill this book! Instead, let's keep it simple …

Hooks

Parts of a hook

By knowing about the components of a hook, you will understand what makes it work and the reasons for using different styles.

Point — Need I say that it must be ultra-sharp? More fish strikes are missed through blunt hooks than for any other reason.

Most hook points are conical. There are variations on that from different manufacturers. In fact, points are often

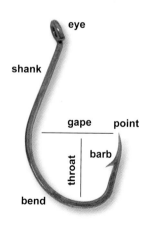

what differentiates different brands, at least in their marketing. Some, where tough fish are involved, may have cutting edges; Owner hooks are a great example of that style. For game-fishing, it is usual for the point to be cut into a diamond shape, which helps drive the point home.

Almost all the hooks we use now (with the exception of large game hooks) are chemically sharpened, a procedure that is part of the manufacturing process. This means that we can typically use a hook straight out of the box and know it's at its best. A sharpener is still essential equipment, though, to maintain the point.

There are three options for the angle of the point —

When seen from the point side of the hook:

A — a kirbed hook has an offset to the left
B — a straight point is parallel with the shank
C — a reversed hook is offset to the right.

Barb — It's easier to pull a hook out than it is to initially drive it home — at least it is if you don't have a barb of some kind. There is a fine balance between enough barb to keep the fish hooked and too much to get through in the first place. Lighter lines will generally need smaller or finer barbs. If a fish is to be released, it's quite normal for the barb to be reduced or even removed; you will need to keep the line tight, though. Often when fishing with popper lures and the like we will squeeze the barbs completely flat on the attached treble hooks. Not only does this make them easier to remove from the fish, but also easier to remove from people who get inadvertently hooked.

Bend — The bend of the hook is one of the most critical components. There are many variations, but two main styles — J hooks and circle hooks. The former is self-explanatory, and is the most common hook style you will see. The latter is a style where the hook curves back on itself, almost right back to the shaft in many styles. They are fished in quite different ways; circle hooks, also known as recurved hooks, are designed to roll into place when a fish turns and swims away. Inevitably, they hook up in the corner of the fish's mouth, right behind the jaw. They are the easiest hook to remove.

J hooks are essential when fishing with lures.

Throat — The depth of the hook from the tip of the point to the inside of the bend is called the throat or bite.

Shank — The shank is the straight part of the hook. The length of the hook shank is dictated by the size of the fish and the size/type of bait. Some styles find favour with particular areas or for those targeting particular species. For example, very-long-shanked hooks have long been popular with those chasing blue cod.

Shanks are either round (most hooks) where the shank is created from drawn wire, or forged (game hooks primarily) where the shank is flattened and becomes much stronger.

Bait holders — Less common now but still seen, the slices on some hook shanks are designed to restrain the bait and stop it slipping down and covering the point.

Gape — The distance between the hook's shank and the point is known as the gape. Depending on the size of the fish, plus the size and type of bait, the most suitable combination of shank length and gape is chosen. Those two characteristics differentiate most of the hook styles available.

Hook eye — There are two components to the hook eye: the style and size of the hole, and any

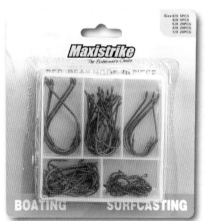

bend in the shank around the hole. The average hook has a large hole constructed in line with the shank. Some have the eye turned back; such a hook makes it easier to snell the hook (when you tie the line directly to the shaft, rather than knotting it to the eye). Although rare, you will also see hooks with a flattened spade instead of an eye. Those are also designed to simplify the snelling of a trace to the hook.

Most hook eyes are ring eyes where the wire is turned to form the eye. On heavy-duty hooks, particularly those used in game-fishing, the eye is welded or brazed on. Some live bait hooks, primarily designed for the commercial market, are also fitted with a ring through the eye which allows the bait to move in a more natural manner.

Coatings on hooks

Hooks are generally coated to protect them from degradation and to make them less visible in some situations.

There are many options used, from simple tinning of the steel to secret formulas such as VMC's Permasteel coating. Even Teflon has been used.

Colours can range from the typical black, bronzed and red to the popular blue, as well as less-obvious colours such as green, purple and even pink!

In general terms, all the major brands — such as (but not limited to) Mustad, Gamakatsu, VMC, Owner, Eagle Claw, Black Magic and Youvella create great high-carbon steel hooks with excellent coatings and proper tempering. There are also many no-name products, which should be treated with a degree of suspicion.

BELOW: *Some of my favourite hook patterns. 1 – Youvella Octy, an affordable beak pattern hook. 2 – Youvella Mutsu, a modern take on the circle hook. 3 – Mustad Big Gun, a very strong model that can double as a live bait hook. 4 – The Kahle hook. This one is a Mustad Big Mouth. 5 – Gamakatsu Octopus in blue. 6 – Youvella Circle hook, another variation on the theme. 7 – Generic circle hook. These are excellent hooks for use with live baits. 8 – Black Magic Live Bait hook. A compact and strong hook ideal for kingfish. 9 – Youvella Longline hook. Also suitable for general fishing use.*

Hook sizing

There is no standard for sizing hooks, so any stated sizes are just a guide. There is no comparison between two hooks of the same stated size but different patterns. They are often substantially different in comparative size.

Hook sizes start with whole numbers before becoming 'bar oh' numbers. So a size 16 is smaller than a size 15. A size 2 is smaller than a size 1. The next size up from a size 1 is a size 1/0 (one bar oh). Then they will typically range up to a 14/0, which is a very large game-fishing hook. Hooks can get bigger than that, though!

Size 4

Size 4/0

Size 7/0

ABOVE: *Hook sizes can be difficult to understand. The pattern above is the Gamakatsu Octopus. Within the limitations of printing the ruler the hooks are shown at their true size.*

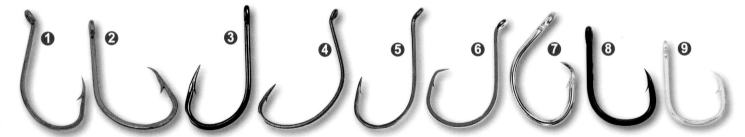

❶ ❷ ❸ ❹ ❺ ❻ ❼ ❽ ❾

Hook patterns

This is one confusing subject if you haven't been around fishing for the last few decades! There are many traditional hook patterns that haven't changed much but may be known by multiple names as manufacturers choose their own way of marketing.

Hook hints ...

- Elephants eat peanuts, so using a hook that is too big may reduce your hook-ups.
- Some species, such as blue cod, tend to savagely swallow baits and it can be hard to safely release them. Using a large hook, a recurved hook or a long-shank hook can help with mitigating damage to small fish.
- Chemically sharpened hooks are great straight out of the packet, but still need regular sharpening.
- Protect your hooks from the elements!
- If a hook looks damaged, replace it. It's a small part of the cost of your day.

Take my favourite hook, the Kahle. This light wire hook looks something like a circle hook. It's also known as a Wide Gap hook. Gamakatsu call it a Shiner. Mustad call it a Big Mouth. It's all pretty much the same hook.

There are so many patterns on the market that it's impossible to cover them all. Instead, and at the risk of upsetting a supplier who feels neglected, I'm going to tell you my favourite patterns. This isn't meant as a list of the best, just those I trust for how I personally fish.

- When fishing cut baits, the Wide Gap hook is still my favourite. The light wire and easy penetration makes for a high conversion factor. I typically use a 4/0 or bigger. They don't suit heavy tackle. I will usually select a red, bronze or gold version.

- The Gamakatsu Octopus is my favourite general fishing hook. A 6/0 is the possibly the best all-around hook you can have. Blue is my first choice of colour, followed by red and black. In my opinion, there is yet to be a better tarakihi hook designed than the 2/0 Gamakatsu Octopus, in either black or red.

- Another essential is the Mustad Big Gun in 10/0. I caught my biggest ever snapper (14.5 kg) on one, but not before three standard Mustad hooks had been demolished by other snapper that day. (Hint — you want to catch a truly large snapper? Go to Norfolk Island.) The 10/0 Big Gun also doubles as a live bait hook.

- Other hooks always in my collection are Youvella Mutsu and Live Bait hooks, Mustad Kirby hooks for blue cod, and a selection of live bait hooks from Black Magic, Gamakatsu and Mustad.

- I usually carry spare assist hooks, which are used on most of our metal lures in various sizes. Usually they are from Gamakatsu or Pro Hunter.

- While game-fishing is mostly beyond the scope of this book, straight hooks in size 9/0, 10/0 and 11/0 cover most game-lure rigging requirements.

LEFT: *Assist hooks come in various sizes and lengths to suit most lures. Always keep some on hand as replacements when lure fishing.*

Sinkers

Sinkers have three uses:

1. to get a bait down into the feeding zone and keep it there
2. to assist in presenting a bait naturally
3. as an aid to casting the bait a distance to where it can reach the feeding zone and to keep it there.

There are so many different shapes of sinker that it can be confusing. The good thing is that, for all practical purposes, we only need to use a small number of them.

Ball sinkers — (1) The ball sinker is one of the most popular styles. Keeping a range of them available is essential for all styles of fishing. Ball sinkers in the smallest sizes are used to weight lines to allow the bait to drift naturally; larger

models are often used in front of live baits. Ball sinkers are also used to get lines to the bottom, the design meaning that they roll and bounce across the seafloor.

The smallest ball sinkers are usually ⅛ ounce, ranging up to 8 ounces or more. Even smaller ball sinkers, with a cut along them rather than a hole, are used to add tiny amounts of weight. They are called 'split shot', and can be easily attached by squeezing the sinker onto the trace or main line.

Using multiple ball sinkers is a good way to add extra weight when bottom fishing. They create a low profile while making it easy to get the correct mass.

Reef sinker — (2) Also known as a snapper lead or bank sinker, this is the number one choice for all styles of bottom fishing. The reef sinker is easy to attach by way of a loop or knot, and is designed with most of the weight in the lower third, meaning that the rig will sink quickly and without tumbling. Its low-profile, elongated shape is also fast to retrieve.

Most general fishing needs are covered by a range of reef sinkers from 4 ounce to 10 ounce. Larger versions are available for hapuku fishing in deep water. Sizes up to 32 ounce are common.

Break-out sinker — (3) Looking like a reef sinker with arms, the break-out or breakaway sinker is the surfcaster's best friend. The long wire attachment means that the weight is concentrated further away, so that it casts like a missile!

The four wire arms can swivel freely but are locked into place before casting. They work to restrain the rig from drifting due to currents and tide, yet the arms are easily released under pressure to reduce snags and gear loss. Also shown is the fixed arm type (4) where the wires are bent to shape.

Other patterns

• *Pyramid* — (5) Either one-hole or two-hole boat sinkers have pretty much been superseded by reef sinkers.

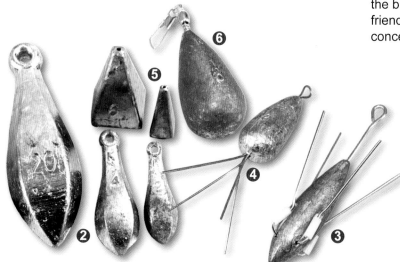

- *Clip-on sinkers* — (6) Very useful when the weight needs to be varied often. They have a swivel with a clip moulded into them; the swivel helps reduce line twist. I always carry a selection.

- Other patterns are specialist ones. *Sandgrip sinkers* don't cast as well, but do hold their place effectively on the sand. There are also sinkers with a loop at each end and with a keel shape; they are designed to troll baits and lures slowly at depth. Special chin sinkers are made for rigging dead baits to swim. *Bean sinkers* are usually used for weights on fishing set nets. *Spoon sinkers* have limited uses now, though they do make a low-profile surfcasting weight.

Sinker hints ...

- When bottom fishing, attach the sinker with a lighter line or a weakened knot — then, in the event of a snag there is a better chance of recovering your rig and, hopefully, fish!
- Pieces of chain make great sinkers, especially for deep water. Chain is low-profile, heavy, less inclined to snag and very environmentally friendly when it does.
- Keep a range of sinker sizes with you at all times.

Swivels

Swivels are designed to reduce line twist. Generally, twist is imparted when a trace is dropped or retrieved. It can also be created when trolling lures or drift fishing. The swivel is attached to the main line, then the trace is tied to the other end.

- The standard basic barrel swivel is relatively inefficient. It is an aid in twist reduction, rather than a total solution. A swivel does create a strong attachment point for the trace, though. The lighter the line, and therefore the lighter the weight attached, the better the swivel will work; friction being the enemy, of course.

- The next step up is the rolling swivel. This style is both stronger and more efficient.

- When true anti-twist protection is required, the solution is a ball-bearing swivel. These tend to be the domain of game fishers where cost isn't an issue. For lure trolling, they are essential. Small ball-bearing swivels are also available to suit very light lines, and are great for any light-tackle trolling or drifting. Sampo are the leading brand in this style.

Red Pigfish (male)

Swivel sizing

Swivels are sized just like hooks, with the same degree of variation between brands! Once again, a size 2 is smaller than a size 1, which is smaller than a size 1/0. Many manufacturers (most accurately those making ball-bearing swivels) will also state the breaking strain of the swivel. New Zealand company Black Magic Tackle rates its swivels by a recommended line strength — 6 kg, 8 kg, 10 kg, 15 kg, etc.

Swivel selection

• When fishing with a dropper rig and sinker on the bottom, it's normally okay to use a larger swivel. As a guide only, if you are using 10 kg line, a size 2 swivel is a good place to begin. Bigger is okay. However, if you are using good-quality swivels, then a size or two smaller is fine.

• When it comes to straylining for snapper, the rules change. The weight of the swivel will affect how the bait drifts; the last thing you want is a heavy swivel sinking faster than the bait. The general rule is to use the smallest size you can get away with. Again, the better the quality, the smaller the swivel you can use.

Colour

A bright-coloured swivel is an attractant to undesirables with teeth … A black or other matt finish is definitely the preferred option.

Other swivel options

• Swivels can also be fitted with clips. For times when bulk and weight aren't an issue, or when rig changes are being made regularly, they are a good option. Fish that spin and twist can force a clip to open, though.

• Three-way swivels were once very popular; in fact, all our early rigs were tied on them. The three-way makes for a strong rig as each knot is individually tied, as well as adding in an extra swivel to the branch line. They still have their place in a tackle box.

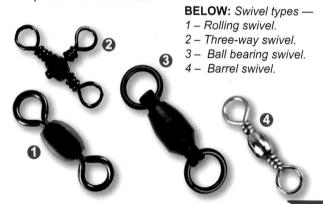

BELOW: *Swivel types —*
1 – Rolling swivel.
2 – Three-way swivel.
3 – Ball bearing swivel.
4 – Barrel swivel.

Clips

The majority of clips you will see, within several variations, look and operate much like a safety pin. They are called interlock snaps and are fine, and surprisingly reliable, for general use. Better models are known as Duo-Lock and Cross Lock snaps. However, when it comes to the highest performance the best is the Coastlock snap. You will find this style to be the most popular, in conjunction with ball-bearing swivels, with game fishers. Interestingly, there are many stories of fish even being caught with the snap open! Not that I recommend that method …

Swivel and clip hints ...

- Use the smallest size possible.
- Knots are always better than clips.
- The darker and smaller the terminal tackle, the less chance it will be found by barracouta.
- Use the best quality you can.

Another style is the McMahon snap, which looks like two opposing hooks. For trolling, avoid it at all costs — they have a propensity to unsnap themselves. Of course, I didn't believe this until the day it happened to me. They are fine, however, for less-critical demands.

There are specialist clips available too, many for surf fishing and beyond the scope of this book. One that is catching on is a very simple U-shaped clip designed for attaching lures. It goes under several names, including Easy Clip. It works well when changing softbait jig heads over regularly, but does add to the weight slightly. There is also some potential to lose the lure, especially when casting. It's a great option as long as you understand the risks.

BELOW: *Some of the common clip styles. 1 – The standard Interlock snap used on most low-cost swivels. 2 – The Duolock snap. 3 – The Coastlock snap. This is the highest performer, which is why it's used for game fishing. 4 – The McMahon snap. It can (and does!) open up. Use with caution. 5 – The Easy Clip, shown with a rolling swivel attached. Lighter versions without the twisted eye are also available.*

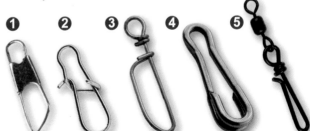

7 ⌒ Fishing Tools and Tackle Boxes

With the rods and reels sorted, there are still many other items to be included in the angler's kit. Each will add to the fun and the efficiency.

Tackle storage

With everything from hooks to sinkers, lures to softbaits to find a place for, thought needs to be given to how all that tackle will be stored. I've owned many plastic tackle boxes, quite a number of soft tackle bags and used dozens of plastic storage boxes, yet I'm still trying to work out the best solution!

In the end, I would suggest it comes down to the following three levels of storage.

Level 1

The basic 'tackle box' (1) with, typically, one to three trays is still a great option. Not all boxes are created equal; the differences come down to waterproofing (not just the seal between lid and box — the handle is often the weak point) and the quality of construction. There used to be problems with chemical reactions between things like rubber lures and the tray plastics, but that is seldom seen now (manufacturers may describe the box as 'worm proof', as it was US-type rubber lures, called worms, that caused the problems).

Keep your hooks, and other items that may rust, in their original packs — otherwise an open tackle box and one wave may cause you an expensive disaster. Look for a box with adjustable dividers so that the trays will accommodate the hook and swivel packets.

At the top end of the tackle-box range are boxes that use drawers rather than trays. They tend to be more waterproof.

Pros

- Simple
- Easy to store
- Easy to transport
- Generally inexpensive (although ultra-high quality, expensive boxes are available)
- Everything is in one place

Cons

- Prone to leakage
- A disaster when one tips over, whether open or closed
- Not pretty when a wave ends up inside an open tackle box
- Limited space for future expansion

Level 2

The second storage option involves the new generation of modular storage systems. Many are soft-sided bags (2), while others are plastic in construction (3), often with access on both sides of the box. Some consist of nothing more than a series of plastic storage boxes stowed in

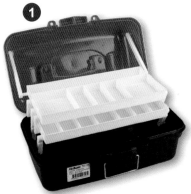

the main bag or box. Others are more of a hybrid system where the box has built-in compartments or drawers plus some removable storage modules. Some have a basic system with additional optional storage boxes available. At the very top end are systems with a range of modules so that you can select the most appropriate for your needs.

The point of difference between brands of soft bags is almost always in the zips. Poor-quality bags using inferior materials will fail every time. I know; I have a collection of them. Conversely, a good tackle bag or modular system is a joy to behold and use, and generally all that will be required for even the most advanced angler.

Level 3

The problem with fishing is that — with the exception of trout fishing, where you know your next fish will be a trout — there is a huge range of methods and species to target, many of which may be experienced on any given day. It can be hard to ensure that you have all the gear needed to cover all eventualities.

In an effort to solve this problem, for a long time my primary tackle box consisted of a full-sized fish box with a proper lid. Using a stainless bolt and wing nut to secure the lid, the fish box became a bullet-proof travel option that would happily live up the front of any boat until its contents were needed. I've also used chilly bins and even a small dive bag to achieve much the same result.

The trick is to have a waterproof plastic box for each range of products. There is now such a choice of affordable waterproof boxes in almost every size that it is easy to put a system together. Once upon a time, we had to sneak Tupperware containers out of the kitchen. No longer!

Low-cost containers are available from the big homeware retailers or even at the supermarket. Companies such as Black Magic make brilliant trace-roll storage and dispensing systems to keep your nylon rolls under control, while another separate box can contain the fishing tools. Re-sealable plastic bags are great for storing pre-made traces and rigs. Softbait storage bags (4) are even better.

The big advantage of this system is that everything is together in one place so you know where it is. Plus it's easy to store.

I use a hybrid system for tackle control now. The big fish box still holds everything, while a soft bag is used for day trips or aboard smaller boats. I fill it with the appropriate boxes from the fish box, and then it's ready to roll!

Tool time

A number of tools and accessories are considered essential. Here's a list:

Hook sharpener — A grooved hook sharpener (5) should be essential item number one. A quick touch-up of the hook point between fish is a good habit to get into.

Pliers — There are so many options that it's hard to know where to start. Fishing pliers (6) are used to remove hooks, trim lines (for good-quality ones), hold fish (nasty ones with spines), bend things, straighten things and all sorts of other tasks. There are also specialist pliers for using and removing split rings, while others are designed for squeezing crimps. A medium-length pair of good quality, with plenty of holding power, is the place to start.

Bait knife — Filleting knives are specific and personal, but a short and powerful bait knife (7) is an essential addition.

Braid scissors — Braid is difficult to cut, so specialist scissors (8) have been developed for the job. Essential for softbait fishing and useful for all styles of line, whether nylon or braid. To be brutally honest, though, I have yet to find a great pair. All the market offerings seem to work fine for a while, but inevitably lose efficiency and then rust. The Berkley models are a good choice, being affordable and as efficient as any.

Gloves — Fishing gloves (9) are a great addition. Generally crafted from neoprene, they are designed to provide warmth, extra grip and a degree of protection from spines. Women love them, kids love them and, used carefully, they can aid in the safe release of fish. There are also special gloves built for protection while filleting (10).

Gimbal belt — While large gimbal belts coupled to impressive harnesses designed to place the load on your lower back are the domain of the game fisher, lighter and smaller belts (11) are a great aid that will take the pain away. Easily fitted models with Velcro belts are common and very affordable. Lightweight harnesses are also available. If you need a heavy gimbal and belt for deep-water fishing with heavy weights, or to use when game-fishing, there is none better than the Black Magic system.

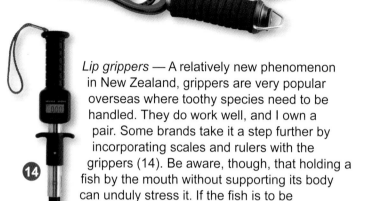

Fish box — A very useful tool that will ensure your catch is kept in pristine condition. Most of us don't need to keep ice frozen for 3–7 days, which can be a prerequisite for bins sold in Australia, but most of the bins on our market (12) will do that anyway. The key thing is that they should be efficient, easy to clean and have a good drainage system. Look at the catches, handles and, even more importantly, the hinges to see the quality of a particular bin. Weight may also be an important factor. Polyethylene bins can also double as a seat in the boat. There is an extensive range of sizes available.

Scales — While you can still buy a set of spring scales, affordable, reliable and accurate digital fishing scales (13) are freely available. I personally have been using a set of Berkley digital scales for several years. They are fantastic for checking luggage weights before heading for the airport, too!

Lip grippers — A relatively new phenomenon in New Zealand, grippers are very popular overseas where toothy species need to be handled. They do work well, and I own a pair. Some brands take it a step further by incorporating scales and rulers with the grippers (14). Be aware, though, that holding a fish by the mouth without supporting its body can unduly stress it. If the fish is to be released, try to keep it in the water while unhooking.

Disgorgers — As soon as you attempt to get the hook out of the throat or gills of a fish there is likely to be damage. If the fish is being kept that isn't a problem, but if you intend to release it then a little more care is required. For that reason there are two basic types of disgorger: one that is made to tear the hook, and another that is designed to remove it carefully.

The first type includes items such as gob sticks (15) — typically a tapered piece of timber around

300 mm long, designed to be inserted into the fish's throat. By wrapping the line around the stick, grasping it and then spinning the fish, the hook will be pulled out. Variations on the theme include models with hooks or slots at the end designed to grasp the fish hook.

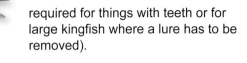

The second type of disgorger is basically a variation on a pair of pliers. Dedicated ones have angled and spring-loaded handles and serrated jaws (16), or a hook that can grasp the hook shank so it can be rolled out. Other models are actually pliers, usually very long ones, with a bent nose to reach the hook.

If you are using a disgorger to aid release, support the fish, keeping it wet and immobile, and then carefully roll the hook out without causing damage. For the health of the fish it may be better to cut the line close to the hook and leave it in place — it will rust out and less damage may occur.

Gaffs — A gaff is an important tool for securing a large fish you intend to keep or for restraining one that may be released. The latter can be achieved by gaffing a fish in the mouth where no permanent damage will be done (usually only

required for things with teeth or for large kingfish where a lure has to be removed).

The size of the gaff is dictated by the species being chased. Once upon a time, we always had a basic 'snapper' gaff aboard; Kilwell Sports must have sold tens of thousands of their wooden-handled model over the decades. It's a very long time since I last gaffed a snapper; we land everything by net now, and only use a gaff for securing hapuku and kingfish.

A solid gaff sporting a hook gape of 75–100 mm, and with a strong aluminium (17) or fibreglass handle, will cover most general needs. If you are targeting bigger fish regularly, chasing tuna or using it as an additional fixed gaff for game-fishing, a 125–150 mm gape will be preferable.

When using a gaff, the rule of thumb is that it should be placed over the back of the fish and then firmly pulled home — don't flail about with it! Better still, if it's possible place the gaff in the mouth of the fish — it will give you better control and none of the flesh will be spoilt.

Nets — Landing nets have morphed from basic fixed models with braided netting designed to catch onto every

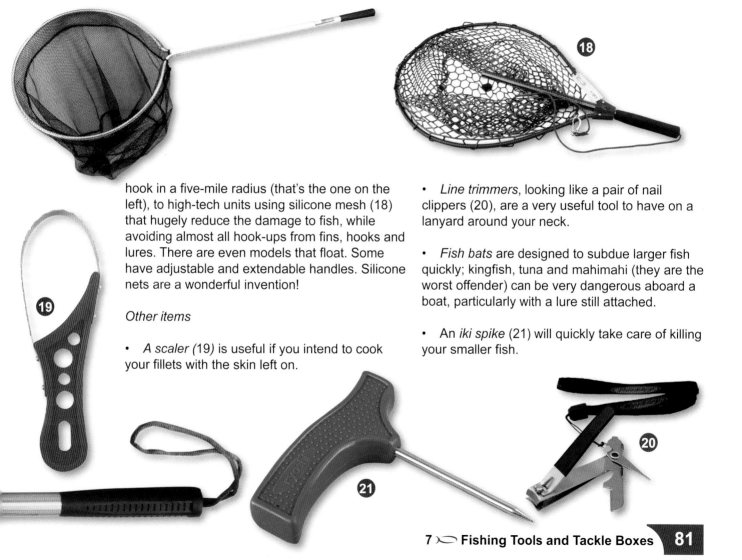

hook in a five-mile radius (that's the one on the left), to high-tech units using silicone mesh (18) that hugely reduce the damage to fish, while avoiding almost all hook-ups from fins, hooks and lures. There are even models that float. Some have adjustable and extendable handles. Silicone nets are a wonderful invention!

Other items

• *A scaler* (19) is useful if you intend to cook your fillets with the skin left on.

• *Line trimmers*, looking like a pair of nail clippers (20), are a very useful tool to have on a lanyard around your neck.

• *Fish bats* are designed to subdue larger fish quickly; kingfish, tuna and mahimahi (they are the worst offender) can be very dangerous aboard a boat, particularly with a lure still attached.

• An *iki spike* (21) will quickly take care of killing your smaller fish.

8 ⌒ Knots and Rigging

Before we can start to construct our first rig, or attach our first hook, it's essential to be proficient in tying a small handful of knots. While the selection available is wide, the number of essentials is very small. Information on tying knots is much easier to obtain now. Any number of books and websites are available to help learn the skills. A great example is the Anglers Mate Waterproof Knot Book. I highly recommend it. With the support of that book's distributor, we have described some of the key knots here for you. Your favourite tackle shop should have a copy of the book for sale.

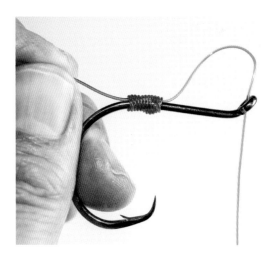

The knots

Knot 1 — The Improved Clinch

A knot for tying line directly to hooks or swivels is the most important to learn. The two options are the Improved Clinch knot and the Uni knot. Learn one thoroughly. My choice is the Improved Clinch — I've been doing it so long that I can tie it in the dark or upside down.

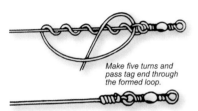

Make five turns and pass tag end through the formed loop.

The knot can also be tied with the line doubled over.

Knot 2 — The Dropper Loop

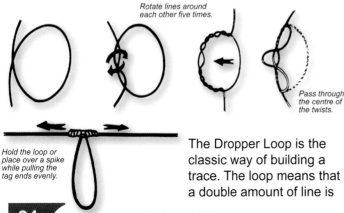

Rotate lines around each other five times.

Pass through the centre of the twists.

Hold the loop or place over a spike while pulling the tag ends evenly.

The Dropper Loop is the classic way of building a trace. The loop means that a double amount of line is

attached to the hook, giving additional protection. Tying your own dropper rigs, even flasher rigs, is an essential skill and a great way to save money. One trick with tying the loops is to use a vertical spike, or even a cleat on the side of the boat, to hold the loop while you pull the knots tight. Works a treat!

With the two knots above you can cover around 60 per cent of all fishing requirements. But wait, there's more! Knots 3, 4 and 5 make up the set required to rig a softbait system.

Knot 3 — The Spider Hitch

There are several ways to tie a double length of line. The Plait and the Bimini Twist are the two best, and knowing at least one of those is essential for every game fisher or

Grasp the doubled line between thumb and forefinger.

Wind around both fingers.

Wind firmly five times away from the loop.

Pass the end of the double through the original loop.

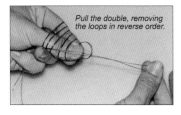

Pull the double, removing the loops in reverse order.

Keep pulling evenly until all the loops are through.

Keep everything even.

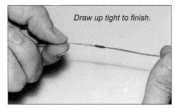

Draw up tight to finish.

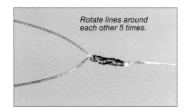

Rotate lines around each other 5 times.

serious sport fisher. However, a third option, the Spider Hitch, is fast and simple, reasonably strong if tied well, and very useful for light tackle straylining and softbait fishing. I always tie a short double in the braid on my softbait rigs. The trick when tying the Spider Hitch is to wrap the line tightly on your fingers so it doesn't run off, creating uneven loops.

Golden Snapper

Alfonsino

Knot 4 — The Five-turn Surgeon's Knot

The introduction of braided lines, and softbait fishing, has seen the need for a slightly wider repertoire of knots.

The Five-turn Surgeon's Knot is a simple and strong way to tie doubled braid to a nylon or fluorocarbon leader. Keep the loops even, and it will all go together well.

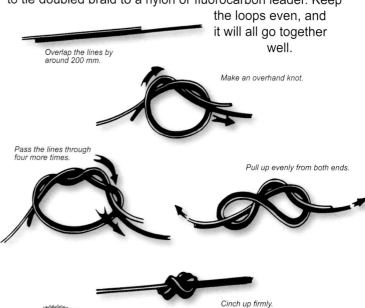

Overlap the lines by around 200 mm.

Make an overhand knot.

Pass the lines through four more times.

Pull up evenly from both ends.

Cinch up firmly.

Note that the knot is shown with one turn only for clarity.

Pink Maomao

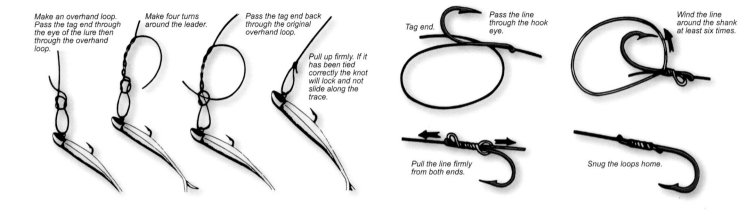

Make an overhand loop. Pass the tag end through the eye of the lure then through the overhand loop.

Make four turns around the leader.

Pass the tag end back through the original overhand loop.

Pull up firmly. If it has been tied correctly the knot will lock and not slide along the trace.

Tag end.

Pass the line through the hook eye.

Wind the line around the shank at least six times.

Pull the line firmly from both ends.

Snug the loops home.

Knot 5 — Lefty's Loop

Presenting a lure or bait naturally is the key to getting more strikes. The Lefty's Loop creates a non-slip loop in the line, allowing the lure to move without restriction. It's very simple to tie.

Knot 6 — The Snood

As an alternative to tying a knot, the action of wrapping and locking off the trace around the hook shaft is called snooding. A Snood is a strong way to attach a hook and an excellent method, particularly when a second hook is required for baits such as whole pilchards.

While it is okay, and sometimes desirable, to have the second hook sliding on a pilchard rig, be aware that many fishing contests have rules where an angler can be disqualified when their rig doesn't comply with IGFA (International Game Fish Association) rules. A sliding hook doesn't comply!

Knot 7 — The Albright

The Albright and its variation, the No-Name Knot, are particularly useful. The best way to fish for big snapper is to strayline with unweighted or lightly weighted baits, using the current to present them naturally. It's all about stealth. With the main line attached directly to the trace, there is no extra hardware to impede the action.

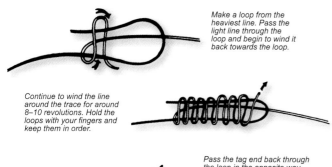

Make a loop from the heaviest line. Pass the light line through the loop and begin to wind it back towards the loop.

Continue to wind the line around the trace for around 8–10 revolutions. Hold the loops with your fingers and keep them in order.

Pass the tag end back through the loop in the opposite way to which it entered then snug the loops home by pulling both ends of the light line.

Don't trim the tag end too short ...

As the drawings show, the Albright is tied using one heavy line, the trace, and a lighter main line. The trace is looped and the main line is simply wrapped around it.
The No-Name Knot is similar but with the line wrapped in the reverse direction.

Keep the loops even while tying and pull up carefully. I usually tie a double in the main line first. Some of the biggest snapper I have caught, including two contest-winners, have been on 6 kg line tied directly to 30-pound trace without a swivel.

Trumpeter

Three basic rigs (and a few variations!)

Every fisher has variations on the basic rigs. Some like a longer loop, or perhaps a greater length between components. There are also options in line weight and hook size, of course. Species, and whether fished from shore or boat, will also add to the mix.

What follows is not necessarily the best way to do it, but rather a mix of suggestions based around how I tie my own rigs.

Rig 1 — The standard dropper rig

This rig is also widely known as a ledger rig or a paternoster rig. It is timeless, and responsible for more snapper, cod and tarakihi fillets than any other. If you buy a commercial flasher rig, it too will be a dropper rig. In its simplest form, the trace consists of a length of line with two loops tied in it (Knot 2). One end is attached to a swivel, while the other end is attached to the sinker by way of a knot or a loop.

Variations include the use of three-way swivels instead of the dropper loops. The top of the trace can be a loop which then allows a snap swivel to be used on the main line, so that rigs can be changed quickly. There have been occasions when I have used a dropper rig attached to the sinker. The trace then drags behind, while the movement

Use an Improved Clinch knot to attach the swivel. The overall length of the trace is typically around 800 mm

The loop length is optional. I like short ones, say 100 mm, for tarakihi fishing but twice that long for snapper.

Tie the loops far enough apart so that they don't reach each other. That will help avoid tangles when dropped.

Tie a weaker knot to the sinker so it breaks away if hooked up.

close to the bottom is a great attractant, particularly for species such as gurnard. It is principally effective when drifting.

Any amount of additional attractant can be added to the rig. Lumo tube can be used behind the hooks. As well as attracting, it will also act as protection from fish teeth. Another option is to use a metal lure on the bottom instead of a sinker. It's an additional shot that will surprise you with its effectiveness. Just be careful not to drag it over rocks and snags.

More than two hooks can be added to the rig; we mostly use three when fishing for tarakihi. Note, though, the comments about IGFA rules and fishing contests above — using more than two hooks may disqualify your catch.

ABOVE: *Flasher rigs are also a version of the dropper rig and are ready to fish!*

Rig 2 — The running rig

The standard running rig is a very simple affair, consisting of a main line attached to the trace via either a knot, such as the Albright, or a swivel. A hook, or two, is attached to the other end of the trace. Ideally, the trace and main line should be as light as conditions and fish size allow. I have now caught several snapper around or over 20 pounds on 20- to 25-pound fluorocarbon trace. If double-hook rigs are being used or the fish tends to swallow the bait, then a trace of 50 to 60 pounds may be appropriate.

Variations include one or two hooks on the trace, attractants such as lumo tube or dressed hooks (the same as used on a flasher rig), and various ways of weighting the rig.

There are several options for introducing weight to the system. A ball sinker can be added either in front of the swivel, where it can run down to the bait; or behind the swivel, where it allows the trace to move through unimpeded. Both have their place. In low

The ball sinker can be fitted either in front of or behind the swivel.

The trace length will vary depending on the style of fishing. As a starting point try 1200–1500 mm.

current I will most likely use the former, as otherwise the sinker can fall faster than the bait and tangles ensue. With lots of current the latter version may be best, as the current will usually keep the bait away from the main line and sinker, making the presentation look more natural. See what works best on the day.

A common trick, particularly when fishing in harbours, is to have the sinker behind the swivel, then feed a large quantity of line over the side with the trace before lowering the sinker. It gives a particularly natural presentation of the bait and works a treat!

Keep the weight to the absolute minimum, such that it allows the bait to move naturally in the current. Sometimes just a swivel is enough weight. Be careful with how the bait is attached, as a spinning bait looks unnatural and may twist the line.

Rig 3 — The live bait rig

This rig is really just a variation on the running rig, but is an important tool if you want to catch species such as kingfish, or even bigger game. Here a much heavier trace is likely to be used, 80 to 150 pounds being a typical starting point. If the fish are being difficult, dropping down to a trace of 50-pound fluorocarbon may do the trick. If marlin and other game fish are also a potential catch and you are using appropriate tackle, then a trace of 200 to 400 pounds may be better.

Typically a balloon is attached, generally to the swivel, via light, breakable cord or sometimes a clip. The balloon helps drift the bait away from the boat or rocks, while keeping it in the strike zone and also indicating when a predator is in the area. There is nothing like watching the balloon tear across the surface as a kingfish attempts to catch up with the bait! Variations on this rig include using just a sinker and no float. Anyone who has ever chartered a boat to fish at White Island or beyond will be familiar with the method. A large ball sinker runs on the line, while the bait, typically a member of the mackerel family, is hooked through the nose. The boat drifts across the zone with the bait deployed at the appropriate depth.

The balloon is attached with a light breakaway thread or a special clip made for the purpose.

The trace length will vary. A starting point would be 2 m of 37 kg nylon or, better still, fluorocarbon. Tie a double in the main line.

The live bait can be attached with a bridle through the eye socket or the nose. Alternatively it can be hooked just below the dorsal fin.

When drifting with a live bait in deeper water and around pinnacles, a ball sinker should be run in front of the hook.

Live baits can also be anchored to the bottom. Snapper and the delectable john dory are the targets for that method with kingfish also a possibility, although a kingfish that is already on the bottom near structure has a huge initial advantage. Few people target john dory often enough (the majority caught are by-catch), which is a shame as they are the best-tasting fish in our waters.

Rig 4 — The trolling rig

The rig for trolling is very simple, and very similar to the live bait rig. (This isn't intended to cover game fish trolling to IGFA rules, where specific minimum and maximum dimensions apply.)

I always start with a double line tied with a Spider Hitch (Knot 3) for non-critical situations or a plait where maximum strength is required. Attach it to a swivel. This is the domain of ball-bearing swivels — lures will twist the line, so you want a swivel that works; don't compromise. You also have the option of using a snap swivel. Run a length of leader from the swivel. For heavy trolling, a loop can be crimped in the trace and then attached to the snap swivel. For light use, a loop can be tied with a knot such as the Lefty's Loop (Knot 5). Alternatively, the trace can be knotted to the swivel.

Knot knowhow ...

- Learn your knots thoroughly, and practise them regularly.
- Check your knots during the day, and re-tie after a big fish or a break-off.
- Tie plenty of traces in advance — why waste good fishing time with your gear in the boat while you tie more?
- Circle hooks are the best option for most live bait fishing.
- When using a sinker on a live bait rig, attach it in such a way that it will fall free if the fish gets away — a fish can easily shed a trace and hook, but towing a sinker isn't going to conclude well.

The lure can be attached by way of another knot or a clip. For many lures, a trace is permanently connected to it and is then clipped on to the snap swivel that was previously attached to the double or main line.

The lure can be tied on or else a snap swivel can be used to attach it.

Ball bearing swivels should be used.

The trace length will vary. 1.5–2.0 m is a starting point for general trolling.

*Ian Dawson with a beautiful
example of a South Island
trumpeter. Stunning colours!*

Mark Roberts created this beautiful crayfish bait that is just perfect for a blue moki!

9 ⌒ Bait and Berley

The subject of bait alone could fill this book! I will thus attempt to simplify the choices and suggest appropriate selections. There are typically three options: fresh, frozen or preserved bait.

Fresh is best!

Fresh bait should always be the first choice and is inevitably the best. However, the practicalities of modern life mean that most bait comes from a service station, tackle shop or supermarket. That said, making the effort to gather or catch bait for your day will result in more fun, better results and the satisfaction that can only be derived from taking our sport back to basics! And don't forget that kids love to catch bait!

Flesh baits

Skipjack tuna. It would be great if we had a ready store of skipjack tuna to catch every time we went to sea. Unfortunately, in our temperate seas that's an option at best for only half the year. That said, there are few better snapper baits than skipjack, so keeping a small lure in the water when at trolling speed is a good idea. Watch out for the typical plops and broken water that give away the presence of tuna. Other tuna species are also very good bait — we used to keep the unused parts of our yellowfin for bait. The biggest snapper I have personally caught in New Zealand was on a piece of fresh albacore. That species does lack the oil of skipjack, but again it proves the fresh is best theory.

Kahawai is an underrated bait species. Scale it first. A big, fresh kahawai fillet can be deadly. They do wash out, though, so change the bait regularly. Kahawai gut is also great for bait.

Trevally makes a brilliant cut bait, too. Once treated as a third-rate fish, they are now a highly prized eating species. Trevally are always my first choice for cut bait after fresh skipjack or mullet.

Mackerel. There are multiple species of mackerel that can be caught and used for bait. They are caught by the use of tiny little flasher rigs called sabikis. Generally we find the bait schools on the sounder, or else we berley next to rocky headlands or pinnacles. Dropping the sabikis into the zone (baited or not) will catch the target species if they are there.

Piper are the premium small-fish bait. Fished whole or in half, a piper will get attention. They can be netted along the beaches and caught on lines with tiny hooks from the wharf. A hint — if there are schooling piper around (usually along ocean beaches), there will almost certainly be john dory in attendance.

Grey mullet is a wonderful bait species. It is very oily and very tough. Snapper love it! Mullet are usually caught by net in estuaries and harbours. Large numbers also run up rivers like the Waikato, where they can even be found as far up as Hamilton.

Squid. If you have the opportunity to catch squid, then you are in for great success. They can often be targeted at night-time from a boat; or, if you are lucky enough to be in an area where the main run of fish is (we have had it happen off Raglan several times in April, for example), then you may be able to target them during the day. In recent years, anglers, mainly from Asia, have shown the locals around Auckland that squid can become a dedicated target from the shore at night-time. It is now a separate fishery in its own right — most of those squid end up on a plate rather than as bait.

Barracouta is also a useful bait species. Slabs of them make popular hapuku bait, while blue cod are happy to eat them, too.

Yellow-eyed mullet can also be used for bait. They are great fun for kids to catch. As a live bait they can be useful, particularly for john dory when fishing around wharves.

Shellfish. Gathering local knowledge on the presence and position of shellfish beds can make all the difference to your results. Knowing what food the target species is eating is one part of the recipe for success; being able to gather that same shellfish as bait is the other part of the formula. For surf fishers, this is often the most critical part of their success. For boat fishers who target snapper, blue cod, gurnard and other popular food fish, it can be less important. For example, when fishing by a mussel farm for snapper, having whole mussels for bait is unlikely to make the difference between success and failure. That said, fresh mussels make great bait and an even better berley. Tarakihi love shellfish, particularly tuatua. Blue moki are also best targeted with shellfish. Parore, an underrated sport fish, are also a fan of shellfish.

FROM FAR LEFT: *Trevally, mussels and even octopus are baits that can be sourced locally at the fishing spot. The adage 'fresh is best' is definitely true when it comes to bait.*

Other fresh baits

Crabs. Found under rocks, in crevices on rocky foreshores and on beaches, almost every species eats crabs.

Octopus are an occasional by-catch and make a great bait when a tough, hard-to-remove attractant is needed.

Flying fish are great whole baits for big kingfish. They can be caught during the summer, under lights at night, around the offshore islands.

Crayfish. Some of the best fishing days I've had at Raglan were when we used crayfish. You might want to look away for this story, but we used to chop fresh crayfish tails into segments and sandwich one with a strip of salted trevally! I have never had fish hit harder than when crayfish tails were involved.

New Zealand pilchards are sold commercially (more on that later) and are occasionally caught by boat anglers when they are chased into meatballs by game fish. Get to the meatball, and scoop them out with a net!

Flounder. If you have watched the fishing show *Big Angry Fish*, then you will have seen presenter Milan Radonich catch many big kingfish. Many of those kings are caught in shallow water in places like the Coromandel. His bait of choice? A fresh, preferably live, flounder. (But I didn't tell you that …)

Frozen bait

The New Zealand bait industry is now a major one, supporting many companies and even more jobs. Much of the bait, particularly skipjack tuna, squid and pilchards, is imported. It's generally processed here for the retail market, either as whole fish or as berley. What follows is a list of the most common species available for purchase seasonally.

Skipjack tuna. Because of a long-term misidentification of the skipjack tuna, the name 'bonito' has come into general use for the bait that is sold. What you buy as bonito will definitely be skipjack tuna. Skipjack is a wide-ranging species that schools in huge numbers. During our summer, they push right in to the coast — I have caught them just a few metres from the shore — and they are the number one bait for all species. If treated badly, however, the bait can become quite soft. Arguably (although there's no doubt for me), salted skipjack tuna is an even better bait — more on that in the section on preserved baits, below).

Strips and cubes of skipjack are my favourite bait. When buying skipjack, the quality will usually be indicated by the condition of the skin. Because skippies (as they are often called) are caught in purse-seine nets there is often some damage; however, a high-quality skipjack will have a bright silver sheen and clearly defined stripes. A badly handled fish, or one that has been in long-term storage, will be less pristine. Also, when purchasing, be aware that smaller fish are better value, as you will often have to trim the fillet thickness down anyway. Don't forget to use the head, either whole or in half, as a big bait. It usually catches the biggest fish.

RIGHT: *Kim with a genuine bonito caught at Norfolk Island. It has different fins and also teeth. That's a skipjack tuna below.*

As a small aside, the true bonito, caught in Australia and throughout the Pacific, looks just like a skipjack except for two things: it's much smaller, and it has teeth! Very occasionally, bonito are available in New Zealand from specialty bait shops.

Pilchards. There must be hundreds of thousands of pilchards fed to fish in New Zealand every year! The majority of those come from Australia, and some from the USA, while in a separate category is the New Zealand pilchard.

New Zealand pilchards are increasingly popular as baits. Being caught locally, the quality is usually fantastic, and they are bigger and a degree tougher than their overseas cousins. The Australian pilchard is generally smaller and they do tend to become mushy faster. Both species do make great snapper bait, though.

Pilchards can be fished as cut baits or cubes; however, they generally last for one bite only — which can be okay if the fish are aggressive, and just time-consuming if you continually have to retrieve your line. When fished as a whole bait, generally with a two-hook rig, they make a fantastic bait. Some anglers improve their offering by using special bait elastic to keep it together. Surfcasters in particular are a fan of this method.

Make sure you buy pilchards that are IQF — individually quick-frozen. Solid blocks are not the way to do it. The quality of imported pilchards is certainly variable. If you find a really cheap price for pilchards I would suggest there is a good reason why. You get what you pay for.

Squid. There are three common types of squid that you will see in the bait freezer:

• The big ones are New Zealand arrow squid. Generally they are fished as cut baits or strips, or may be used as whole baits for species such as hapuku and bass. Or monster snapper.

• The most common baits found are sold as baby squid and are just the right size to use as a whole bait for most species.

• The third type is called a Loligo and comes from the USA. They are a food-grade squid, and will be immediately recognisable as they are much whiter than the common squid.

Blue mackerel. Generally caught in New Zealand, these are usually sold as whole 'baby blues' or packaged as blue mackerel fillets. This is an underrated bait that often works well on the day because of its high oil content, although it quickly gets soft if not properly looked after.

Sanma. The Pacific saury is sold as sanma and it's a wonderful bait. Fished in chunks or as a whole fish, or even rigged as a slow-trolled dead bait, it's a great choice for many species. They look something like a piper without the bill, are a beautiful deep metallic blue and silver, and every game fish in the ocean loves them!

Piper. Piper are reasonably freely available to buy frozen (with apparent seasonal variations). This is a good thing, as they are such a wonderful whole fish to use. Piper are tougher than pilchards, although more expensive. Treat them like gold!

Trevally. Generally trevally isn't sold as packaged bait in the way other fish are. Back in the 1960s when I started my fishing career, the usual bait was a small block of either frozen trevally or frozen squid, purchased from the local dairy. Those packs are still available in some places today, albeit in a better form than in the 'good old days'. A solid mass of frozen trevally is a last resort. Personal experience suggests that it is also one species that suffers badly from freezer burn.

Grey mullet. With their tough skin and particularly oily flesh, mullet make a great bait at any time. They handle freezing well, so have no concerns about buying frozen ones from your tackle shop. It's my first choice for set lines.

Baby salmon. Relatively new to the market and not widely available, baby salmon are a great addition to the range.

While not something I have much personal experience with, the stories I hear suggest that they are well worth trying out.

Tuatua. These can be difficult to find, but if you get the chance to chase tarakihi make sure you have a pack of frozen tuatua with you. One bag will go a long way, particularly as we use strips of squid to help keep the tuatua on the hook.

Preserved baits

The need for convenience has seen a growth in the range of preserved fishing baits available. There are basically two styles: salted then frozen fillets, or fully preserved fish needing no refrigeration.

During the 1970s my parents owned a bach at Raglan. My job was to keep the bait supply under control. The method was simple: wait for the trawlers to arrive at the wharf, then take down an empty fish box and pay to get it filled with trevally. The fish were filleted and then salted into a bucket.

To salt fish, start with an empty, dry bucket. It's never going to be able to soak your clothes again, so make sure it's expendable! Sprinkle the bottom of the bucket with a good layer of plain salt — do not use iodised. Then, place a layer of fillets flesh up and cover well with more salt. Repeat the process. Once finished, cover the bucket or store in a fly-proof container (it doesn't smell, but the flies seem to want to commit harakiri in the container). Within hours, the bucket will be full of liquid.

We would leave the fish in the liquid and take the bucket out in the boat with us. If it wasn't used over the ensuing weeks, it would get progressively tougher. We would enhance the product by adding fish oil to the mix.

Commercially, many species — including skipjack or 'bonito' — can be purchased in salted form. You will find salted skippy fillets in the bait freezer. They are fantastic, as they are pliable directly from the freezer and can safely be returned there if not used. To make your own, use the method described above but remove the fillets from the brine after an overnight soak. Pack in plastic bags (preferably seal using a vacuum packer) and store in the freezer.

You will also find salted flesh baits available for purchase in sealed buckets. It is the same product we used to make at the bach.

RIGHT: *Ian Hunt with a few examples of preserved bait that are both high quality and easily stored.*

Berley

There are many commercial berley options available, or you can make your own very easily. A good friend of mine who fishes at Kawhia has a session or two every year making his own. He minces skipjack tuna plus any leftover bait he keeps for the purpose, adds an extra bit of fish oil and then freezes it inside plastic buckets. The frozen blocks fit inside his berley container and are deployed on the bottom.

Just about anything can be added to the berley, from bread to sand, depending on where you want the berley to finish up in the water column. Shellfish, such as mussels, are great in berley. The broken shell and leftover mussel will drift beautifully in the trail.

Commercial versions are available in many sizes, and there is bound to be one that will fit your commercial berley pot. There are generally lots of choices, from flesh-based berleys to shellfish and kina ones, even salmon berley. The pest that is the koi carp has also been turned into berley (and bait, under the name Dorado).

Most commercial berleys are frozen into a mesh bag. The bag can be tied to the back of the boat or hung over into the wash next to the rocks. Alternatively, home-made and commercial pots can be used. They range from old 10 litre paint pails to weighted pots like the galvanised steel wobbly pot, to clever designs where the flow can be controlled, such as the Rayz berley pot.

Baited Rigs

This bait is best rigged with one hook. Take a half-hitch of trace around the end of the bait to secure it.

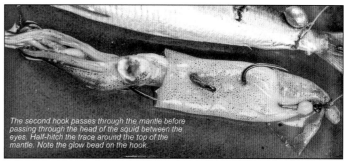

The second hook passes through the mantle before passing through the head of the squid between the eyes. Half-hitch the trace around the top of the mantle. Note the glow bead on the hook.

1: Strip bait with a single hook — make sure the hook point is kept well clear of the bait. Note the tapered shape, which gives movement to the bait.

3: Double-hook squid rig — there are multiple ways to do this one; just ensure that the bottom hook goes through the head of the squid.

The second hook is on the other side of the bait. Note the small ball sinker fitted. It slides down against the bait before the trace is half-hitched around the tail.

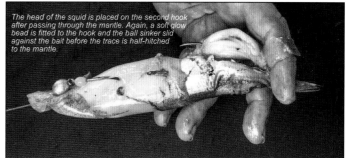

The head of the squid is placed on the second hook after passing through the mantle. Again, a soft glow bead is fitted to the hook and the ball sinker slid against the bait before the trace is half-hitched to the mantle.

2: Pilchard double-hook rig — half-hitch the trace around the tail to take the strain off the hooks.

4: Squid tube and pilchard sandwich — deadly! My favourite big bait. The squid tube protects the pilchard, yet allows all the juices to flow.

10 ⌒ Wharf, Beach and Rock Fishing Basics

Most of us start our fishing careers from either the local wharf or the shore. Many move on to fish from the rocks while others become boat fishers; sometimes both. The skills learnt ashore are critical to your success no matter where you fish — the ability to tie competent knots, bait hooks, select the appropriate tackle and adapt to conditions can all be learnt ashore.

Before going any further, I must again stress the need for safety to be paramount. This is even more important with kids. There is a fine line between wrapping them in cotton wool and not taking proper precautions — I know I did things on the Raglan wharf as a kid that my parents knew nothing about, that would have had fatal consequences if anything had gone wrong and that I'd never let my own kid do — but I did learn how to mitigate risks. Just use common sense and never, ever presume anything.

Rocks present an even greater danger. As I write this, yet another group of new New Zealanders are requiring the help of a rescue helicopter and local rescue groups to get back to shore, after being stranded in conditions in which most of us would not have fished, and clearly with insufficient knowledge of tide heights and movements. While the problems aren't restricted to just that group, new New Zealanders are over-represented in such rescue situations. Recently, I wrote an article on TV fishing host Milan Radonich, where he described to me an incident on the rocks early in his career. Again, he shouldn't have been there — and was probably lucky to get away with only a very badly damaged foot. Milan is a very sensible and practical fisherman, which shows that any of us can make a bad call. Please learn from the mistakes of others: it's less painful than making your own.

Please be careful, and prepare well for any eventuality.

Wharf fishing

So much of our fishing is about structure. A wharf is a structure, which is why you'll see schools of mullet sitting around the piles and timbers, sometimes with predators like kingfish, kahawai and john dory in attendance. Often, beyond what is visible, other species lie in wait for food to drift down to them.

There are a number of ways to catch the small fish that typically school around wharves throughout the country. First let me say that they aren't sprats or herrings — they are actually yellow-eyed mullet, although other species occasionally get in the mix. We don't have herrings in

Yellow-eyed Mullet

New Zealand although the genuine sprat, of which we have two species, is caught offshore at various times as well as in the southern South Island harbours.

Yellow-eyed mullet can be caught in three easy ways.

• The first is to use a small baited hook, plus just about any tiny bait, and fish it either weighted or unweighted beside the wharf or structure.

• The second option is to use a sabiki rig or dedicated bait-catching flasher rig. They can be either baited or unbaited, although the former is best. This will usually catch multiple fish at once. I recommend chopping commercial rigs in half for the kids, as two or three hooks is more than enough and will reduce tangles!

• Option three is to use a plastic 'baitcatcher' trap. Fill it with bread and lower it over the side. The fish will enter to feed, but are unable to escape.

Any of these options will keep the kids amused for hours. However, with a bit more effort and thought, there is the option to tangle with something bigger ... read on.

Safety preparations ...

- Wear an inflatable lifejacket.
- Dress appropriately, with proper footwear and also clothing that won't weigh you down.
- Carry an EPIRB in remote areas.
- Carry a throw-rope with a float attached.
- Check the weather forecast and the tides.
- Ask the locals; they usually know their conditions best.
- Keep a close eye on the kids.

South Island and lower North Island

Fishing with a larger bait on heavier gear, or a live bait anchored away from the wharf, opens up the possibility for several species. Red and blue cod are targets, as are warehou, barracouta plus kahawai, snapper and kingfish further north. Sea-run trout, and salmon, are also a potential catch. Be aware that different fishing regulations may apply for these last two species.

North Island

Most northern wharves will produce snapper — the further north you travel, generally the higher the incidence. Having a big bait anchored is always a great option. Kahawai are regular visitors to most wharves. A whole mullet or pilchard works well for them. I remember vividly a session on the steps of the Raglan wharf many years ago. I splashed a number of rigged dead yellow-eyed mullet on the surface under the wharf, and kahawai kept smashing them! It was great fun and a good lesson.

The john dory would be the most appreciated 'by-catch', being our best-tasting species. They needn't be just a by-catch, however — places such as Whitianga, Cooks Beach and Houhora are famous for their populations of john dory. Setting a live bait gives you a very high chance of catching one. You can also specifically target them — fish with live bait weighted to the bottom. Softbaits also produce john dory from our wharves.

The same live bait set for a john dory may also account for a kingfish. Unfortunately, most battles with kingfish include the wharf pilings and end badly. Some wharves, however, particularly in the Far North, are known kingfish haunts and kings can be specifically targeted from them.

Parore are an underrated potential target — most wharves have good populations. They only occasionally take a flesh bait, much preferring to eat well-presented green weed baits. Shellfish can also be their downfall.

Beach fishing

For this section I'd like to thank my good friend, Mark Roberts, for his assistance. Mark, a skilled and dedicated surf fisher, is based south of Napier. He is also a very talented photographer. When it comes to fishing from the sand, I always seek his advice first.

It is incredible just how many 12-foot surf rods and reels are sold in New Zealand every year. Every household must have at least one! While a 12-foot rod is still typical, there is a tendency for more 13-foot and even 14-foot rods to be sold now. Stronger, lighter materials have made such lengths usable for even the inexperienced fisher. If you fish infrequently, or want to find your way without large expenditure, then looking in your favourite tackle store for a surf rod/reel combo of 12 or 13 feet, typically around the $99 to $149 price point, will get you started. Spending more will give you a rod of better-quality materials with higher-quality guides. The more expensive reels typically have better seals and more ball bearings.

Spooling the reel with a nylon line of around 20-pounds breaking strain is the place to start. Using heavier line would need heavier casting weights, and also creates issues due to drag from tide and current. To the main line attach a shock leader that is long enough to leave around six turns on the reel when you have things ready to cast; something around two rod lengths is about right.

Shock leader.

The trace to the sinker is tied at a length of around 100 mm. It is able to slide freely along the shock leader.

The main trace is tied at a length of 250–300 mm.

ABOVE: *An example of a high-tech surfcasting bait rig, using a shield to hold and protect the bait.*

Thirty pound line is ideal for the purpose. The shock leader does just what it says — it's designed to take the load, rather than stressing the main line, when the sinker is despatched. A strong cast would otherwise break the 20-pound line. The shock leader and main line can be joined with double Uni knots.

When it comes to terminal tackle, surf fishers have developed a complete industry around their needs. Clever and sophisticated hardware is used to deliver the bait securely out to sea. While commercial rigs are available, initially you won't need to go down that track — but reading and research is recommended if you want to further develop your abilities. Mark suggests using circle hooks for all of your fishing, matching hook size to the bait being used. Generally he uses breakaway sinkers (the ones with

the wires incorporated to retain their position), as they hold well on sandy bottoms yet release quickly when necessary.

The standard surfcasting rig is a running rig.

1 – Start by passing your main line through the eye of a swivel, leaving it free to slide. Then tie on a second swivel.
2 – To the end swivel attach your trace and hook; the trace would typically be 250–300 mm long.
3 – To the free end of the sliding swivel, tie another trace. This one wants to be around 100 mm or so longer than the main trace. To that, attach your sinker. The dimensions can be adjusted, but the sinker trace must be longer than the baited trace to reduce tangles and to protect the bait. The trace will be able to run freely when the sinker reaches the bottom.

Mark uses a softbait wallet (which looks like an upmarket CD-holder) to carry pre-made spare traces. It saves time re-rigging on the beach, and means that a range of trace options can be carried ready to go.
Because it's often quite a walk to where you will fish, it's important to be self-sufficient. As well as the requisite spare trace material and bait, you should carry a fish measure, bait knife, short gaff, pliers, spare and warm clothes, plenty to drink and also a torch if it could be dark before you return. And remember to let someone know where you are going.

Beachcraft and baits

Reading a beach is a key skill to develop if you want to be consistently successful.

•   A good place to start is to visit the beach at low tide to see if shellfish beds are visible or any signs of fish feeding are discernible. Note those for later. Often the fish will leave the channels and travel into those feeding zones under cover of darkness or in suitable sea conditions.
•   Look for rips. Don't fish the rip itself, but rather to the side. The rip can stir up the bottom and deposit food for fish to scavenge.
•   Look for structure. Some may possibly show on local marine charts. At either end of the beach there may be a headland. Fishing the margin where beach meets rock is always a good place to start.

Watch where others are fishing along the beach and what results they are experiencing. Remember that every beach is different, and results will vary depending upon tide, moon phase, time of year, time of day and lots of other variables. Do not be despondent if at first you do not succeed; success or failure, every bit of information adds to your knowledge store.

I asked Mark for his thoughts on best times and tides. His preference is to fish the bigger tides of the new and full moons. The greater water movement will generally stir things up. He also likes to fish the last two hours before high tide. That will vary, though, according to the beach. Many beaches are better fished closer to low tide, to access the best areas without having to wade dangerously into the surf. As with most fishing, early morning and evening will generally produce the best results as well as the best conditions.

Bait selection can be very important. Because you may be fishing in wash and wave action and also because the bait needs to be cast, either a firm bait or one that is wrapped well with bait elastic should be used. Mark tells me that octopus and squid are his favoured baits, but notes that gurnard seem less partial to them. He buys eating-grade squid from the supermarket to get the best quality. Salted skipjack tuna ('bonito') is another favourite, as are pilchards, although they do need special attention to stay on the hook. They are also more likely to receive the attention of 'pickers' (fish too small to take the bait).

Shellfish are important as bait, too. Blue moki is a great fish to target from the shore for those in the South Island or the lower half of the North Island. They love shellfish, crabs and crayfish. Sometimes shellfish can be sourced right where you are fishing. Mussels from the supermarket also make a great bait, but like all shellfish will definitely need to be held on with bait elastic.

Beach fishing is a wonderful way to experience our great outdoors, spend time with the family and learn the basic skills for catching fish.

Rock fishing

Fishing from the rocks introduces the need for a whole new skill-set. Rocks are structure. How they form and how the gutters below the water create feeding zones and highways for the fish dictate the best spots to target. So does access and safety. The greatest emphasis should be placed on the last two.

Berley is a key component in creating success from the rocks. A bag of frozen berley, pellets or even a fish tied by the tail and left to wash against the rocks will do the job. Tossing out handfuls of chopped up pilchards will also add to the attraction.

When fishing for snapper from the rocks, usually the best way to fish is to cast unweighted or very lightly weighted baits into the berley trail. It's kind of the reverse of what we do fishing a trail from the boat. Snapper will rise to the surface to feed on the berley; a bait slowly drifting down through the trail will get attention. Heavily weighted baits in rocky areas can get snagged on the bottom and are more likely to attract less-desirable species. The trick is to keep the bait moving.

In areas where you can cast onto sand, the rules change a bit. Baits fished on the bottom can attract all the other common species, from cod to gurnard, john dory to elephant fish, depending on where you fish. Big trevally are another possible catch, particularly in the Far North, and will fall to the same methods used for snapper. Kahawai are a common catch and can also be caught from the rocks on cast lures or even softbaits fished down a berley trail. Schools of blue maomao also cruise along the rocks.

Kingfish are one of the major targets for rock-fishing specialists. For many, it is their sole focus! Numerous large kingfish have been caught from the rocks on live baits, and by large I mean fish approaching the magical 100-pound mark (that's just over 45 kg!). It really is a specialised field, with heavy rods — often extended game rods with lever drag reels — heavy traces and big baits used. Blow-up paddling pools can be used as holders for live bait and huge amounts of berley are expended in setting up the trail to attract the smaller fish to bring the predators around.

Tackle

While rock fishing does require specialist equipment in some areas, often your existing tackle may be incorporated. For short casts in safe, easily accessed areas, a 7-foot rod, such as you would use with your favourite baitrunner-style reel, will do the job. Typically, though, a dedicated rock fishing rod is around 10 feet long. That gives enough length to help guide fish around rocks and obstructions. Many fishers use their 12-foot surf rods instead. It all comes down to the rocks you are fishing, your height above water, how close you are to the water's edge and the species chased. Choose a reel with plenty of capacity (you may be unable to follow any large fish you hook), and one that can take unplanned knocks.

The terminal tackle used is also subject to those same issues. The trace may be in constant contact with rock and weed when being retrieved, making fluorocarbon an ideal choice. A long leader may be required to help lift fish from the water when fishing well above the surface. Circle hooks again become a good choice. Having the hook lodged behind the jaw when lifting it from the water means fewer pulled hooks or lost and damaged fish. Use good-quality swivels and hardware, as they will be subject to more load than when fishing from the shore.

Long-handled gaffs, or specific rock-fishing ones made to slide down a line to grab the fish, are required for this style of fishing. High-quality footwear and an inflatable lifejacket should also be considered part of the fishing tackle. A good backpack, plenty of prepared traces, a bait knife, pliers and a fish measure make up the rest of the basic kit.

Don't forget to take something to use to carry your fish/fillets back to the car. A small first aid kit is also highly recommended. Take plenty of water and also a throw-rope and float. The life it saves may be yours.

Finally, you can carry it in so you can carry it out — don't leave your rubbish on the rocks.

LEFT: *Milan Radonich, host of* PlaceMakers Big Angry Fish, *with a huge trevally caught from the shore in the Far North.*

11 ⟁ Boat Fishing Basics

From the humble dinghy to a fully equipped launch, a boat gives anglers the ability to locate fish and place themselves in the best position to catch them. A boat is a very important fishing tool. Fishing from a boat requires different skills and techniques than fishing from the shore. Water depth, fishing structure not visible to the eye, a moving platform — all these things change how the bait is presented. Safety is again paramount. Check the weather forecast and conditions, don't overload the boat, let someone know where you are going, carry several forms of communication and ensure that there is a reserve fuel supply.

Where to begin — know your target

Faced with an expanse of water and shoreline, it can be hard to know where to begin. Don't worry, you aren't alone; we have all been through it. The place to start is by understanding your quarry. Hapuku won't be found in a west-coast harbour, while snapper can vary where they will be depending on time of year, tide and water temperature. You are unlikely to fill a fish box with blue cod in the Hauraki Gulf.

Knowing what species is in the area you intend to fish or, conversely, knowing the habitat of your target species is step one. From there, think structure. From reefs to channels, mussel farms to rocky coastlines, all are structure that will potentially hold fish at some time or affect the water flow.

Research further by talking to fishing club members and other locals, searching websites, studying charts and visiting local tackle shops.

Electronics and fishing

Over the last few decades, the qualities and features found in marine electronic gear have changed the face of boat fishing. The advent of GPS has been the greatest advance. No longer do I line up the red roof with the edge of the headland (actually one of my favourite tarakihi spots) — now I punch in instructions to head to waypoint 31. Secret spots are secret no longer. GPS also adds to safety — however, it is not a replacement for basic navigation skills; further education is essential if you cannot plot a course, position by dead-reckoning or understand how to calculate distances and position using longitude and latitude.

Sounders, or fish-finders as they are often called, have also gone through a major renaissance. The drivers for this have been both the improved quality of LCD display screens and the excellence of the software written to interpret the information returned. The basic operation of a sounder hasn't changed much: a pulse of sound at a set frequency is transmitted via the transducer. By measuring the time it takes to hear that signal return, after bouncing off anything in the way, the depth can be calculated. By displaying the strength and pattern of the returning

signal it is possible to reveal the bottom type, any structure and even the species of fish below the boat.

Colour screens, once the domain of the rich or the dedicated, are now available for just a few hundred dollars. Colour indicates signal strength by a variation in the colour used. To a skilled operator, it's the nearest thing to having a camera on the bottom. The way the signal is interpreted, often with a digital component to the processing, has allowed greater efficiency in pulling the important information out of the noise.

ABOVE: *Good electronics really help to improve your fishing. We caught snapper to 8 kg on this spot.*
1 – Baitfish. 2 – A slow jig sitting a couple of metres off the bottom.
3 – Snapper groups on the bottom.

A little less than two decades ago, I started a marine electronics business. At the time the challenge was to get first a hand-held and then a basic GPS — without even a plotter screen — at a price below $2000. Now, the GPS is probably included in your cell phone for no extra charge. How things have changed.

The basic sounders we sold then had mono screens only 60 pixels high. They typically sold for $200 to $300. Now, for little more than $300 you can buy a full-colour sounder with 320 vertical pixels. Something of that performance used to cost more than $2000. Fuel may have gone up in price but the cost of electronics has plummeted, even more so compared with average incomes. However, one thing hasn't changed — you still need to be able to interpret what the screen is telling you. Perhaps a subject for another book …

Drift fishing

Rather than waiting for the fish to find you, or for the berley to draw them to you, one of the very best ways to find fish is to drift. By drifting you can repeatedly place the bait or lure right where the fish are holding, known as the 'strike zone'. Drifting is also a great way to prospect to find the fish in the first place.

The challenge with drifting is to keep control of the boat, particularly its speed. In perfect conditions that isn't a problem; unfortunately, perfect conditions are the exception to the rule. The answer in most situations is to use a sea anchor, an item that looks a bit like a parachute (which it sometimes gets called). The sea anchor is generally attached to a corner of the boat astern (conditions permitting — you don't want a wave to come over the back of the boat). By careful manipulation of the placement and length, and also by turning the angle of the motor or rudder, it's possible to control the direction of the drift, to a point.

Where to drift

Typically, I will drift for the following reasons or in the following places:

ABOVE: *Drift fishing is productive! These great blue cod and snapper were caught off D'Urville Island.*

- In a new area, and without the ability to locate structure, drifting is a way to prospect for your quarry.

- To chase species such as gurnard. They are usually located on flat sand or muddy areas, and drifting can be the best way to find and catch them.

- In the area surrounding any rock or reef. Snapper are regularly located on the sand just off the edge of reefs and other foul ground. So are blue cod. Drifting such margins is one of my favourite ways to fish.

- To chase hapuku, bass or bluenose. Often the water depth can range from 150 to 300 metres. Anchoring isn't an option.

- Any time a work-up is spotted. These are fishing honey-pots. Fishing under work-ups with jigs and softbaits is the second-best way to go fishing (or the best until the day you experience your first marlin bite).

- Fishing with live baits and jigs over structure to catch kingfish.

- Just about all softbait fishing (covered in more detail in a later chapter).

- Definitely all jig fishing.

- When all else fails.

About the last point — one of my most memorable fishing sessions occurred on a day when everything that we knew should work, didn't. In desperation I noted a small reef on the chart in only 5 metres of water just off the beach, and decided to drift nearby. From the first drop on, we caught snapper. So good was the fishing that we were drifting right into the surf line, where we could see the bottom, yet we were still hooking fish in a depth of only a couple of metres. Only the breaking waves in front of us ended each drift. We repeated the exercise and spent the rest of the day catching great snapper. Never stop trying!

Drift fishing tackle

Generally, no special tackle is required for drift fishing (apart from the sea anchor); however, there are a few points to keep in mind.

- First, the movement of the drift will create extra drag on the line — so the thinner it can be, the lighter the sinker weight you will need. Braid is a good choice.

- Keep in touch with your bait, and feed line out regularly to keep it on the bottom. I find that a fast-taper rod with a sensitive tip gives the best feel. Retrieve and re-deploy your bait regularly so the line angle doesn't get too steep. With braid, you will feel the sinker bouncing on the bottom.

- Because of the movement that drifting imparts, there can

LEFT: *Gurnard respond well to drifting baits. Flasher rigs work particularly well.* **OPPOSITE:** *Look for places to strayline where there is water movement to carry the food.*

be benefits in mixing things up — using a lure instead of a sinker on the bottom can open up additional opportunities. Attaching a running rig below the sinker, in addition to the standard dropper or flasher rig, also works a treat.

• When drift fishing I always fish with at least one, and often two, slow jigs as well. They are set either side of the boat, with the jig a metre or so off the bottom. The movement of the boat gives the lure all the action it needs. Softbait rods will usually handle the job; short kayak rods are even better. Adjustable rod holders are perfect, as they will hold the rod almost horizontal and the tip well out from the boat. Most days, it will account for the biggest fish.

• A GPS plotter is a fantastic tool for drift fishing. Often the drift is affected by tides and currents, not just the wind — the plotter will show that. By marking any strikes, you can align subsequent drifts to hit the best spots.

An explanation on how to drift around work-ups is covered in the softbait fishing chapter.

Fishing at anchor

Before dropping your anchor, you need to answer the question, *why am I anchoring on this spot?*

• Is it because I can see fish on the sounder?
• Is it because I expect fish to pass this spot?
• Or is it because I am positioned to allow my bait to be straylined back into structure?

A yes to any of the last three is a reason to stop the boat.

1 — Spotting fish

I love to chase tarakihi. At times they can be the most frustrating fish to catch, because you need to anchor on them with pinpoint accuracy. If you know what you are doing, it's possible to recognise schools of tarakihi on the sounder. They are generally to be found on low, broken or foul ground, gravel patches and mud areas. I will re-anchor multiple times if necessary to get the boat exactly on the right spot. A GPS plotter will help you get your anchoring right.

Snapper can be notoriously difficult to see on a sounder, particularly when scattered. When schooling, that can change. I often see snapper show up in groups, looking like inverted ice-cream cones in shape. I was lucky enough once to see the same behaviour while diving. If you can recognise such displays on the sounder, you can anchor amongst them and expect action.

2 — Waiting for fish

Sometimes you have to place yourself in the right position for the fish to find you. A typical example would be fishing by a mussel farm. You are unlikely to see schools of snapper show on the sounder (although it does happen); rather, it's a case of picking a likely area of the farm and fishing various depths while waiting for the groups of fish to swim past. Berley will help get them to your bait if the water flow allows.

In harbours, we generally choose to fish the edges of channels while anchored. We regularly do the same at places such as Coromandel, where we will select areas with good water flow between islands or around rocks. In deeper water, we often anchor based on a depth we know the fish to be at.

A typical example would be during the west-coast spawning season from around October to December. Often we will hear about the depth that the fish are holding. If 52 metres is the gossip, then we will anchor at the indicated depth — often without fish visible on the sounder — and wait until the bite starts or radio chatter suggests a different depth. There is no structure; it's all flat bottom, so knowing where the fish are is critical.

Some anchoring uses experience coupled with local knowledge. For example, at my tarakihi spot waypoint 31, described earlier, I will usually motor around the area looking for the groups of tarakihi. Depending on the tide or other factors, they can be loosely scattered. In that case I will anchor up for a period of time in the general area. We will usually catch a few fish; however, I know that if we motor around again after waiting for an hour or so, we will likely find the bigger groups we are looking for.

Fishing for species such as blue cod can be less stressful — getting the anchor in the general area can often be good enough.

For me, another favoured anchor-fishing spot over the years is in a place called Crayfish Point, north of Raglan. It doesn't always fire, and being in a depth of 12 to 15 metres the conditions usually dictate whether we can fish there. When it does produce, it is almost always tide-dependent. Sometimes the bite can be as short as 20 minutes. Clearly, the fish are travelling inshore to feed.

Keeping a fishing diary will help you recognise the patterns happening in your own area so you can draw on that knowledge when you fish new ground.

3 — Straylining for fish

Primarily a method for catching snapper, fishing an unweighted bait into structure is great fun. Anchoring is critical, because generally berley is used to draw the fish to the area and it needs to travel towards the structure, not away from it. The idea is to locate an area you know or believe to be holding fish, then anchor up-current of it, allowing both bait and berley to travel towards the structure.

The technique can work anywhere, although the trick is to get the combination of anchor placement, wind and current right so that you aren't wasting your time fishing barren areas. There can be other factors too — one spot I like to fish is an island just outside the Coromandel Harbour. Early in the morning the rising sun casts an extensive shadow across the water; in winter this lasts until around 10 a.m. Straylining back towards the edge of the reef surrounding the island, where the fish are hunting under the cover of darkness, is very effective until the sun hits the water.

For strayline fishing you will use Rig 2 discussed in the knots and rigging chapter; the running rig. The key is to use the minimum amount of weight possible — the bait should always be moving, so if it reaches the bottom and stays there then it's not at its most effective. Start with a small sinker, or even none, and add weight until the bait runs naturally. I prefer to keep the reel in hand, which is the reason baitcaster reels are ideal for the job, and feel

RIGHT: *Always keep your options open; Jake van Selm caught this fine hapuku on the bottom while the boys were straylining at Never Fail Rock off the Mercury Islands.*

the fish take the bait before striking. Casting the bait well behind the boat and allowing it to slowly sink into the strike zone can also work well. Generally, I fish two rods, one cast well out the back and the second kept in hand.

Baitrunner/feeder style reels are popular for this type of fishing. They have the advantage of two drags, the one that sets the initial pressure on the bait and the second that is activated when the bail arm is engaged, just like any other spinning reel. While undoubtedly popular and effective at times, they need larger rods to balance them. I really believe that if you scale your tackle to the target, you will catch more fish. An example of this happened to me one day at Coromandel. I was in a 12-foot dinghy fishing solo. I chose to fish a reef that almost breaks the surface, just south of the harbour. I anchored up-current of the reef

and fished with a couple of baitcasters loaded with 4 kg line. While the tide flow was high I used a couple of small pinch-on sinkers, probably each an eighth of an ounce, and drifted strips of salted tuna in to the reef. I reduced the sinker size as the current slowed. With the change of tide I anchored on the other side of the reef, and repeated the exercise. At one stage another aluminium boat roared up and anchored nearby. The sole occupant proceeded to cast a whole pilchard on a running rig that had a sinker of at least 4 ounces (based on the splash it made each time it landed on the water). After 25 minutes — I timed him — he had caught nothing and moved on. I caught three fish while he was there, took a box of snapper home and released many more.

It's very much like a cooking show — give them good flavours but, most of all, present it well.

Tackle for anchored fishing

While the typical 'boat rod' will handle the duties when fishing the bottom from an anchored boat, using dedicated rods designed for strayline fishing will improve your chances when fishing that way. They are described in the rod and reel chapter.

LEFT: *Another great snapper for Kim. However, notice the rod holders; this rack is made by New Zealand company Railblaza. They can be removed from the rack and used on extra mounts along the gunwales.*

There are a number of items of tackle that can also add to your success.

• An efficient and reliable anchor is essential. If fishing rocky areas, make sure you have an anchor, such as a grapnel, that can break free if snagged. Around mussel farms a dedicated hook is used. The hook is attached to a short rope and then latched to one of the main ropes between the buoys. It is then an easy matter to release the boat without damaging any of the mussel ropes. Never drop an anchor in a mussel farm.

• Rod holders are an essential part of the kit. A range of both fixed and adjustable styles, plus a 'rocket launcher' to store spare rods, will make the fishing space more efficient.

• Delivering berley effectively can also be a key to success. Mounting a berley pot on the stern of the boat is an option for delivering berley there; however, often it is preferable to release the berley closer to the bottom. While you could make your own system to do that, commercially there are two popular products for the job. The first looks like an over-sized metal spring inside a mesh bag. It goes by a number of names, the best known being the 'Wobbly Pot'. Because it is heavy, it sinks quickly and holds position well. It will also hold the larger commercial sizes of frozen berley. The second is the Rayz pot. It has a weight in the bottom but also has a unique way of adjusting the water flow through the pot, ensuring that the right amount of berley is delivered to suit the conditions.

Trolling

First, be clear — it's trolling, not trawling. The latter is what commercial fishing boats do when they drag a net. Trolling is the art of towing a lure behind a boat, and covers everything from weighted lines pulled slowly in a lake to dragging surface lures to attract marlin.

While both of those examples are specialised fields outside the scope of this book, many of the techniques are the same.

Kahawai

The first species most people get to catch on trolling lures is the underrated kahawai. Because they school and often hang around the edges of reefs and washes, they are easy to target.

Trolling a work-up

Before I cover the lures required, I first need to talk about the technique needed when trolling around a work-up. If you want to show that you have no experience, then just drive your boat through the middle of the next work-up you see. I assure you that the raised fingers you see won't be indicating that the passengers in nearby boats have only caught one or two fish …

The trick is to watch for a moment, and work out which way the school of fish is moving. The birds will indicate where they are, but not necessarily where they will move to. Once you are sure where they are heading, then troll around the fringe of, but away, from the school, turning so the lures travel along the leading edge of the school. If another boat is already there then they have first rights, so travel in the same direction they are. If the school sounds (dives below the surface), then stop and wait for them to resume their feeding. That's a good time to drop metal lures to the bottom.

Lures

At times kahawai will hit any trolled lure; at other times they are incredibly frustrating. If there is any one lure to keep in the tackle box, it is the white bone lure. Of course they are no longer made of bone, just plastic; however, this most basic of jigs is still incredibly effective. Dragged behind the boat at a fast walking pace, it will also account for albacore, skipjack and even kingfish. The next snapper to grab a bone jig won't be the first, either.

An option is to use a paravane or diving board in front of the lure to take it below the surface. Usually, running one lure on the surface and one below is the way to begin. Bibbed minnows also offer a way to troll deeply, with the added advantage of being attractive to kingfish.

At times, kahawai get really fussy and it's then time to pull out the secret weapon — a white fly the same size as a whitebait! Any pattern will generally do, and a good tackle shop will help you. Ask for a white deceiver fly and to see any other bait fish imitations they sell.

LEFT: *Before trolling any work-up it's important to check on the direction the school is travelling — a simple matter with this patch of trevally!*

Softbaits and metal lures can also be trolled for short distances between drifts.

Albacore and skipjack tuna

As mentioned earlier, tuna will take a bone jig; but they are better targeted with small feather or vinyl lures. At times, these need to be very small; at other times, albacore will jump all over big marlin lures. A good thing to do is to buy a packet or two of small vinyl lure skirts and a box of tapered weights to suit. That way you can always make up a cheap and ready-to-use lure at a moment's notice.

ABOVE: *Keeping a pre-rigged hand line close to hand, with lure attached and set to go, is the way to be ready when you spot a work-up.* **BELOW:** *The white plastic bone jig is a must-have lure for every boat.*

Large saltwater flies are also a great option, for skipjack in particular. At times they can be ridiculously fussy with what they will take, and even trolling around schools of them won't generate bites. That's when it's time to pull out the flies.

In many places later in the season, they seem to have bellies full of what appears to be a red krill. That will explain why I have found pink lures to be particularly effective as the summer comes to a close.

Kingfish

Kingfish will at times take anything that's moving, and at other times will ignore all offerings. Trolling isn't the best way to catch them — jigs and live baits are — however, they will often respond to a bibbed lure or even a popper slowly trolled around structure. A rigged slow-trolled bait, like a piper, can be a deadly way to catch them, too. Make sure your tackle is up to the job, because kings are usually found around structure and they generally head back there when hooked …

Trolling tackle

Your standard boat rod and reel will happily double for trolling duty for light use, but dedicated trolling tackle is best for kingfish and all other game species. Nylon is preferable for all trolling, as braid is unforgiving and doesn't handle the impact of a strike well.

A basic trolling rig will consist of the main line tied to a swivel and then a heavier trace attached to that. For a short troll, a standard swivel may suffice; for longer periods and serious trolling, a ball-bearing swivel is a must. A double line before the swivel can also help protect the rig.

Make sure the drag is set properly — you don't want it cranked up too tight, as either something will break or the lure will be ripped out of the fish's mouth. Too loose, and an overrun and resulting bird's nest will follow. Set it so that you can comfortably pull line off the reel. Remember that there will be additional load when line is dragged over the rod.

When catching skipjack for bait rather than sport, a bungee line is a good option. The usual method is to have a line of heavy mono or light cord, with trace and lure attached. At the boat end, the main line is attached to a bungee cord. When a skippy hits the lure the bungee soaks up the impact and straightens. The fish can then be quickly dragged aboard, usually without stopping the boat.

Trolling speed

Speed is a hard one to describe, because it's all about the lure action.

- For tuna (and marlin) we typically troll at a speed of 7–8 knots.

- Kahawai trolling is generally at a slightly lower speed, perhaps 4–7 knots depending on lure type.

- If you are pulling bibbed lures for kingfish, you will travel even slower.

You will feel the vibration of the lure when it's right, while excess speed will probably cause it to jump out of the water.

As a rule (and an often-broken one, I should add), it's probably true that it's better to troll too fast than too slow — remember, fish are aggressive and don't want the food to escape. But if the lure is bouncing from wave to wave or tumbling and spinning, then you are travelling too fast.

An interesting point to note, though, is that marlin have been hooked on lures travelling at 18 to 20 knots or more!

Apparently it is an incredibly impressive sight when a big fish hits a lure at that speed …

One trick that I use when the fish are being difficult is to hand-hold the trolling rod with the tip parallel to the water, and jerk the rod smoothly to make the lure look like it is attempting to flee. It usually works like a charm on fussy fish.

This snapper was taken while drifting and straylining a skipjack bait at the Bay of Islands. It weighed a whisker under 20 lb. The outfit used is an ideal one for both jobs. It's an Abu Garcia baitcaster fitted to a Berkley Gorilla Stick.

12 ∽ Other Options

Fishers are ingenious. If the same amount of time spent solving fishing problems was expended on other things, we'd have been to Mars and also found a cure for cancer! From early solutions such as the kontiki or 'galloping gertie', anglers are always looking for new and better ways of getting a bait into the strike zone. Over recent years there have been three worth commenting on.

Fishing kites

Fishing with kites from our surf beaches is a popular and affordable way to catch fish. With the way the best exponents operate, it is both a science and an art! The basics are fairly simple, though. A specialised kite is deployed, attached to a line that drags (typically) 25 baited hooks a kilometre or so out to sea.

A series of sinkers and floats is used to ensure that the hooks end up on the bottom. The kite is able to be set to deploy at an angle so that it will drag the line directly offshore. The main line is attached to a large reel, either manual or electric, for later retrieval.

There are variations on the theme, including the option of using a kite to set a line attached directly to a fishing rod and reel. Regardless, it's essential to set on a clean bottom, otherwise the hooks will snag and the main line and kite will likely be lost.

Kite fishing remains a great option when you are able to fish to the conditions. The kite cannot be deployed if the wind is onshore or too light, which means there are days that would otherwise be ideal that become unfishable.

Parore

Torpedoes

Because so many good fishing days were lost to kontiki and kite fishers through onshore winds, one of those ingenious fishermen decided there had to be a better way. The clever part was deciding to use the propulsion unit from an electric outboard and then waterproofing it into a design capable of towing the line and baited hooks out to sea. What started as a home industry has now developed into several successful companies marketing their products, in some cases internationally.

The torpedo part of the system usually consists of a moulded plastic tube, designed to hold the batteries and electronics. Attached to that, and hanging below, is the electric outboard motor and propeller. The control systems have been reworked as the designs have improved. At its most basic, there is a control to set the motor running time.

Various systems have been used to make the torpedo run straight, usually incorporating a trim tab or rudder of some kind. The latest deluxe models have a GPS fitted which takes over the direction-control side of the problem, sending the torpedo right to where it should be.

LEFT AND RIGHT: *Recently, my brother Craig has been using a torpedo off the Kaipara. He has an organised system complete with quad bike! The results look pretty good ...*

As with kite fishing, a reel is required on the beach to store and retrieve the main line. There are various options, starting with manual ones that look something like an electric fence unit through to electric models that take all the pain out of retrieving the line. Beach trolleys have also been developed to get the torpedo to the fishing site. Even electric versions of those are available!

A noticeable comment made by torpedo users is just how extensive some species are and how many fish there are relatively close to our surf beaches. South Island users have found snapper as far south as Hokitika, and elephant fish have become a regular target. Along the North Island coast snapper and gurnard are the main catch, but the quantities and size have surprised many users.

I'm yet to hear of any unhappy or unsuccessful torpedo users.

Kayak fishing

Of all the changes and trends in fishing over the last decade, the art of fishing from kayaks has seen the greatest advance. Kayak fishing has become a sport of its own, with dedicated clubs, businesses, contests and more. Kayaking seems to tick all the boxes — it's beautiful in its simplicity but can be as technical as you want to make it, and it's healthy, relatively cheap and, with the advantage of stealth, very, very efficient.

A little under a decade ago, I met an early adopter of this sport while at a fishing contest. His name is Rob Fort and since that day, through his writings and actions, Rob has developed into arguably New Zealand's foremost exponent of fishing from kayaks. He makes his living teaching and guiding in the beautiful Coromandel and also manufacturing kayak accessories. Over the ensuing years I have seen Rob towed by a kingfish at speeds a water skier would be proud of, catch snapper at sizes anyone would be proud of, and all the while contributing further to our general fishing skills. I have drifted beside him in a boat catching huge snapper, at times being out-fished.

Sometimes we were developing techniques in parallel, such as the way we fish slow jigs in a hybrid style of fishing with softbaits; at other times Rob forged ahead with his own findings. He, more than anyone else, has developed the technique of fishing very small softbaits and working in very shallow water where more fish exist than we had realised. All those techniques have flowed into general fishing.

Fishing kayaks are a specialist item. Yes, you can fish from a domestic-type sit-in kayak — however, the dedicated sit-on fishing models are incredibly stable and designed with all the features a fisher requires. For example, there

BELOW AND RIGHT: *Kayak fishing has its own range of specialised products — anchor packs and sea anchors, plus nets and gaffs with floats make up just part of the range. Rob Fort (below) is shown with a typical Coromandel snapper. Note the equipment fitted to his kayak, which includes rod holders, electronics, security leashes and much more. For further information contact him at Coromandel Kayak Adventures.*

are hatches designed to keep important gear away from the water. Proper rod holders, cable systems to control the anchor, mounts for electronics, storage for the catch to keep blood out of the water, a seat with a back, a steerable rudder, places to tie off equipment on, and much more, make up the typical equipment list.

When I talked to Rob about what makes a great fishing kayak, his first comments related to safety. Apart from being a means of flotation and support in the water, the PFD (personal floatation device) becomes an integral part of the

system. Dedicated models have pockets for storing tools and equipment and even a means of securing drinks. There needs to be several means of communication: running a VHF radio is the first choice, particularly with the availability of waterproof and affordable hand-held models, while fully waterproof cases are available so a cell phone can also be used.

Another point Rob made concerned the choice of paddle. The design and length is important, and choosing the blade type and design and matching that to each individual around the need for power or range will make all the difference to comfort and safety.

BELOW: *Rob Fort does even more with his kayak. He's also an accomplished spearfisherman who uses his kayak to access remote spots. The snapper weighed around 27 pounds!*

Proper clothing is another important part of kayaking. Because you will be wet from spray and also having to deal with variable temperatures, sweat and fish handling, technical clothing designed to breathe and take the knocks is essential. Rob uses Sharkskin products in particular; their suits and tops are designed for outdoor water sports, and are windproof and also sunproof to SPF30+.

As for the boat, the best option is to research the brands and their suitable models. Talk to those using the boats and gauge their opinions. Be aware that many retailers and personalities do have particular brand affiliations, though, so pick through the information carefully! It's a bit like buying a car. Check what equipment is standard and find out what will entail an additional cost. Rob makes the suggestion that you should paddle as many boats as possible before buying.

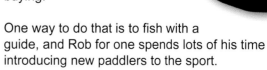

One way to do that is to fish with a guide, and Rob for one spends lots of his time introducing new paddlers to the sport.

13 ∽ Fishing Rules and the Environment

These two things are really inseparable. We rely on the authorities to ensure that regulations are fair to all and give a guarantee of a resource available for the future. Our part is to respect those rules, respect the resource, keep rubbish out of the environment and take only what is needed.

When you are new to fishing, the rules and regulations around the taking of fish may seem confusing. In reality, it's very straightforward and the information you need is easily obtainable.

The information below is provided as a guide and a starting point, and does not constitute the most recent requirements for your area — these change regularly. Please ensure that you know the rules!

Red Gurnard

The Ministry for Primary Industries

This is the section of government currently responsible for the protection of the fisheries resource. They set the rules and enforce them. The ministry has a very good website that makes a wealth of information available. As well as all the detail on fishing regulations, there is information on releasing fish, safety, fish identification, net design and much more.

To access the site, go to **www.fish.govt.nz**.

A recent addition to the site is an app for smartphones that brings all the rules and information quickly to hand. It is easily downloaded from the website.

The basics — fish measurement

While all the information you need is available from the ministry site, there are a number of key points to be aware of. The first, and most critical, is how to measure a fish.

It is essential to remember that:

• a fish is measured from the V of the tail to the tip of the nose.

• It should be laid on a flat surface with the measuring device underneath the fish.

If you are taking fish you believe to be on or near the minimum size, remember that the only official measurement is the one the fisheries officer will be using.

Printed measures and inaccurate rulers have been found wanting in the past.

• For shellfish, the rules are similar. Measure scallops and paua in a flat line, not over the curve of the shell.

• Crayfish are different again. Spiny lobsters are measured between the tips of the spines on the second segment, while packhorse crayfish are measured by tail length. For spiny lobster (our common red crayfish), there are different measurements for males and females. (The crayfish, that is — not the person doing the measuring!)

The basics — fish numbers

Your maximum catch, known as the bag limit, can often be made up of a combination of various species. Some of those species may have an individual limit, or just be part of an overall limit made up of several species. For example, in the north you may have a limit consisting of a combination of species that may include kahawai, tarakihi and trevally. You then have a separate number of snapper you may take and yet another separate limit for hapuku and/or kingfish.

The numbers in each category, and for various species, may be different in each area. The ministry website explains the requirements clearly.

ABOVE: *Make sure you measure your fish properly — a direct line from the nose to the V of the tail is the official way.*

The rights of a fisheries officer

There are two types of fisheries officer you are likely to come across.

• The first is the full-time officer, and he or she has similar powers to a police officer — including the power of arrest. These officers can stop, search and detain in exactly the same way. You are entitled to see identification but if instructed to stop, you must.

• The second type of officer you will encounter is the honorary fisheries officer (or HFO). Contrary to the belief of some, the HFO has exactly the same powers as a full-time officer except for the power of arrest. You are entitled to see their identification. Treat an HFO exactly as you would a full-time officer and follow their instructions.

Officers of both types have extensive powers, and while TV programmes like *Coastwatch* have shown the worst of offending and human greed, the fact is that almost without exception the officers have a huge regard for both the sport and the resource and prefer to educate rather than prosecute. Obey the law and work with them, and we will have a wonderful resource for the generations to come.

ABOVE: *Well-known magazine editor Keith Ingram is also an honorary fisheries officer.*

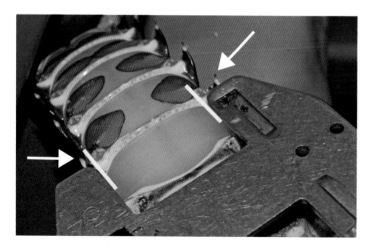

LEFT: *A male crayfish being measured. The spines on the second segment are marked with a white arrow. The inside of the measuring gauge is shown with a pair of yellow lines. This cray is easily big enough.*

The environment and fish handling

When I think about the practices we employed back in the 1970s when we first started fishing seriously, things have improved markedly. For example, we know how to catch many more fish than we did then, we know how to release them safely, we don't throw rubbish overboard, we use tackle that is safer for fish, we are better able to target our desired species and we are cognisant of the need to take only what we need.

The Quota Management System

The Quota Management System (QMS) has been touted as making many improvements to our fishing by restricting the commercial take to pre-ordained safe limits. It's not perfect, but it has certainly helped in the recovery of species in some areas, notably the snapper populations in the Hauraki Gulf.

Unfortunately the QMS is biased towards commercial take, and the simmering dispute between commercial and recreational anglers continues despite the efforts of many good men and women. It should be noted that some of the best fishing improvements have been made when industry members have taken ownership themselves; nowhere is that better illustrated than in the southern rock lobster fishery where quota-holders took the pain while it rebuilt and are now making a profit from their efforts. And they deserve to.

From a personal point of view, I believe commercial fishing isn't bad and commercial fishers aren't the enemy; however, there are many who would argue that powerful fishing companies, those who own most of the quota, are. As I write, the threat of snapper quota cuts for recreational fishers in the north has made the news — yet commercial operators are likely to have no cuts to their quotas. That situation is clearly wrong. Commercial fishers need to reinvent their industry with environmentally sustainable practices — which return higher values — favoured over the more destructive ones (such as trawling).

However, the war will never be over until the day a government recognises the value of recreational fishing financially: as a tourist draw, as a high-participant sport and, perhaps most importantly, as a part of the social fabric that levels out people of all races and social standings. On that day we can start to build the greatest fishery in the world. After all, paraphrasing what the character Ray Kinsella said in the film *Field of Dreams*: 'Build it, and the people will come.' It's just unfortunate that, so far, the government has made the fish resource that should belong to all New Zealanders and be operated on their behalf into a property right owned by individuals and able to be traded. That's enough politics!

Hapuku

Bass

Tackle and fish handling

One important component of the plan for the future of recreational fishing has been buy-in from industry. Some of that is driven by their customers, and some by the ethics of the particular company. Sometimes the downstream spin-off for these companies can be huge.

Take, for example, the world's largest tackle company, Pure

Fishing. Over recent years they have been enthusiastic in their support for more environmentally sustainable practices. Perhaps the most conspicuous of the resulting products is Gulp! softbait. Being a biodegradable product, Gulp! doesn't impact on the environment the way lures made from petrochemicals do. Not only that, but softbaits encourage fish to strike the jig head, meaning that most are hooked

behind the jaw which enables easy and safe release.

Another great example of the way Pure Fishing works for the environment I noted the first time they handed me one of their silicone landing nets. Designed to protect the scales and coating on the fish, the net is a quantum leap forward in safe handling. Another serious advantage is that hooks and jigs hook up less and if they do they are quick to release, which all adds to reducing the stress on a fish you are going to release.

Lip grippers, too, are sold by Berkley and aid safe release. By holding the business end of a fish and keeping it in the water while the hook is removed, its survival is assured. If the fish has to be lifted before being released, it's important that this is done with support so that its spine isn't stretched.

It's important that we support those companies that support our efforts to protect and enhance our resource.

Taking only what you need

The greatest recent advance in knowledge arguably involves the way we keep fish after capture. We once stored fish in wet sacks. The first fish box I ever used was a plastic rubbish bin. Now, we have fully insulated fish bins that are effective and affordable. Saltwater ice is freely available for packing fish, and the quality of the product we take home now is immeasurably better so nothing is wasted.

Perhaps the most important thing to learn is to know just what you need to keep. There are some days where I release everything I catch, and some where I give part of my catch to others. On other days, I will keep a bag limit. I make no apologies for that, and nor should I have to. I use everything I keep.

There has been a tendency by some fishing media people and forum contributors to almost place themselves above the general populace because they don't keep a limit or they release all their big fish. That is just nonsense.

You have to use common sense when making the decision. And while it's a fantastic feeling to release a big fish (I've released several snapper weighing over 20 pounds), I don't begrudge anyone catching and keeping their big fish. As long as nothing is wasted and you stay within legal limits, then the decision is yours — and yours alone — to make.

The commonly used phrase 'limit your catch, don't catch your limit' should be a guide, not a rule. Just expect my wrath, and that of all my mates, if you exceed the numbers, mistreat the catch, sell it or waste it …

Tips for proper fish handling ...

- Fish with an appropriate hook size. Use larger hooks in preference, to avoid undersized fish.
- When appropriate, methods such as lures and softbaits potentially do less damage to fish that will be released.
- Choose biodegradable softbaits such as Berkley Gulp! over tails made from petrochemicals.
- Choose silicone rubber or knotless mesh nets for release fishing.
- Handle fish with wet hands or a wet towel to protect their scales and mucous covering.
- Don't lift a fish to be released from the water. If it must be lifted, use a net or support the body of the fish to protect the spine and internal organs.
- Don't throw a released fish from a height into the water.
- If you see fishers taking undersized or excess fish, attempt to educate them in their error — if you can do so safely. If they suddenly no longer speak English or become aggressive, then call 0800 4 POACHER (0800 476 224).

The author with a snapper of over 6 kg taken on a slow jig. So often we find the slow jig will account for the best snapper of the day.

14 ⌒ Lures and How to Fish Them

This chapter specifically refers to using lures other than softbaits — those follow next chapter. The reason for covering lures first is that the use of metal lures has grown in popularity once again. Many new styles, most with a Japanese influence, have found their way to our shores. While I love to fish just with metal lures, we more often use a hybrid system incorporating softbaits and metal lures. An understanding of 'metal lure theory' will help you get the best out of all situations.

Top water lures

Top water lures are those designed primarily to generate strikes on the surface. The most familiar is the popper. This style usually incorporates a cupped (concave) face designed to catch the water, creating noise and commotion. Poppers are great for catching kingfish in our waters and are essential if you travel through the Pacific — from experience, I can tell you there is nothing like the sight and feel of more than 100 pounds of giant trevally crashing a popper! Poppers are fished using a jerking, 'popping' motion designed to simulate an injured bait fish. The more noise you can make, the better. The action is made with the rod. High-speed retrieves aren't required; strong spin rods with matching reels are, though.

A second style of top water lure has recently become popular. It's called a stick bait and is fished in a similar way to a popper, both on the surface and just below it. The shape also allows high-speed retrieves. Stick baits range from affordable to stunning works of art costing hundreds of dollars. They appeal not just to kingfish — snapper and many tuna species are suckers too, and I've heard rumours of marlin falling for their allure.

Trolling lures

Typically, most anglers' first experience with trolling will be to drag a small 'bone' lure for kahawai. Kahawai are great to catch and the easiest species to target throughout most of New Zealand. While it's called a bone lure, referring to the material used to manufacture the lure in times past, today they are made of plastic, but there is still much in common with the original designs.

Trolling is well covered in the boat fishing chapter, so here I just will cover the types of lures used for trolling.

BELOW: *From left; Pro Hunter GT Minnow stick baits, Pro Hunter Crystal Killer popper, Pro Hunter Ko-Jack minnow.*

Saltwater flies — Also great as a trolling lure. A few should always be kept in your collection.

Feather lure

Saltwater fly

Feather lures — Trolling feathers have accounted for huge numbers of fish throughout the world. From tuna such as skipjack, albacore and yellowfin, through to massive bluefin and marlin, feather jigs are a very versatile lure. Kingfish, kahawai and anything else that takes a lure are also potential targets. Feather lures also create a beautiful pulsing motion if you jerk then drop back the rod tip when trolling.

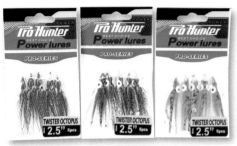

LEFT: *My personal favourite is the 2.5 inch pink vinyl squid. Lead weights are available that insert inside the squid. A small ball sinker will also work.*

Vinyl skirts — Smaller versions of the skirts used on larger lures aimed at marlin make great trolling lures. They can be purchased in various sizes, rigged and ready; however, the best way is to have a box of the tapered lead jig heads made for the purpose plus a selection of vinyl skirts in various sizes and colours. That way you will be ready to match any situation. Use a straight trolling hook — any bend or kirb in the hook will cause it to spin.

Minnow lures — There is a huge range of trolling minnow styles on the market. From surface plugs such as the stick baits mentioned earlier, to lures with huge bibs designed to pull deeply into the water, there will be something to cover your need. Because we have a comparatively limited range of species to target with such lures, they are used less than in other areas of the Pacific. Kingfish primarily, followed by tuna and kahawai, are almost all we have to chase with them. I say almost, as snapper too are known to grab minnow lures. Taking that a step further, Pure Fishing has introduced Sebile lures to our market and is currently developing a range and fishing style to target snapper in particular. The results are promising!

Other trolling lures — Softbaits can be trolled for short distances between work-ups and I have found them to be effective on skipjack at times. Metal spinners that would normally be cast with a spinning rod or trolled for trout are also useful. Larger resin lures become the domain of the game fisher, a subject that needs a book all of its own …

Paravanes and downriggers

Sometimes it's best to get the lure a little deeper. There are two options for that: paravanes and downriggers. A paravane (also

ABOVE: *This Sebile lure is weighted for casting but can also be slow trolled.* **RIGHT:** *A paravane is a great way to get a lure a little deeper. This one can be adjusted to make the lure swim to the side as well as deeper.*

known as a trolling board) is fitted before the lure and is designed to drag the lure down. There are two popular types: one is a basic curved board with limited range; while the common plastic model, the one shaped like a paper dart, has adjustments for depth and for dragging the lure sideways. There is also a third kind of board, harder to find here, that consists of a stainless steel plate with a sliding ring and weight. The advantage it has is that the board is tripped when a fish strikes, causing it to return to the surface.

I highly recommend using a paravane when trolling for kahawai. Just remember that if you troll it from a rod, it will need to be a strong rod due to the extra drag. Whatever you do, make sure that the drag is set properly and don't suddenly accelerate the boat or you might end up with a two-piece rod or a broken line.

Downriggers take the lure (or bait) even deeper. A thin wire is attached to a lead ball (typically weighing nearly 5 kg), and a release clip holds the trolled line. The wire is stored on a large spool and released via a brake. Better downriggers have a line counter to show the depth, while economy models may use the spool diameter to register the depth.

Downriggers are a fantastic additional tool, but are best for slow-speed use and need to be used judiciously around any structure that could cause the wire or weight to snag.

Lures for casting with light tackle

Casting a lure from a wharf, off a beach, from a boat or at a river mouth is great fun. Just about any lure with enough weight to be cast can be used. Typically, a metal lure, often called a spoon, is used. Some are indeed shaped like a spoon, and over the years many teaspoons have been transformed into fish-catching wonders! My earliest spinning attempts

ABOVE: *Downriggers, such as this model from Scotty, will take a lure or bait even deeper than a paravane.*
RIGHT: *Spoon lures remain a great casting option for most species.*

consisted of cutting up pieces of copper sheet (one advantage of being a plumber's son), attaching hooks and turning them into lures to catch the perch in Hamilton's lake.

The lures most likely to be used now are a hex lure, looking something like a solid piece of metal cut at an angle front and back; a small bait-fish-shaped lure of the type we use for jigging on the bottom; or a spoon/wobbler type lure of which the Toby is the best known. The Toby is arguably the most popular trout spinning lure in New Zealand and is just as effective when used in salt water; it can also be slow-trolled. Softbaits also make great casting lures.

Please keep in mind that casting spinners in this way can result in not only saltwater fish being caught but also sea-run trout and salmon. Different fishing regulations, and local variations, will likely apply.

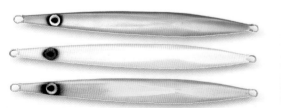

Lures for bottom fishing

Over the last few decades, fishing with lures on the bottom has gone through several peaks and troughs. Back in the 1970s we began jigging for kingfish at Raglan with heavy metal lures called Mavericks and Irons. I still remember the very first day I tried the techniques, which I had read about in Australian and American magazines. From having never caught a kingfish we had accounted for more than 50 by the end of day one. It was a lesson, not just in lure fishing but in embracing different techniques and tackle. I have been in love with lure fishing ever since.

Big metal jigs

Our early efforts at jigging may have been the first on the west coast, but jigs had already been introduced to the waters around White Island. What we were all primarily doing was speed jigging — cranking the lures as fast as possible to the surface and waiting for the crash strike. While that still works, over the past decade or so a new technique has been brought to our shores. Japanese anglers introduced us to a radical new jig method

LEFT: *There is an extensive range of long jigs available, with the positioning of the weight in the lure being the main difference. Assist hooks are essential for the best results.*

using long, heavy, thin and flat lures that were 'jerked' to create the strike rather than cranked at speed. The immediate advantage was that it was possible to jig for hours, rather than minutes, without an arm falling off or an elbow locking up.

Long jigs, or knife jigs as they are also known, have another difference, too: rather than having a hook attached to the bottom, a hook, usually two, is tied to a special Kevlar cord and attached at the top of the lure. It's called an assist hook. Many are attached with a simple loop to the

Lure size ...

With the range of options you'll see in any well-stocked tackle shop it can be hard to choose what to use. Carrying a range is important, but you need a starting point.

Poppers — These come in floating and sinking models. Start at around 150 mm or 200 mm. If long casts are required, a narrow and end-weighted popper is needed; they are often described as pencil poppers. A size around 150 mm is ideal for stick baits, too. Big is best for both these styles.

Minnow lures — Aim for bait fish in size. Of course, a bait fish could be a 500 mm long kahawai … Typically, a body length of 100–150 mm is a good place to begin. Think about the average size of a pilchard or a mullet.

Long jigs — The size of these will depend on the rating of the rod used and the depth of the water. A weight of 200 g is probably a typical starting point. Lure length is pretty much irrelevant — it's all about weight here.

Small metal jigs — Three factors count: depth, drift speed (those two are connected) and bait-fish size. The basic rule is as small and light as possible. Typically, 60/80/100 g lure is what you will start with. I carry sizes from 40 g to 150 g on a normal trip.

jig; however, when chasing the largest predators, such as big kingfish, properly rigged assist hooks are actually attached to the main line with a solid ring while the lure is attached with a split ring, allowing the lure to be changed without re-rigging. And solid rings don't straighten out, either.

There are two general styles of long jig: centre-weighted and bottom-weighted. The former tend to flutter more on descent and are particularly suited to shallow water. Bottom-weighted jigs drop faster and deeper, and are particularly good if hapuku and bass are being targeted. As with all lure fishing, keep a selection of several styles, weights and colours, as you never know what will be best on any given day. The standard sizes for the jigs are described by weight: 200, 300 and 400 g are the usual, although you will see both heavier and lighter ones on the market.

The rods used, as described in an earlier chapter, are very specialised. Short, strong and using only the best

*LEFT: Its not just big fish that grab long jigs! Snapper are incredibly aggressive and are also a target. **TOP RIGHT:** Kevin Green, owner of Allied Outdoors Ltd, takes his job seriously! Here he is hooked up to a good kingfish on a Pro Hunter Salty Dancer long jig that he was testing. **RIGHT:** Tony Dawson with a Bay of Islands kingfish caught on a long jig. Note the selection on the baitboard!*

of hardware, they are rated by lure weight or, more often, line class. Because they are designed exclusively for braided lines, the PE rating is used (see page 58 for a full explanation). The rods are matched with either very powerful spin reels or narrow-spool overhead reels.

Getting the best from long jigs is all about the action. The specialists make it look easy: the technique, called mechanical jigging, involves putting the rod butt under your arm and holding the foregrip. Then, with the rod tip down and the reel handle up, lift the rod while simultaneously rotating the reel handle down. Then, drop the rod tip while turning the reel handle up. Repeat until the jig is hit or it's lifted too far from the structure. It gives a beautifully erratic action that predators love! Better still, it's economical on energy expenditure — at least until a big kingfish grabs the jig. Feel free to mix the standard retrieve up with fast retrieves or other actions.

LEFT: *My partner Kim Standfield is more than a match for me with a fishing rod; why do it one at a time when there are two hooks on the slow jig!*

While kingfish are the typical target for long jigs over structure, they are also loved by deep-water predators such as bass, hapuku and trumpeter. Use shorter retrieves and keep the lure as close to the bottom as possible for those species. Snapper and big blue cod will also grab the lure.

Small metal jigs

Once upon a time, in a previous century, thinking fishermen found that our two most popular species, snapper and blue cod, would eat lures. While I'm sure that many of these initial captures were accidental, those clever early adopters realised that there was potential for more. Following the success of techniques developed overseas using metal lures such as Stingsildas, a whole new sport was developed.

Through the 1980s, lures such as Grim Reapers and Lethal Lures, both made here in New Zealand, dominated the market. Much of the fishery was based around the Hauraki Gulf where snapper school, feed under work-ups and travel through channels and corridors. From that point of view not much has changed; however, the range of species found to eat metal, the huge improvement in lure type and action and the skill of the anglers using them have all grown astronomically.

My favourites

The lures we use now are represented by many patterns, styles and brands. One brand I have worked alongside in recent years has created arguably the most suitable lure of any available in our market. Pro Hunter has developed a massive range of lures, and from that range the importer has carefully selected those that best suit our species. Perhaps the lure that has done most to reignite the metal jigging craze is one called the Prowler.

The Prowler is my go-to lure anywhere I'm fishing. Over recent years I have caught huge red emperor on them at the remote Chesterfield Reef (Aussies get more excited over a big emperor than we do over a big snapper) and caught multiple species on them in Tonga, but, more importantly, I've caught lots of snapper on Prowlers here in New Zealand.

The Prowler, as you can see from the picture, is end-weighted. Its stubby shape makes it sink quickly when attached at the tail, while attaching at the head increases the flutter action. The two assist hooks have a vinyl skirt and lumo bead to add even more attraction. It is the flexibility of the design — with three attachment points — that makes it so versatile. Prowlers come in weights from 40 g to 300 g, making it a pattern that can cover everything from pan-sized snapper and cod through to kingfish and hapuku.

Whenever I see a work-up that may hold snapper below and the water is deeper than 25 metres (and often when it's not), I will fish a Prowler first. That is even more important with less-than-ideal wind and sea conditions; the Prowler will hold position better in adverse conditions, as heavier lures can be used because the design has more weight in a smaller lure length than comparative lures.

When fishing in a more traditional manner with metal lures, and by that I mean drifting and exploring channels, shellfish beds, the edges of structure and work-ups in shallow water, the lures I choose will likely be more like a bait fish in design. The two I usually select are the Octo Angler and the Fanky. Both are Pro Hunter lures.

LEFT: *The Prowler is one of my favourite lures and if I had to select just one lure, it's this one!* **RIGHT:** *That's a Prowler hanging out of the jaw of that very big red emperor.*

- The Octo Angler is a typical bait-fish shape but slightly end-weighted, making it cast well too. Like all the lures we use, it has assist hooks with a vinyl skirt. The Octo Angler is definitely the lure I would prefer to select first every time.

- Over the last year or so, the Fanky lure has been used extensively for our snapper missions. While it's available in sizes up to 200 g it's the smaller models, from 20 g to 80 g, that really excite me. Being more symmetrically weighted, it has a tendency to flutter and that's an action snapper love. I wouldn't go jig fishing without a range of Fanky lures in my kit.

Of all the changes that have been made to lures, perhaps the biggest improvement has been the simplest — the dumping of treble hooks in favour of single hooks and then assist hooks. We get a massively higher strike rate than we ever did with trebles, we no longer lose 30 per cent of the

THIS PAGE: *Two of my favourites; at the bottom of the page is the Fanky lure. It seems to have just the right action for snapper in particular. Above is the Octo Angler. The way the weight is designed into it, and the way it moves, makes the Octo Angler my preferred first choice for most conditions.*

fish we hook, and we no longer damage fish that are to be released. Better for the fish, better for the fisher — how good is that?

Other factors

While the lures have changed, so too has the tackle. Braid has transformed our jig fishing; I couldn't imagine using nylon now. After trying all sorts of options I have come to the conclusion that our typical softbait rods, ranging in length from 6 feet to 7 feet, are the ideal tools for fishing metal lures in depths to around 35 metres. The action, the simplicity and

How things have changed ...

In this chapter I described our first-ever attempt at jigging kingfish and the 50 fish we caught. While we could legally have kept them all, we didn't. Obviously we kept a few big ones, but mainly killed the smaller ones for smoking. At our second jigging attempt we were just as successful, this time keeping only the smallest fish for the smoker and releasing around 40 fish. But as the day progressed, it was what happened with other fishers that blew us away.

Raglan's Jackson's Reef, particularly at those times with limited electronics available, was the sort of place where if you saw someone catching fish you would move and anchor near them. If you ever saw two boats together, the chances are you'd quickly become the third boat. See three boats and you knew something was up, so there would soon be 10 around you. It was an effective system.

That particular day was hot and sunny and the snapper weren't biting. However, on our boat it was continuous hook-ups with kingfish crashing the Maverick and Iron lures. Before long the watching gallery consisted of more than a dozen boats. The anglers in the other boats had no idea at all what we were doing. Then it started — we were abused! Every time we released a kingfish, another round of abuse would begin. We couldn't believe it.

I don't have the slightest problem with keeping a bag limit of fish on occasions, or releasing everything on other days, but that choice is mine to make. The fact that some of the other anglers nearby felt that everything should be killed really disturbed us. And while that incident was 35 years ago and hasn't been the only time I've experienced the angling equivalent of road rage, it's really good to know that in the twenty-first century the attitude of the vast majority is geared around preserving the resource while harvesting a renewable amount.

I'm so pleased that things have changed!

the surprising strength of the rods dedicated to that style of fishing are just as good with small metal lures. Once the depth increases and the lures grow heavier, then the extra capacity and ease of use afforded by an overhead reel is the answer, meaning that a slightly different rod is better suited. As an example, Pure Fishing has Berkley and Abu Garcia rods in their range that complement their matching softbait rods. Typically these will be 5-foot-6 to 6-foot long and slightly faster in taper than the more parabolic softbait rods.

When fishing small metal jigs, extremes of action aren't necessary; in fact, I've caught many fish with the rod sitting in a rod-holder. Because braid is used, almost all the action applied to the rod is sent to the lure. Typically, a moderately fast lift-and-drop motion is used, with most strikes happening on the drop. The trick is to keep the lure on or near the bottom, meaning that when drifting, line needs to be fed out regularly. Once the angle starts to get steeper, it's time to retrieve and start again.

Drop the tip quickly and wait for the line to straighten (making sure it doesn't wrap around the rod tip), and be ready for the bite. I often wait several seconds before lifting again, as sometimes the strike comes well after the lure stops and it will feel like a fish biting on a normal bait. If at any time you notice slack line as you drop the jig, then lock up and strike — a fish has picked up the lure! While I mostly fish the lures directly below the

boat, I will also mix things up by casting the lure away and working it back along the bottom.

Fishing around work-ups is covered in the softbait chapter.

Slow jigs

A further category of lure was introduced to our market a decade ago. Collectively known as slow jigs, these lures are designed to be fished in a very slow motion allowing the pulsing action of the fine silicone skirt to do the work. On more days than not we catch our biggest snapper on a slow jig.

The best way to fish them is not to! Drop the lure to the bottom, wind it up a metre or so, then put the rod in a rod-holder with the drag set slightly lighter than you normally would. You will know if a fish has found it: either the rod will double over or it will bounce and look like a fish is eating the lure like a bait, which is exactly what it is doing. Don't rush to pick it up, as the lure will do the work for you.

Alternatively, fish the slow jig like a normal metal jig but make the rod lift-and-drops very, very slow. Another method is to wind the lure up very slowly. All the options will work. There are a couple of styles of slow jig — one has a longer head and may have two attachment points to vary the action. The Pro Hunter Crazy Charlie is an example of that. The other has a ball or oval head with a single, slightly offset, connection point; the Pro Hunter Salty Ghost is that type of jig.

I fish both styles, but probably favour those with the ball-shaped head. My favourite way to fish slow jigs is in a hybrid system alongside softbaits. It's explained in the softbait chapter.

When it comes to tackle, I have some personal thoughts on what is best. Probably most of the fish I have taken on slow jigs have been on softbait rods, mainly through necessity. They are fine if you are hand-holding the rod, but when left in the rod-holder there is too much whippy movement, particularly in less-than-ideal sea conditions. My preference is to use a baitcaster with a slightly heavier action, which is the same rod I would use in deep water with small metal lures.

I've actually also taken that a step further by using a kayak rod with my slow jigs. The short butt and tip still keep the lure far enough away from the boat, yet the shorter overall length means the action isn't too violent. A rod 5-foot or 5-foot-6 long is ideal.

Lure colour

So many options are available that it can be hard to know where to start. To be honest, often colour is the least important of the variables — size, weight, depth fished and movement can be more important. That said, the following are my own findings from several decades of lure fishing. They aren't necessarily right or wrong, just what has worked for me.

Poppers — The red head (with a white body) is the first to choose in almost any situation. I haven't fished stick baits a lot, but my first choice has been a very dark colour to create a visible silhouette.

Minnow lures — Personally I prefer any bait-fish colour, so a blue/white/silver colouration will be first choice.

Spinning/casting — A sliced stainless hex lure or a Toby lure, always in black!

Long jigs — I don't have a preference really, although blue, silver-white, black and pink will usually feature in my colour choices, in that order. Far more importantly I have found that if a kingfish strikes and misses a lure, you will often get follows without bites. Changing to a completely different colour will often immediately trigger a strike.

Small metal jigs — For the Prowler lures I have had the best success with pink/white patterns. There is a photo on page 152 of a red/orange Prowler, a colour not currently available, which has now been smashed to pieces by many fish. It is now my favourite!

For bait-fish-style lures like the Octo Angler I will choose a bait-fish colour first, a combination of blue/silver/ pink. I'm happy to change if it isn't producing results. There is an orange/green Fanky lure that I love. It's my first-choice colour in that style.

While all the metal lures mentioned are already lumo in their finish, if you are fishing deeper water for hapuku and bass there is nothing to stop you adding extra lumo tube in front of the lure. I have even heard of anglers joining two lure bodies together in line to create extra weight, movement and noise.

Slow jigs — Absolutely no question: the green with orange flash, often called a Fire Tiger, is fished before any other colour every time. Note the comments about the slow jig often catching the biggest fish!

Trolling lures — The bone lure in white is essential, with green or silver as an interchange. A white saltwater fly is also irreplaceable. With small feathers and vinyl lures trolled for tuna, a green/white, pink/white or blue/white combo is the norm. However, later in the season I find that a pink/red colour is far and away the best for skipjack tuna.

ABOVE: *The stainless steel bone jig is a favourite of many anglers.* **BELOW:** *Snapper love Fanky jigs! The author with a Coromandel snapper that fell to a metal jig.* **OPPOSITE:** *I went fishing with Danny (L) and Darryll (R) from Marine Direct Ltd, to show them how to use softbaits. Instead, every fish we caught that day took a metal jig. Which is why you should cover all the bases!*

Measures that we use ...

You will have noticed by now that there is a mixture of imperial and metric units throughout the book.

I make no apology for that!

The fact is that there is no replacement for a twenty pound snapper! A nine point something kilo snapper just isn't the same ...

The industry still has a mix of measurements, such as 15 kg or 30 lb line, while lures are usually sold by weight in grams, sinkers in ounces, rods in either feet and inches or metres.

For that reason we have both metric and imperial too.

15 ⌒ Softbaits

It's nearly a decade since the night the first ever Gulp! softbait was fished in New Zealand. I know, because I was there! It caught a snapper and from that moment my fishing was changed forever. A short time later, April 2006 to be exact, I was aboard a boat at Great Barrier Island with the New Zealand Gulp! importer. I stood with my camera for literally five minutes and in that time five snapper were caught, the biggest weighing 16 pounds. After six minutes I picked up a rod, and caught my first snapper on the very first cast. By the end of that first day I had accounted for the first-ever snapper weighing over 20 pounds caught in New Zealand on a softbait. And that was just the beginning. What follows is just the entry point into your own softbait fishing adventure ...

The difference

Flexible plastic lures are not new. They have been mainstays in the American bass market for years, and still catch many fish. Most plastic baits are made from petrochemicals and as such are not designed to be biodegradable. Some incorporate a scent that will leach from the bait.

Softbaits — and Gulp! is far and away the market leader — are made from a food-grade material that does break down but still incorporates all the flexibility of soft plastic baits. Further still, they absorb the special Gulp! 'juice' and disperse it in the water.

OPPOSITE: *One of the most enjoyable days of softbait fishing I've ever had happened at Coromandel. Being just before Christmas we kept a few bigger fish for the smoker while releasing probably 50 more. It was made even better by sharing it with good people; my partner Kim and good friend Tony Dawson.*

The biodegradability of the bait is what separates a softbait from the soft plastics. This chapter is concerned only with softbaits.

Getting started

To fish softbaits you will need the following:

- a suitable rod and reel combo with braid
- a selection of jig heads in various weights
- a selection of softbaits in different colours and styles
- braid scissors
- a fluorocarbon leader
- a sea anchor on the boat.

And that is it. Fishing softbaits is incredibly simple when reduced to its essence.

Rods and reels

Selecting the correct rod and reel is critical to success. The standard softbait rod will cover 80 per cent of your needs, with deep-water fishing requiring specialist tackle. The typical rod is around 7-foot and rated at 6 to 10 kg, or possibly lighter. It will usually have a parabolic action, meaning that it bends through most of the blank. If you haven't used or picked up a softbait rod before, you may initially think it's far too light to catch a big fish. You would be wrong. While the rods are light, they are incredibly powerful with a large amount of reserve power in the butt. They are designed to be light because you will be holding and casting with the rod for extended periods.

Because braid is the only way to fish softbaits, and it has no stretch, the rod is required to absorb extra load. The parabolic action does that during the fight and on a strike. It also helps to keep the lure in place by applying extra pressure.

The range of suitable rods has widened over recent years and it can be confusing to walk into a tackle shop and select one.

Here's what I recommend: ask to see a 7-foot Berkley Dropshot rod. The Dropshot was the original rod designed to suit our conditions, and has seen more improvements since first being introduced. Once you have handled one, you will know what a suitable rod should feel like. Then you can compare other rods until you find the one you want. While you can't beat the purity and feel of a great one-piece rod, most you will see are two-piece and that is the best choice for storage and travel. The other key things to look at are the guides and the grips. Remember that you will be holding the rod most of the day and casting repeatedly, so go for the best components.

Small, powerful spin reels are used for softbait fishing, and the changes in spin reel technology over recent years are astonishing. Powerful drags, high-quality bearings and waterproof construction have made the spin reels of today almost indistinguishable from those of the past.

Line capacity requirements aren't great. Typically a size 30 or 40 reel is used, and depending on the spool itself it may hold anywhere between 120 and 300 metres of suitable line. We generally use either a full 300-metre spool of braid or else a 125-metre roll with a backing line behind it. Nylon is fine as a backing line, but you need to

OPPOSITE FAR LEFT: *Blue cod love softbaits too!* **LEFT:** *The Berkley Dropshot rod is still the one the others are compared to. The graphics and grip materials change most seasons but the design has only improved.* **ABOVE:** *It's easy to see the parabolic action of a properly designed softbait rod in this photo. The position of the rod is about as high as it needs to be lifted. More risks 'high sticking' and breakage.* **RIGHT:** *The Shakespeare brand is another in the Pure Fishing stable. The Deceiver is a very affordable spin reel option that I know (from experience) to perform well.*

wrap the knot between the backing and the braid so that it doesn't push through the line above, causing jams. Light braided fly line is a good alternative backing line to nylon. A full spool of braid is the best option.

Line and trace

There are now a number of suitable braids on the market; however, FireLine is the original line designed for this style of fishing and, in my opinion, still the best for casting. FireLine is quite a stiff braid and for that reason won't easily hang up or catch on the rod guides. This is critically important when casting repeatedly. Softer braids are absolutely fine, and even preferable, for deep-water fishing.

Don't think about using anything other than braid because your results will be very, very disappointing. Apart from the direct connection afforded because braid has almost zero stretch, its minimal diameter is critical to the results. The reason is that there is little resistance so the jig head can drop faster, be cast further and have less drag when drifting. The breaking strains of braid are a minefield, though. There are no true standards. Diameter will give you a guide, although it's not infallible either. See the chapter on lines for more on this.

Continuing on from what we covered in that chapter on lines, the most common braid I use is 6-pound FireLine original; sometimes we will use 8-pound. Work with a line-testing machine tells us that 6-pound FireLine breaks at close to 20 pounds. The sizing given on the spool is intended to indicate the equivalent nylon diameter, not the breaking strain: 6-pound FireLine is 0.15 mm in diameter. However, to confuse us further, the newer FireLine Exceed braid rated at 6 pounds is 0.09 mm in diameter, reflecting a figure closer to its breaking strain.

The only specific advice I can give you is that our 6-pound and 0.15 mm line does the job perfectly on the standard softbait rig. Whatever brand or style of braid you are looking at, start at around that same diameter.

Braid, while incredibly strong in itself, has very little resistance to damage. For that reason a leader is essential — and, even more importantly, a fluorocarbon leader. As mentioned previously, fluorocarbon has incredible wear characteristics and our testing shows that it has more than double the protection of nylon. To add to that, fluorocarbon has almost the same refractive index as water, making it almost invisible. Finally, it sinks (nylon floats), which

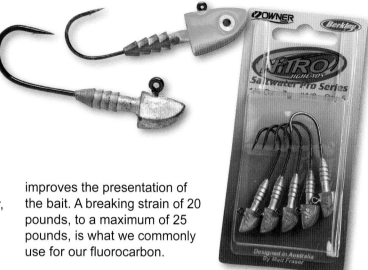

improves the presentation of the bait. A breaking strain of 20 pounds, to a maximum of 25 pounds, is what we commonly use for our fluorocarbon.

Jig heads

The softbait is attached to a jig head. Jig heads come in a range of weights and hook sizes. For best results, the bait needs to be balanced to the size of the head. That's not a difficult thing to do; the challenge is in selecting the right combination of bait size, jig head, line weight and trace to present the bait naturally. A light jig head is maybe a ¼ ounce in weight. The typical weight we will fish is from a ½ ounce to ⅝ ounce. Once you get over ¾ ounce, the heads are getting pretty heavy. Jig heads from ⅜ ounce to ⅝ ounce suit the standard 5-inch jerk shad style of softbait well. The shape of the head helps add action to the bait as it falls.

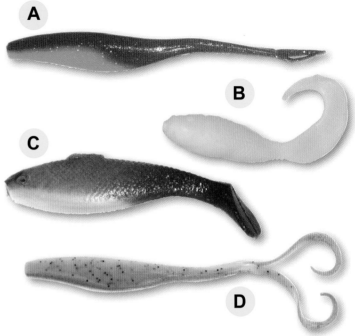

ABOVE: *Four of the best! A – Jerkshad in Nuclear Chicken colour. B – Swimming Mullet in Chartreuse. C – The Pogy in Anchovy coloration. D – The Crazy Legs in Lime Tiger.*
LEFT: *A properly rigged bait; the hook exits through the top of the bait at a predetermined point.*

The style of head and colour is less important than the quality of the hook. As with all fishing, check the hook point regularly. One trick we have learnt is that using small baits and matching jig heads doesn't reduce casting distance.

Baits

Softbaits can be moulded into just about any shape, but two dominate the market.

• The first is a traditional bait-fish shape called a jerk shad. It works best when action is imparted with the rod. It's our first choice for any fishing where we are casting the baits. We usually use a 5-inch jerk shad.

• The second type of bait is traditionally called a grub. The Gulp! Swimming Mullet is the one we know best. It has a curly tail that vibrates when the bait moves. It doesn't need a lot of movement — even the action of the boat drifting or the bait sinking gets it doing its thing. A 3-inch or 4-inch curly tail grub is the place to start.

There are multiple other shapes available as well. Some are bait-fish patterns, with or without tails. Others are unique designs that can look like anything from squid to crabs to worms. The range is extensive.

When it comes to colour, well, anything goes. There are a few things to know, though. The first is that the Nuclear Chicken you may hear about is a colour, not a pattern. It's red and green and it does catch fish! More snapper have been caught on a softbait in Nuclear Chicken colour than any other — and that is because more baits in Nuclear Chicken colour are fished than any other! Most patterns will be available in that shade.

I have only ever struck the situation where colour was critical once. Until I changed to the New Penny colour everyone else was using that time, I couldn't hook one of the big snapper that were savaging the baits. With the colour change, I immediately hooked up — and then, for the first time ever, I had a snapper completely spool me. I've never since experienced a situation where colour was so critical.

My preferred shades are usually natural fish colorations — Blue Pepper Neon (blue/silver), Sardine (black/silver), Lime Tiger (orange and green), anything in pink and, finally, chartreuse. One colour never to be without is called

Glow. It's a clear/white colour with lots of lumo attraction. A curly tail bait in Glow is deadly in low light, dirty water and when fished into dark.

Rigging a bait is a simple matter with a little practice. The hook point enters the centre front of the bait and the hook exits at a point when the bait lies flat on the hook shaft, not bunched up. The photo shows how it should be. When using a jig head the bait is fished with the hook point up. Most baits have an obvious up side (usually the darker colour is on top) and many have a slot in the bottom. The slot is used with special 'worm' hooks developed for fishing with soft plastics. For most of our fishing a jig head is the best option and we seldom use worm hooks.

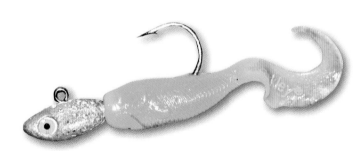

ABOVE: *Another look at a rigged bait. The pockmarks all over the head of the jig are bites from snapper teeth!*

The how and where

Softbaits are primarily fished in three ways. One is called wash fishing, where baits are cast into shallow areas, particularly into white water. The second is by drifting; this can be around structure, in open areas or under work-ups. The third method is fishing at anchor.

Wash fishing

Wash fishing is the most exciting way to catch fish that you can imagine! The boat is kept within casting range of rocks or a reef (extreme caution and skilled boat-handling may be required), and the baits are allowed to sink into the

gutters and wash where snapper and other predators are feeding. The challenge is to keep the bait within the feeding zones as long as possible, between casts, without hooking the bottom. This is achieved by matching the size and bulk of the bait to the weight of the jig head.

The thing that most amazes us is just how aggressive snapper are. They will smash softbaits on the surface and actively compete with each other to get at the bait. The bite from a big snapper in the wash is something you have to experience — they take no prisoners! Before we started softbaiting, we had little idea just how ferocious snapper could be.

Drifting

Drift fishing, especially when presenting baits under work-ups, is the most successful way to catch fish on softbaits. Any work-up at any time needs to be prospected. Many factors will indicate whether snapper, in particular, are present — such as the speed the work-up moves, how long it's been there, the time of year and what bird species are over it. A good sounder removes a lot of the guesswork.

Anywhere there is structure, there is fishing potential. Drifting the sand margins close to reefs is a favourite for

ABOVE: *The fish that sold a million packets of Gulp! The author caught the first ever snapper over 20 lb on Gulp! in New Zealand on his very first day fishing them. Pure Fishing had sent their Australian Pro Team over to show us how to do it. We all learnt fast and had a day we will never forget! The snapper weighed around 22 lb and was released.*

me; snapper and blue cod love those areas. Any foul patch is a given. Gravel patches along shorelines have been the most surprising place we have found good numbers of snapper. Drifting beside breaking reefs means you may be able to cast at the wash while simultaneously fishing baits on the bottom.

LEFT: *Perfect wash fishing territory! Big snapper were caught right on the spot shown. The white water provides cover as well as transport for food.*

As previously covered in the boat fishing chapter, a sea anchor is critical for drift fishing. I have three, in different sizes, and will choose which to use according to the tide and wind speed. Sometimes I will run two together.

At anchor

I have successfully fished softbaits while at anchor on many occasions. Generally, if you are catching fish on baits you will catch bigger ones on softbaits. One memorable session happened while filming for the *Gone Fishin'* TV show. We anchored near a reef close to Great Barrier Island. The berley was started and I sat back and waited for 10 minutes or so. While the others drifted, or cast, flesh baits behind the boat, I was able to cast further and more accurately right where the berley was heading. The hits were immediate, and the fish got continuously bigger until I eventually got all but spooled by a big fish (the hook pulled with only a few metres to go and the anchor only half way up …).

Again, it is the aggressiveness of snapper that makes this method work so well. Plus, you can cast the bait to the strike zone rather than battling wind and tide. Try it for yourself!

ABOVE: *Graeme Sinclair caught this fine 8 kg snapper while filming directly outside the world famous Hole in the Rock at the Bay of Islands. Like so many other snapper it fell for a Gulp! jerkshad in the nuclear chicken colour. Of course, the author felt no pressure to make sure he netted it cleanly while the cameras rolled!* **OPPOSITE:** *Mussel barges send out lots of berley when they are working; there are few better places to guarantee a feed of snapper!*

Working the baits

When working softbaits, keep in mind that there are three triggers: vision, scent and action. My belief is that vision is the least important. That needs explaining ... when fishing the washes, we sometimes get a hit straight after the lure splashes down. That is a vision trigger. As the bait falls down the rock face, or drifts along with the boat, the movement in the bait causes the bite. Simultaneously, the bait is leaving the special Gulp! juice in the water and that too triggers a bite. That explains why we can put the rod in the holder, leave it, and still catch fish.

Here's how I work the baits:

Wash fishing — cast into the wash, particularly into channels and gutters. Let the bait sink for a few seconds. How long depends on the depth; don't let it get to the bottom. If there is no bite, jerk the rod sharply a couple of times, then drop the tip. After a couple of seconds, take up a couple of turns of line and jerk it again. Repeat the process until the lure is away from the structure, then cast again. I will usually free-spool a couple of times as well to keep the bait in the strike zone.

Drifting — (1) Drop the bait directly to the bottom. Jerk the bait a couple of times, then drop the tip. Let more line out. Repeat. When the line starts to angle too much, wind in and repeat. (2). Cast the bait forward of and to the side of the boat, feed out extra line and let the boat drift towards the bait. If the line comes tight or goes unusually slack, wind in fast and hang on, because you have hooked up! Otherwise, stay in touch with the bait and feed out more line, working it the same way as in (1). Wind in and cast again.

Anchored — cast well back into the berley and let the bait sink through the trail. Most hook-ups will happen then. Before it reaches the bottom, jerk the bait a couple of times and wind in a metre of line. Repeat the process, which will have the effect of pulling the bait upwards through the berley.

ABOVE: *Methods continue to develop; the Pro Hunter Ecstasy Hunter is a hybrid lure with the feel of a slow jig but with the ability to bait it with a softbait or even cut bait.* **BELOW:** *The Pro Hunter Monster jig head is new and is designed to reduce tail bite offs by adding a second hook to the rig.*

Working the work-ups

Whether fishing with softbaits or with metal lures, work-ups are the place you want to be. While kingfish, kahawai and trevally are most likely in the upper part of the water column, snapper are typically on or near the bottom. Here's how we fish a work-up:

• Motor at low speed towards the anticipated travel direction of the work-up. Don't drive into it.

• Watch the sounder; often the groups of fish are away from the main work-up. Fish them if you see them.

• Stop in front of the work-up and drift. Let the work-up go past you. Depending on the wind and current, you may have to go round and stop in a different position.

• Often the snapper are well behind the work-up, so drift a little longer when the birds have passed.

• Use the GPS plotter to mark the position of any fish seen on the sounder. Often they will still be in the general vicinity well after the work-up has gone.

Hybrid fishing

Our best success when drift fishing, whether or not we are in a work-up, is by using a hybrid system consisting of slow jigs and softbaits (and metal jigs too). The system consists of at least one, and often two, slow jigs. They are set either side of the boat with the jig a metre or so off the bottom.

The movement of the boat gives the lure all the action it needs. As described earlier, softbait rods will usually handle the job but short baitcaster or even kayak rods are better still. A rod-holder is needed on each side of the boat, preferably far enough forward to stay out of the way of other rods being used. Adjustable rod-holders are perfect, as they will hold the rod almost horizontal with the tip well out from the boat at a suitable angle.

With the jigs set, we then fish softbaits and/or metal jigs as usual. The slow jigs need little attention other than adjusting the depth during the drift. If there is a fish interested, I can guarantee you will know all about it! Don't set the drags too tight, as some of the strikes are huge and the combination of braid and a loaded rod can be very unforgiving. Most days, the slow jig will account for the biggest fish.

Finally …

For all our success, softbait fishing is still in its infancy and we are continuing to learn more while developing new techniques, particularly around deep-water fishing. Try different things — there are no wrong methods. You may just discover new places that hold fish or new ways of getting baits to them.

LEFT: *Under the category of 'once in a lifetime' was an amazing day I spent with Carl Muir (pictured) from Epic Adventures at Tairua. We were doing a story on his charter out from the Aldermens. We had jigged kingfish with long jigs when something hit a lure near the surface. I cast a softbait to see what was around. We were shocked, but thrilled, to hook and land a great mahimahi. To catch one in New Zealand is special, but wait, there's more! For the next two hours we were able to hook a mahimahi at nearly every cast! It was fabulous sport and they are fantastic to eat. In the end only fatigue and the chance to catch a marlin brought the session to an end. A day I will long remember …*

16 ⤬ Filleting Your Catch

There was once a time when filleting a fish was a skill as basic as changing a tyre or repairing a fence. Watching TV cooking shows today is proof that few now have even basic skills in fish preparation. Fish fillets come plastic-wrapped from the supermarket …

Catching a fish comes with responsibilities; that fish needs to be either safely released or properly processed and eaten. We don't have the space in this book to cover all possibilities and methods for handling every species, so I have concentrated on the two most important: snapper and blue cod. Most other species are filleted in a similar way.

Before filleting

The way the fish is handled before ever seeing a knife is, arguably, more important than the filleting itself. Once upon a time, albeit 40 years ago, our fish box was a wet sack. We are very fortunate now that we have affordable, easily obtained insulated fish bins available. Even better,

saltwater ice is available at almost all tackle shops and service stations. Saltwater ice stays frozen for many more hours than does freshwater ice. Not only that, but it doesn't start to break down the flesh in the way freshwater ice does. Which brings us to the golden rule:

- **Keep ALL fresh water away from your fish at ALL times.**

The one and only time I will let fresh water near fish flesh is as a final rinse before cooking, and then only if I have to. When a fish is caught, it should be killed immediately with a spike to its head. The spike is called an iki stick. Generally the fish will stiffen when you hit the right spot.

After spiking the fish, place it in the fish bin with the ice. Many people correctly create a slurry of salt water and saltwater ice to place the fish in — a slurry will chill the core of the fish quickly. Many anglers add frozen water-filled drink bottles to the slurry to keep things cold. Personally, I don't make a slurry. Instead I pack the fish in ice and leave the extra ice in the bags, adding more around the fish as needed.

Treated this way you will have a product that no one, not even the most organised commercial fisher, can match. You won't believe the difference in taste or the ease in filleting with the flesh still in good condition!

BELOW: *The quality of the finished product is only as good as the care taken with the fish after capture. Saltwater ice is the answer to keeping fish in pristine condition.*

Choosing a knife

A filleting knife is the most personal and important tool you can have. It may take you a while to get the right one, but make the search a priority. If filleting is a new skill you are developing, here is where I suggest you start:

1 – Get a large, solid filleting board. Fish filleting tables are available for purchase, which is wonderful — but regardless of whether you fillet on the side of the boat, a table or even in the kitchen (so you live alone, then?),

Don't gut your fish ...

As long as your catch is packed in ice and prepared as soon as you get home, there is no need to gut the fish at all; all you will do is spend a lot of time and effort for no reward.

The same applies with scaling. Unless you plan to cook the fish whole or leave the skin on for cooking, both of which require a scaled fish, then the skinning process will take care of the scales. There are exceptions, notably flounder and dogfish; while parore need to have the black stomach cavity lining removed.

ABOVE: *From left: the Anglers Mate floating fillet knife is a low-cost option and a great spare knife. The knives in the middle are part of a set from Anglers Mate and have a range of blades, plus a sharpening steel. The Tramontina white-handled filleting knife is a very good option and the ideal blade shape.*

the best thing you can do is to buy a heavy filleting board. If you don't scrimp on the choice, it will be a once-in-a-lifetime purchase. A laminated kauri or teak board at least 500 mm long, but preferably bigger, is the best option. I found my perfect board at a home show 15 years ago.

LEFT: *Filleting tables, such as this model from Anglers Mate, make processing and cleaning much faster while keeping the mess out of the kitchen!*

Don't use a light plastic cutting board, as it will slide around and make the job much harder. A good board will make you a better filleter immediately.

ABOVE: *The Lansky hand-held knife sharpener is a fast and inexpensive way to keep an edge. I use mine regularly while filleting.*

2 – The ideal filleting knife for me has a blade length of 200–225 mm (8–9 inches) with an overall length of 350 mm (14 inches). Anything under 7 inches isn't a filleting knife. The blade will be flexible, fairly narrow in the shoulder and usually at least slightly curved. There will be a very pronounced curve from the tip to the main part of the blade. The blade doesn't want to be too flexible, however, as it still has to deal with bone. A very flexible blade is great for skinning, though, and is the reason why many anglers have various knives for different uses. For example, a slightly beefier knife around 200 mm in blade length is ideal for boning or making cutlets.

A new twist on flounder ...

Under the category of 'you won't believe it until you try it', some years ago one of my writers told me about filleting flounder before eating them. For decades we had speared flounder and cooked them whole in a frying pan. I tried filleting a bunch one day and was blown away. I'd thought there would have been quite a loss of flesh, but instead when the fillets were cooked they seemed to puff out and grow in volume. Not only that, but the cooked fillets tasted more like john dory than flounder!

Bleed your kahawai?

Kahawai is a great fish to eat either fresh or after smoking, but it was always said that the flesh is so much better if you immediately bleed the fish after catching it. The easiest way is to cut the throat latch. Ensure that the blood is draining away and if not, cut a little deeper towards the gills.

However, in the opinion of many experienced fishers it tastes just a good if you immediately ice the fish without bleeding. It must be very quickly chilled, though. And there's no mess!

3 – Sharpening is really important. The quality of the steel used in the knife will dictate how good the knife is, as well as how successfully it holds its edge. While it's a huge topic beyond the scope of this book, learning how to sharpen a knife properly is the key to getting the best results. The best way to get a knife properly sharp is to use a system like a Lansky sharpener or the ultimate knife sharpener, a Warthog system. With a properly sharpened knife to start with, a standard steel will suffice to keep the edge between fish. A hand-held sharpener with ceramic or tungsten blades, designed to be drawn over the blade, is a great way to quickly maintain an edge.

LEFT: *The author filleting fish on a beautiful Bay of Islands afternoon. Note the glove on the left hand. Filleting gloves are available from Berkley and Anglers Mate. They provide a degree of protection to the hand and better grip on the fillet.*

ABOVE RIGHT: *The Warthog sharpening system is the ultimate way to go! I hadn't seen one until a couple of years ago. It works by applying sharpening pressure at the correct preset angle. All you have to do is draw the knife repeatedly through the V formed by the sharpeners! I found them at www.top-gear.co.nz.*

Filleting Snapper

This method of filleting adds in one more change of knife direction than a professional filleter would make. But that's okay — we aren't pros and we want to make the job as simple and efficient as possible!

1: The first cut is made behind the head and gills. Note the angle of the knife which cuts back towards the head.

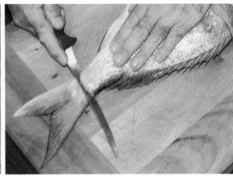

2: Make the second cut just forward of the tail, again angled towards the head.

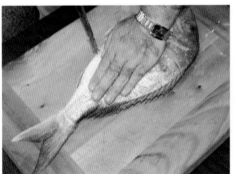

3: Continue to cut through the skin until you reach the anal vent.

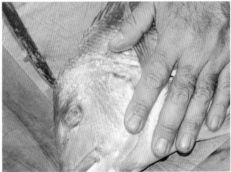

4: Return to the head of the fish. Cut forward until the knife stops then twist it towards the tail and cut through the skin.

5: Continue cutting through the skin all the way to the tail then take the knife back up to the head again.

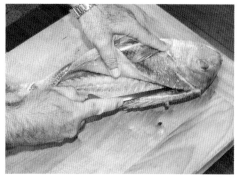

6: Continually lift the fillet and work the knife hard along the backbone in a slicing manner to free the flesh from the bones.

7: Continue slicing along the frame and over the backbone until the knife is butting up all around the ribcage.

8: This is the tricky part – pull the fillet away from the head and lift it at that point until you expose the bones right on the backbone.

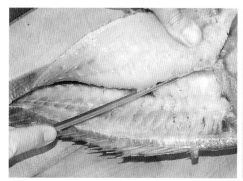

9: Cut through those bones (they are the pin bones you remove during filleting), then let the knife run up and over the ribcage – don't cut into it!

10: Run the knife in a slicing manner over the ribcage and down the other side.

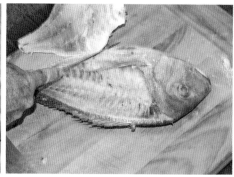

11: Cut through the skin and you will then be left with a perfect fillet! Because you haven't broken into the gut cavity there is far less mess and contamination.

Skinning Snapper

The method shown here is used for most similar-shaped fish species including common ones such as tarakihi, kahawai and trevally. Watch for extra bones along the V with golden snapper.

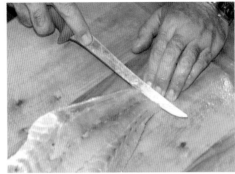

1: Hold the tail end of the fillet. The first cut is made on an angle down and forward as far as the skin.

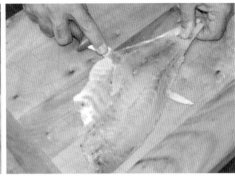

2: Hold the fillet (personally, I hold my hand flat down, sandwiching the skin to the board) and using a sawing motion work the knife forward.

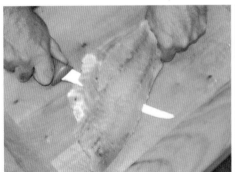

3: Keep sawing the knife forward and on an angle downward. It is almost a scraping action which will have the effect of removing the flesh hard down to the skin.

4: At that point the flesh and the skin are separate. Be aware when skinning fish with thin skin or small scales that it is much easier to accidentally cut through the skin.

5: Feel the line of bones along the centre of the fillet. Make a cut to one side of the bones roughly along the line where the knife is sitting in the photo. They start around halfway along the fillet.

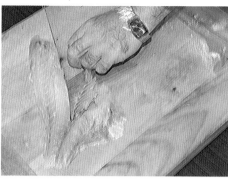

6: Repeat by cutting on the other side of the bones along the centre. The cut isn't vertical but rather on a slight angle to recover the maximum amount of flesh.

7: That should leave a thin strip of flesh containing all the bones. Check with your fingertip to make sure you haven't missed any.

8: What remains is a perfectly boneless fillet ready to cook.

Something you should never do ...

In my opinion it is a travesty to skin a john dory before cooking. JDs are the finest eating fish in our sea and need only be filleted, not scaled or skinned, before cooking. The skin retains the moisture and the flavour is exquisite. Fillets of john dory should only ever be cooked in butter after dusting with a little flour. No additional flavours are required!

Filleting Blue Cod

Blue cod are simple to fillet as the method skins and debones the fish all in one operation. The resulting fillet is ready to send to the kitchen for cooking ...

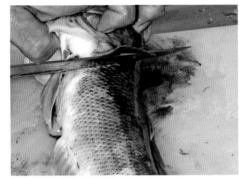

1: Make the first cut behind the head and gills. The knife angles forward to get the most flesh recovery.

2: Cut down to the backbone then run the knife hard along the backbone, cutting towards the tail.

3: Stop just short of the tail. The clutter around the fish is the skin from the other side of the fish which has already been filleted.

4: Flip the fillet over and make a cut under the fillet and along the skin as if you were about to skin it in the normal manner.

5: Stop around 50 mm or so in, just far enough to be able to get a good grasp on both the fillet and the skin.

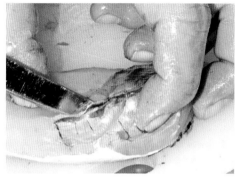

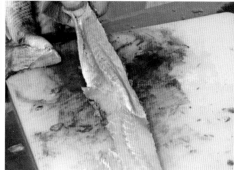

6: Make a single cut behind the ribcage. Some also make a cut down the centreline of the fillet but that isn't strictly necessary.

7: Grasp the fish and skin in one hand and hold the fillet with the other, then peel them apart.

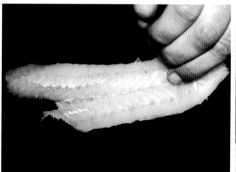

8: The skin should look like this with the centre pin bones plus the ribcage attached and still intact.

9: That should leave you with a perfectly formed, completely boneless fillet.

ABOVE: *Ang Govier with a fine example of a Marlborough Sounds blue cod. It was so hungry it ate two baits ...*

17 ⌒ Smoking Fish

Smoking fish, and other foods, is an art all on its own. For more detail, I recommend The Kiwi Sizzler Smoking Book, *which takes the subject further than I can here.*

Smoking 101

There are several ways of smoking fish. The methods we employ are forms of cooking, as opposed to true cold-smoking which is a process using cool temperatures and several days of smoke. Let me first explain the different options.

Portable hot-smokers

The compact portable smokers you are probably familiar with, the ones that use meths to heat the sawdust, are smoker/cookers that take around 20 minutes to complete the process. They create a tasty result that can be eaten hot or cold, but isn't designed to be kept for more than a short period of time.

Treat it as a product to be consumed immediately or stored in the fridge overnight.

Hot-smokers work by having a layer of sawdust spread over the bottom and a rack for the fish above. With the lid fitted and the meths heater (there may be two) underneath ignited, all you have to do is wait until the flames go out.

And that's it!

Gas or electric smokers

In recent years, the art of smoking has seen a renaissance due in no small part to the development of small gas and electrically operated smoking boxes. There are two that currently dominate our market: the Bradley electric smoker and the Kiwi Sizzler gas model. A third option is the UFO steamer, a great machine in its own right which can also be configured to smoke. All three suit the smoking of not just fish but also meat and vegetables. Each has its strengths and weaknesses. I use all three, depending on what I'm smoking.

- The Bradley is unique in that it operates with special timber bisquettes that are loaded into the burner. The unit operates semi-automatically, feeding another timber bisquette through every 20 minutes. The temperature is thermostatically set and the digital version has complete control over heat, time and smoke generation. It is certainly easy to control the cooking results with a Bradley; however, the trade-off is that you need to purchase the special bisquettes. An advantage is that Bradley makes the bisquettes from various types of timber to match particular foods.

- The Kiwi Sizzler gas smoker is a cost-efficient way to smoke a couple of fillets through to the whole catch. The first advantage is that it is cheap to run. The burner connects to a standard gas bottle and burns timber chunks and sawdust, both of which are freely available. It's very simple to operate. The downside in comparison with the Bradley system is that it is a little more difficult to accurately control the temperature, plus the smoke box needs to be topped up with timber or sawdust regularly. Those are very minor concerns, particularly when adding in the substantially lower initial purchase cost and widely available smoking materials.

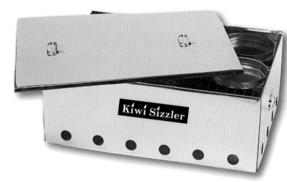

Red Cod   **Blue Cod**

Built-in smokers

The very first smoker I ever used was one Dad and I built in a weekend. First we poured a small concrete pad that incorporated a horizontal fibrolite pipe. The pipe was approximately 600 mm long and was fed from a firebox dug into the ground. The firebox was lined with bricks. On the pad was built the smoker body, using veneer blocks. A timber door frame was fitted and a fibrolite door installed.

LEFT: *All around New Zealand there are great smokers gracing backyards and baches. This one lives at the top of the South Island. The gas smoke box is lower than the fish box, giving the smoke a chance to cool. The vent controls the flow. A cool unit!*

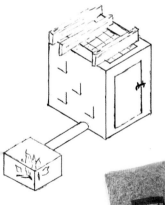

LEFT: *By sheer luck, when I wasn't even looking for it, I found the sketch for our original block smoker. It couldn't be simpler ...*
BELOW: *Kiwi Sizzler has a range of smoke timbers, including manuka, pohutukawa and oak wine.*

A single steel mesh was hung at the top of the smoker and 'S' hooks were made from number 8 wire to hang the fillets from. The roof of the smoker consisted of lengths of 4 by 2 and the smoke flow was controlled by turning them on their edge. Wet sacks could be added to keep even more smoke within the box. Overall the smoker was around five blocks high (1 metre) and around 700 mm by 700 mm outside size.

A pile of manuka logs and a sack of sawdust were kept stored in the boat shed, ready for action. I still miss smoking fish that way; even though the wind direction (we lived atop a hill — next stop Raglan) could affect the heat and smoke draw, the extra effort was worth the results. Even through the rose-tinted glasses of time, the results were almost always fabulous and I'd still smoke that way today if I had the option.

For many years, old fridge cabinets, 44-gallon drums and even old stoves got turned in to smoker cabinets. They still work! Larger walk-in block smokers are commonly used by commercial smokers. Some have a separate firebox; others have the fire built on the floor of the smoker. Shelves can be fitted and the fish chunks or fillets allowed to sit on them while smoking.

The best commercial smoker I ever saw had a stainless smoke-box and a hollow outside shell to where the smoke first travelled and cooled. It was all controlled by an air fan. It also had a liquid spray injector to moisturise the air, particularly for use when smoking hams and bacon. The same thing can be made from concrete blocks by having a hollow ceiling and then passing the smoke down a block cavity and having it enter the chamber at the bottom. A fan can control the flow.

Species to smoke

All fish can be smoked, but some are better than others. In order, these are my favourites:

Salmon — There's nothing like it. Be very careful that it doesn't dry out, though. Basting with maple syrup or brown sugar during the smoking process can enhance it further.

Striped marlin — Magnifique! There is no better smoked fish to eat while still hot or in a white sauce.

Kingfish — Almost as good as striped marlin. Smokes beautifully.

Kahawai — Our most common smoked fish. At its best when kept on ice and then well brined before smoking. Hard to beat.

Trevally — Tastes great but be careful not to over-smoke or over-cook, as it dries quickly.

Hapuku cheeks and wings — Often underutilised, these fatty parts of the hapuku are a real delicacy. The same applies with snapper wings.

Grey mullet — An oily fish that smokes well.

Gemfish — Often seen in supermarkets, I have only smoked them once but thoroughly enjoyed the result.

I have only ever smoked trout in a quick-smoker. The results are usually as good as the product you start with — muddy-tasting trout tastes just as muddy when smoked. On the other hand, a sea-run brown trout will likely be nearly as good as a salmon … clean-water trout tastes great.

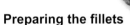

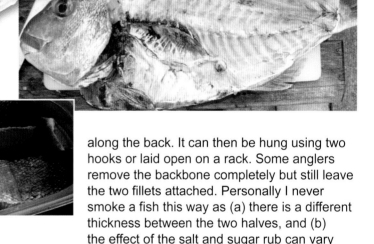

Preparing the fillets

Whole fish for smoking are usually prepared in one of three ways:

1 – Fillet the fish. There's no need to be particularly fancy with this; we typically cut through the pin bones and leave the stomach flap on the fillet. If the fish is being hung to smoke rather than placed on a rack, it is better to cut it just behind the gills, leaving the pectoral fin and bone around it intact to support the weight.

2 – Option two sees the head removed and the fish filleted on one side but with the two halves remaining attached along the back. It can then be hung using two hooks or laid open on a rack. Some anglers remove the backbone completely but still leave the two fillets attached. Personally I never smoke a fish this way as (a) there is a different thickness between the two halves, and (b) the effect of the salt and sugar rub can vary between the two sides.

3 – Chunks. Kingfish, marlin, tuna and large salmon can be smoked in chunks. Chop the fish into cutlets and place on the racks.

The brine process

There are many variations on how to do this, and you will undoubtedly develop your own. There are two main methods: either placing the fillets in a liquid brine, or rubbing/sprinkling with a mixture of salt and brown sugar plus any other flavourings required.

When using a hot-smoker, the fish can be cooked immediately after sprinkling with salt and brown sugar. It works fine, but the results are even better if the fish is brined for a period first. (Some people don't even sprinkle the fish at all and get great results — I know, as I've tasted them!)

There are so many brining options that it's hard to know where to start. Personally, I get a mixture of 50/50 salt and brown sugar and mix it dry. Sprinkle some in the bottom of a container, then place a layer of fillets skin down before sprinkling with more of the mixture. Repeat with additional layers, cover, place somewhere cool and leave overnight. The next day, you will find the container full of liquid. Remove the fillets, wash them thoroughly and dry them.

Alternatively, a liquid brine can be made. Everyone has their own mixture, but a starting point is half a cup of brown sugar and half a cup of salt mixed into a litre of water. Some people have a sugar to salt ratio of two to one or more. Other things can be added, such as bay leaves, rum, soy sauce, Worcestershire sauce, peppercorns and just about anything you like.

The critical thing is that it is a balance between time in the brine, thickness of the fillets and the degree of salt added that dictates when it is ready to smoke. You might need to do a few trials to get it right.

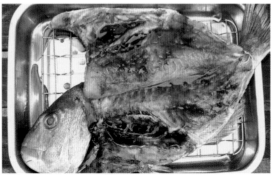

FAR LEFT: *Salmon brined and about to be sealed up before being placed in the fridge over night.*
LEFT: *Salted and sugared split snapper that has been left for a period of time for it to form a liquid. Ready to smoke!*
RIGHT: *The same split snapper after being hot smoked.*

Drying the fish

Except when cooking in the quick-smoker, the fillets have to be properly dried before smoking. They need to hang in a cool, fly-proof container until the surface of the fillet is tacky dry. It's called forming a pellicle, and is essential to the quality of the final product. Generally, I put the fillets into the smoker, after drying them with paper towels, seal all the gaps and then run a fan hard up against one of the vents. Note that, depending on the weather, it may take from two to six hours to get the pellicle formed. The biggest problem is keeping the gaps sealed enough to keep the flies out.

The timber

The single most common smoking timber in New Zealand is manuka. It creates wonderful results. Pohutukawa is also available commercially, and tastes wonderful. Another smoking timber that is very popular is made from the oak barrels used in the wine industry. You will find both chunks and sawdust available for sale. With the Kiwi Sizzler gas smoker I use both: a bowl of wood chips is soaked in clean water and these are used as the

Freezing also kills bacteria ...

Instead of heating to above 70°C, freezing prior to smoking will also destroy the bacteria in fish. A temperature of -18°C for two weeks apparently does the job.

main fuel in the smoker box. To generate additional smoke, a handful of sawdust is added as required. A combination of both gives complete control over the smoking and cooking process.

If you are sourcing your own smoking timber, remember that it must be the natural product — not processed or preserved in any way. Avoid resinous timbers like pine.

The smoking process

Typically, the smoking process will take six to eight hours. It can be longer with a larger smoker where the heat is better able to be controlled. With the Kiwi Sizzler I generally get the smoke going early in the process if the fish has dried properly. If the fish pieces are big or I'm not totally happy with how well they have dried, then I will put a low heat through for the first hour.

Technical articles I've read say that it's important to raise the internal temperature of the fish to 70°C for about 30 minutes to properly kill most bacteria. I usually aim to do that at around hour 4. For the first four hours I keep generating smoke, then after the heating stage I may add additional smoke depending on how well the fillets have coloured up. It's not a scientific way of judging the taste results, but you soon get a feel for it after making a batch or two. Remember that you aren't using the smoke just to preserve the fish — you'd have to smoke it for a week for that to happen. Rather, the smoke adds flavour.

Except when the heat stage is being performed, I try to keep the smoker temperature at around 50–60°C. I also swap the trays around regularly to keep the heat even through the fillets. The Kiwi Sizzler gas smoker has a built-in thermostat on the smoker door, so it's possible to keep a good eye on how things are progressing. By hour 5 you need to be checking the fish regularly and you may even find that smaller pieces can be removed. By hour 8, even the biggest pieces will be ready. When smoking salmon, I find that it's usually ready by the fifth hour and smoking for longer will often completely dry the fillets. I've never managed to keep smoked salmon away from

the vultures for more than two days in my household, so preserving it is the least of my worries!

Post smoking

The first thing to do when the first fillet is ready, before anything else, is to open a cold bottle of your favourite beer to consume while you demolish the first smoked fillet. If you don't and you can't appreciate that doing so is one of the greatest pleasures known to man or woman, then you are either a vegetarian or dead.

Once the fish is removed from the smoker, allow it to cool down to room temperature in a place where it can have full air flow. The killer for smoked fish is condensation causing mould, so the last thing you want to do is to put the hot fish into a cold fridge with all the pieces stacked together.

Once cooled, the fish can be stored. The length of time for each method is dependent on how well preserved it is — and also who you believe — but I tend to err on the side of caution. I will usually put some fillets in a plastic container to consume over the following three or four days. The rest get vacuum-packed and will be happy in the fridge for at least a week. If any of the fish is to be frozen, it too is vacuum-packed and then frozen as soon as possible. Three to six months is the life of the product, although I only ever use frozen smoked fish for pies and the like.

An alternative way to smoke

One of the best things I added to my last boat was a Kiwi Sizzler gas barbecue. It's a great unit on its own, and we happily cooked fish, scallops, crayfish, steaks and a lot of bacon and eggs on it while at sea. It also got used back on shore, too, as it's an ideal size to mount on a small patio or deck. I always considered it part of my emergency kit, along with spare water and dried food.

However, the Kiwi Sizzler didn't just get used as a barbecue. Early in the piece we discovered that it also made a fantastic smoker! We kept a roasting dish just for the purpose (it's not much use for anything else after burning sawdust), with a wire rack fitted inside it.

A sprinkle of sawdust was placed in the dish and a couple of fish fillets were put on the rack. They were prepared in the same way described for a portable hot-smoker. Close the lid and wait 30 minutes or so, and you get to enjoy beautiful hot-smoked fish! There is nothing like smoking fresh fish and then enjoying the results while still at sea.

But wait, there's more!

New on the market is a cast smoke box that will fit any barbecue with a hood and turn it into a smoker. Smoked fish is now an option anywhere and at any time.

Blue moki from the shore.

18 ✏ Fish Identification

The following pages provide you with a guide to the most common species found in New Zealand. Further information can be sourced by going to the Web NZ Fish Guide at www.fishguide.co.nz.

Albacore Tuna	**196**	Frostfish	**210**	Leatherjacket	**206**	Red Rock Cod	**218**
Alfonsino	**198**	Gemfish	**210**	Ling	**212**	Sand Flounder	**228**
Banded Wrasse	**237**	Golden Snapper	**198**	Marblefish	**226**	Sandager's Wrasse	**236**
Barracouta	**200**	G/father Hapuku	**218**	Monkfish	**214**	Scarlet Wrasse	**236**
Bass	**202**	Grey Mullet	**220**	Parore	**226**	Sea Perch	**218**
Blue Cod	**204**	Hake	**212**	Pilchard	**220**	Skipjack Tuna	**196**
Blue Mackerel	**196**	Hapuku/Groper	**202**	Pink Maomao	**198**	Snapper	**232**
Blue Maomao	**206**	Hoki	**212**	Piper	**234**	Sole	**228**
Blue Moki	**208**	Horse Mackerel	**222**	Porae	**230**	Spotty	**237**
Blue Warehou	**214**	Jack Mackerel	**222**	Ray's Bream	**210**	Sweep	**206**
Bluenose	**202**	John Dory	**216**	Red Cod	**212**	Tarakihi	**230**
Butterfish	**204**	Kahawai	**224**	R/Banded Perch	**218**	Trevally	**232**
Butterfly Perch	**200**	Kelpfish	**226**	Red Gurnard	**216**	Trumpeter	**208**
Demoiselle	**200**	Kingfish	**224**	Red Moki	**208**	Y/belly Flounder	**228**
Elephant Fish	**214**	Koheru	**222**	Red Pigfish	**234**	Y/eyed Mullet	**220**

ALBACORE TUNA

Description: A beautiful silver fish that is great to eat and great to catch! While they can grow to huge sizes, think over 40kg, the typical albacore we catch is 2–10 kg. Easily distinguishable from skipjack tuna by the long pectoral fins (the first thing you will notice) and by the lack of stripes. The flesh is white and suits many cooking styles.

SKIPJACK TUNA

Description: Skipjack are easily recognised by the horizontal lines along their silver flanks. They have a very dark blue/black back with hints of purple and blue visibly reflected in the light. Skipjack also have very short pectorals, an obvious attribute when compared to albacore. The flesh of a skipjack is dark red. A typical skipjack caught in New Zealand is 2–3 kg. Anything from 6–10 kg is big. The world all tackle record is over 20 kg however, they have been recorded at over 30 kg. That is a very large amount of bait…

BLUE MACKEREL

Description: With the traditional mackerel pattern on their back, the blue mackerel is a distinctive fish that is readily identified. They have a body shape not too dissimilar to that of a kahawai and are actually a member of the tuna family.

Where: Found throughout the North Island and the upper South Island during the summer. The first visitors are huge albacore that turn up off the Bay of Plenty in early spring. Generally found in schools so if you hook one, expect more. Less often encountered in shallow coastal waters (unlike skipjack tuna).

How: Trolling is the usual method although albacore will take a drifted bait and cast fly. Any small trolling vinyl or feather lure, and also trolled saltwater flies, will work. At times large albacore will take big lures set for marlin and other big game fish. Look for splashes and birds working offshore during the summer to locate the schools.

Where: Skipjack generally move into our waters in late November or December and some stay well into June. Some of the early arrivals can be in very large schools. At least until the purse seine vessels find them. While skipjack are generally seen in schools or 'plopping' on the surface, they can be caught down to 200 m. When warm currents arrive they will push right in to the coastline. Generally seen only in the North Island although with the right currents will turn up off the top of the South Island.

How: I recently had a fabulous session casting softbaits to skipjack and it was incredible sport! They can spool a reel very quickly. Skipjack can be anywhere during the summer and are not always visible so it pays to keep a lure in the water whenever you can. The same techniques used for catching albacore apply. Small red lures seem to be the best option for skipjack late in the season. A popular food fish in many cultures and some Hawaiians prefer them to yellowfin in certain dishes. I have eaten them stuffed and baked (they taste like turkey where albacore are more akin to chicken) and they are great consumed that way with a summer salad. The fact is though, they are superb bait and are going to be recycled into snapper or tarakihi fillets more often than eaten!

Where: Generally found north of Banks Peninsula, the northern east coast is their major habitat, although I've caught them on the west coast too and large schools turn up south of Taranaki. At times schools of blue mackerel foam at the surface, creating a huge noise.

How: Usually a by-catch when bottom fishing, although they can be targeted with small lures and baits. Saltwater flies work well as do flasher rigs. An oily flesh said to be good for smoking but less so for other forms of cooking. They need processing and freezing as soon as possible. A popular cut or whole bait too that can be purchased commercially.

ALFONSINO

Description: An unusual catch but not rare. Typically living in depths of 200–800 metres, alfonsino are distributed all around the world. At first glance you may think you have caught a golden snapper, if you're not familiar with them; however, the alfonsino is distinctly different. While both have a large eye, the smaller scales and crimson colour are obvious in the alfonsino.

GOLDEN SNAPPER

Description: Sometimes called red snapper, this species is unrelated to our common snapper. A beautiful fish, but one to take care with as the gills, head spikes and scales can all cause cuts and damage to the unwary. The orange-red and silver coloration, plus the big eye, are distinctive.

PINK MAOMAO

Description: A beautiful fish exhibiting genuine pink-crimson coloration on its back and flanks with a silver belly, although there are colour variations. They grow to a little over half a metre and a couple of kilos or so. Not related to blue maomao.

Where: Generally caught off the North Island and northern South Island. I have personally caught two: one at Raglan's Gannet Island in 50 m and one off Mayor Island. They are a commercial species and taste great.

How: Purely a by-catch, taken when targeting deepwater species. There is a good reason to run a small hook or two on a dropper rig when targeting hapuku — big tarakihi and alfonsino are two of the potential species you may catch.

Where: A northern species, seldom encountered much further south than East Cape. The large eye shows that they enjoy the darkness. I have caught them inside caves in only 5 m of water during the day, but typically catch them around rocks and pinnacles in depths over 50 m. In the Far North I have caught them in shallow water while catching snapper at night.

How: Golden snapper spin when hooked, often messing up flasher rigs in the process. To target goldens, look for schools of fish on the sounder on top of pinnacles in water deeper than 50 m. Often they are in mid-water. Baited flasher rigs, small lures and softbaits will work. We've even had large goldens take long jigs. Golden snapper are a slow-growing fish so big ones are now relatively rare. They taste great; just watch for the double row of pin bones when you are filleting them.

Where: Found in the upper two-thirds of the North Island, most prolific around the Bay of Plenty north. Personally, I have never caught one off the west coast. I have cast unweighted baits to them around offshore islands and caught them when bottom fishing for tarakihi in 100 m. Potentially found in depths to 200 m.

How: Pink maomao are a good fish to eat, although the flesh can be watery if not looked after well. They can be targeted around deeper rocks and reefs and typically will make up part of a mixed catch that can include golden snapper, tarakihi and snapper, which all inhabit similar areas. The best and biggest fish I have caught have been taken that way off Tauranga and Mayor Island. Pink maomao will take small cut baits, baited flasher rigs are even better, and will also respond to very small lures and softbaits.

BARRACOUTA

Description: Despised by fishers everywhere but loved by the tackle trade. Barracouta are not related to the tropical barracuda; however, their teeth are capable of destroying any tackle in their way, often without the fisher even realising it has happened. Easily recognised by their long, thin shape and nasty dentures. Silver-blue in colour. Big ones are a couple of metres long and may weigh over 6 kg. They are edible, not that I recommend it, and there is a commercial industry for them. Many, when caught, are found to have worms in their flesh. Barracouta make great bait, particularly for hapuku and bass.

BUTTERFLY PERCH

Description: One of the most common species you will see in the water anywhere in the country. They get bigger as you head south with the potential to reach 300 mm. Very pretty, the butterfly perch has a distinctive black patch at the rear of its flank.

DEMOISELLE

Description: There is more than one species of demoiselle; however, the two spot demoiselle is the common one. It is dark in colour over most of its body with two distinctive spots. Usually seen in schools, with individuals typically 100–200 mm long.

Where: Barracouta can be caught anywhere in New Zealand, although the middle of the country is their spiritual home. There is no particular depth they inhabit. Barracouta move into the northern waters of the North Island during the winter, creating havoc for fishers everywhere. I have caught them everywhere I have fished in New Zealand. The most memorable were babies around 400 mm long, which we caught in the entrance to Coromandel Harbour. They were a beautiful fish even if they did destroy our softbaits!

How: Can be caught by trolling and they are often associated with birds working, particularly in the south. Large schools can be found on your sounder at any time of year; however, those in winter seem much more distinct — big red balls in mid-water are a definite indicator of the likely species. Most barracouta are a by-catch for anglers fishing on the bottom or drift fishing. Barracouta love flasher rigs and will gladly destroy them in seconds. Avoid shiny hardware (use black swivels) and keep the rig simple and streamlined to help reduce the attraction. Sometimes throwing a handful of bait cubes in the opposite direction while dropping your bait will work. But only sometimes!

Where: Reefs, drop-offs, wrecks and walls will usually hold populations of butterfly perch. You don't have to go very far to find them!

How: I have only ever caught one legitimately in the mouth (and several others foul hooked) even though many of our regular spots hold huge populations of them. Bigger ones are edible, although there are better and easier fish to target.

Where: Seen in the upper half of the North Island, always around rock and reef areas. One of the most common of the reef fishes.

How: Not a recreational fishing target in any way, just a very unusual by-catch when foul-hooked.

BASS

HAPUKU (GROPER)

Description: Bass and hapuku (groper) are generally included together in any discussion; however, there is a clear distinction between them. Bass grow much bigger, and generally are much deeper in the body and lack the under-slung jaw that characterises a hapuku. Both have a bronze or dark coloration on the flanks, a very dark back and light belly. The elongated shape shown in the photos helps to clarify the difference.

BLUENOSE

Description: Correctly called a bluenose warehou, everyone knows them as bluenose. A schooling fish normally caught when chasing hapuku and bass. Similar to a maomao in profile, the blue-green back and silver flanks are distinctive, as is the large eye and big mouth. So is their size — potentially more than 50 kg. A more typical size is 5–15 kg.

Where: In northern waters both species can be caught together. Bass are primarily found in northern waters while further south hapuku predominate. Hapuku are caught in all our waters. Groper is the name given to hapuku by most southern locals. While they can be caught in very shallow water most populations have been well fished. Hapuku move into shallow water in the Bay of Plenty and Taranaki over winter where savvy anglers with local knowledge are able to target them. Most big hapuku and bass are caught in deep water around structure. Cook Strait, White Island, the Three Kings, Mayor Island and the Ranfurly Bank would be the acknowledged hotspots. Depths will range from 50 m (although rarely now) to 200–300 m. Any deepwater structure is a potential holder of both species.

How: Powerful reels and braid have made deepwater fishing a much more pleasant experience! Braid gives feel while nylon stretches. Typically, a couple of large baits on a dropper rig is deployed. Generally, they work well but to really have the best shot at catching a hapuku, especially in well-fished areas, a live bait is the answer. We have caught hapuku in our tarakihi spots by leaving a live bait on the bottom. A real bonus! Hapuku and bass will also take jigs. They are targeted on long jigs in the Bay of Plenty and Far North. Regardless of method, use every available lumo option to help make your offering visible. Both species are great to eat! I prefer to prepare them into cutlets rather than steaking, as was once traditional.

Where: Potentially found all around the country, most recreational catches come from the Bay of Plenty, deep reefs in the Far North and particularly from Cook Strait. Now seldom found in depths under 100 m, except when schooling above deeper structure.

How: Normally a by-catch when hapuku fishing so typically taken on the same heavy tackle. Lighter tackle can be used if you can keep away from the larger predators or if you are lucky enough to know where and when they school to spawn in shallower water. Bluenose have a propensity for spinning and tangling when more than one fish is hooked. Drifting the tops of deeper reefs is the usual method. The fish will show on the sounder schooling above the reef. Any flesh baits will work, squid in particular, and they will take jigs too. Great to eat and the fillet looks just like one from a big snapper.

BLUE COD (1)

BLUE COD (2)

Description: When it comes to national fish, the blue cod is second only to the snapper. A beautiful and powerful fish, they can be ravenous and aggressive. A big blue cod will exceed 5 kg but they are rare at that size and restricted to remote areas of the South Island. Typical cod will weigh a kilo or so. Fish caught in the North Island are often a brown colour (1) with a touch of blue-green around the eye. Because they are a less common catch, inexperienced northern fishers have found themselves in possession of undersized blue cod when later stopped by fisheries officers. A lesson in why you need careful fish identification! In the South Island the fish tend to have a beautiful blue-green sheen to their back (2). They are stunning to look at and to eat.

BUTTERFISH

Description: Also known as greenbone, a descriptive term for obvious reasons. A distinctive fish with its long, trailing dorsal fin and large tail. Bronze-olive in colour, sometimes with shades of blue and green. They can exceed 5 kg in weight, but more typically are 300–500 mm long and a kilo or two

Where: Blue cod can turn up anywhere but the best places to catch them are the margins around reefs, weed and foul ground. In the South Island they are also caught in harbour entrances. In fact, they can be just about anywhere. In the North Island they are a regular part of the catch south of a line through East Cape but less reliable further north. Pockets of them will be found on foul patches north of the line, although I know few northern anglers who would expect to target them.

How: Blue cod will eat any cut bait. A firm flesh bait is best as they will repeatedly attack the bait and the feeding frenzy will attract more fish to the area. Squid and salted bonito would be my first choice but barracouta will do too. A two-hook dropper or flasher rig is ideal. Traditionally, South Island fishers have used long shank hooks, sometimes just called cod hooks, as they have a tendency to wolf the bait and be hooked deeply. Alternatively, particularly around the top of the South Island where a limited and slot fishery exists for blue cod (read the local fishing regulations for more detail), big hooks are the answer, as are circle hooks. Blue cod love softbaits! When it comes to table quality it is like having two species; North Island cod are okay, South Island cod are stunning! I personally think the cold water is the reason. Still, if the scientists tell us one day that there are two species I won't be surprised.

Where: Found all around the country, shallow kelp areas are the places to look. The large tail is required because of the surge areas it inhabits, while the long dorsal likely helps with camouflage in the kelp.

How: Butterfish are not generally a target for capture on rod and reel. They are a popular target for spearfishers. Some fishers have caught butterfish on very small weed or shellfish baits drifted above or in the kelp beds. A genuine challenge! Butterfish are very good to eat.

BLUE MAOMAO

Description: Schools of these pretty fish are common on the surface in the Far North and any underwater archway or overhang will likely hold schools of them. The blue on its back ranges in colour from dark to electric. The sweep also gets called a maomao but is a distinctly grey colour. Once you've seen a blue maomao there is no confusion.

SWEEP

Description: Related to blue maomao and sometimes called grey maomao, sweep are very similar in appearance but with a dark green-gunmetal back, sometimes bronze, with a bright silver belly.

LEATHERJACKET

Description: Hard to confuse this species. The single large spike in front of the dorsal fin is distinctive and so is the tough sandpaper-like skin. It has a tiny mouth full of nasty, sharp teeth. Grows to about 400 mm.

Where: While they can be found as far south as Wellington the blue maomao is predominately a northern North Island species. Millions live at the Poor Knights. Driving around the rocky shorelines of the outer Bay of Islands is a guaranteed way of finding them.

How: Those whose opinion I respect tell me that blue maomao taste great! They do respond to berley and any small hook or sabiki will likely be their undoing. Many get hooked in the eye when they venture too close to the bait. Usually they are a by-catch, but they can certainly be targeted.

Where: Found throughout New Zealand. Sweep grow to around 350 mm and can weigh about a kilo. Typically caught in water under 30 m deep.

How: Sweep can school in big numbers, sometimes becoming a nuisance when other species are being targeted. Many end up being foul hooked. On the rare occasions we have processed them to eat they have been quite acceptable tucker. If you want to target them, use a smaller hook size. Berley really gets them going.

Where: Found all around the country in depths to around 200 m. Most common in shallow, rocky, weedy areas.

How: I hate leatherjackets! Since we have started softbait fishing they have become the bane of our lives. They will destroy softbaits in seconds, nipping away the tail of the bait while avoiding the hook. Take the hint, if your baits are being nipped, move on as there are no snapper there. I once watched a pack of more than 50 leatherjackets harassing my softbaits off the Whitianga coastline. Leatherjackets are often sold as creamfish and they have a reputation as a fine fish to eat, reminiscent of flounder. They can be caught on small longshank hooks.

BLUE MOKI

Description: Blue moki is a powerful predator that can grow to over 10 kg and be a handful for anyone lucky enough to hook one of that size. Typically a blue-grey colour, although tinges and patches of bronze are also common. Similar in shape to the related trumpeter. Has a small mouth.

RED MOKI

Description: A pretty red and bronze fish of the same family as the tarakihi and porae. The colours vary and I've seen species which are intense red while others are lighter or more bronze overall. The large powerful tail indicates where you will find them living. Potential growth, I believe, is a metre and weight in excess of 6 kg.

TRUMPETER

Description: Related to the blue moki but a distinctive olive-grey colour with obvious horizontal bands on the upper body clearly defines it from other species. The fins and body are tinged with yellow. Trumpeter can easily exceed a metre in length and grow to over 20 kg in weight.

Where: Blue moki are found from the Three Kings to the Chathams, but the majority of the population and fishing effort occurs from East Cape south. They are a key species for fishers in the Wellington region. While found from the shallows to 200 m and sometimes over mud, the best place to find them is around rocky shorelines and beaches with adjoining foul patches.

How: Shellfish are the moki's favourite food and the first choice for bait. Crayfish is another option, while small baited flashers also account for the occasional moki. Surfcasters have turned catching moki into an art form. They make a great table fish, particularly those from the cooler southern waters. While I have seen them when diving in the north I've never caught one, probably because we use large baits or whole pilchards in the areas where they reside. They are a fish that needs to be specifically targeted for regular success.

Where: Red moki are territorial and long-lived — as long as 60 years. Distribution is mainly around the North Island and the top of the South. They are one of the most common species seen by divers in the north and probably the first fish speared by most newbies to that sport. In some areas they are present in very large numbers. I know from years of diving around the Raglan coastline that at times I would be swimming with lots of red moki. They are generally found in depths of less than 50 m with the majority located in much shallower water — the reason for the powerful tail.

How: Red moki are average as a table species. They seldom take a bait. In fact, for all the hours I've spent fishing at Raglan where I know there are in large quantities, we have only ever hooked one legitimately in the mouth. Small shellfish baits may attract their attention.

Where: Found in depths from around 10 m, particularly in the South Island, to waters over 300 m deep. Large specimens are caught on deeper reefs when targeting hapuku and bass in the north. Trumpeter are distributed throughout New Zealand, but they increase in numbers further south where they become an important part of the recreational catch.

How: Trumpeter love to eat crustaceans and shellfish; however, most are caught on strip baits. Flasher rigs are better still, while lures and softbaits will also get their attention. Large specimens are quickly removed from any fishing area as trumpeter are aggressive feeders. Great sport and fabulous to eat.

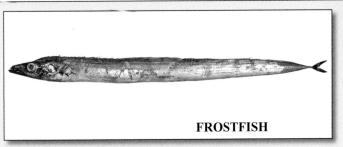

FROSTFISH

Description: Looking something like a length of polished chromium steel with teeth, the frostfish was originally known by recreational anglers from examples that wash up (or just beach themselves) where they were picked up to be eaten! You can't miss the distinguishing characteristics: very, very thin, a very small tail and skin that comes off when touched. Plus those teeth ...

GEMFISH

Description: A beautiful iridescent silver fish that looks similar to a barracouta but is immediately identifiable by the deep belly and large eye. There is also a noticeable dark patch across the first three dorsal spines. It can grow to over 15 kg; however, the average ones caught are usually 3–6 kg.

RAY'S BREAM

Description: At least two species are found in New Zealand. Ray's bream are similar to a maomao in shape but with a deeply forked tail and large eye. The colour of a freshly caught fish, resembling something akin to a piece of polished stainless steel with a dark blue-purple back, is very distinctive. Ray's bream have a growth potential of a metre and weight of 6 kg; however, most caught are well under 2 kg.

Where: Found throughout the country without being common anywhere, they are a by-catch for mid-water trawl fisheries. They are an occasional by-catch for deepwater anglers on rod and reel, particularly in the Bay of Plenty and South Island.

How: Usually taken on hapuku gear or on jigs fished in deep water. Nasty teeth like barracouta that can create similar carnage. While difficult to target, some anglers have caught them in numbers on jigs. If you catch one, break out the jigs and try for more. Said to taste great when either filleted or steaked and cooked in butter.

Where: Found throughout New Zealand and an important commercial species. Normally taken as a by-catch around deepwater reefs and rocks when chasing hapuku and bluenose in depths of 50–600 m.

How: Any of the usual flesh baits fished in deep water will account for gemfish. They will take lures, too. A great fish to eat, particularly when smoked. Some anglers have been known to discard them, thinking they are barracouta. What a waste!

Where: Found everywhere, sometimes in huge schools, mostly in mid-water well offshore. Recreational anglers usually meet with Ray's bream when they are taken as a by-catch while targeting hapuku and bluenose.

How: Savvy anglers have recognised that Ray's bream are able to be targeted when found. Typically, they will show as a large school in mid-water on the sounder. The fish are aggressive and will take lures and cut baits presented in front of them. Ray's bream have the reputation of being superb table fare.

RED COD

Description: In total there are currently 15 known species of cod in New Zealand. The most important, commercially and recreationally, is the red cod. The red cod has a pink-red general coloration with a silver-white belly and green-bronze back. Without using fin ray counts, the red cod is easily distinguished from other cod by the dark patch beside the pectoral fins and the square tail. Red cod can grow to over a metre and to around 7 kg. This species is related to the northern hemisphere cods. The blue cod is completely unrelated.

LING

Description: Ling is an important commercial species. It is easy to separate from species such as red cod as a ling has a pointed tail similar to an eel. In fact, it looks very similar to an eel when placed beside one. The mottled pink and white coloration is also distinctive. There are barbels below the lower jaw. Capable of growing up to 2 m long and weighing up to 30 kg.

HAKE

HOKI

Where: Found throughout the country, primarily over mud and sand bottoms. Numbers increase as you head south and the greatest quantities are caught off Canterbury and Westland. While taken at depths of over 800 m, large numbers are caught from beaches and in harbours.

How: It's fair to say that most North Island fishers treat red cod with disdain. Conversely, on the east coast of the South Island, they make up a large percentage of the targeted catch. The problems with red cod are three in number: firstly, they don't fight at all; secondly, they are slimy and they stink if you break into the gut cavity; and thirdly, the flesh is described as watery and tasteless. The first two qualities can't be changed; however, the quality of the flesh can be improved by chilling it for 24 hours, then rubbing it with salt several hours before cooking. If you don't, the flesh tends to break down, particularly when fried. It does smoke well. It is a common sight to see red cod for sale in supermarkets. They will voraciously eat just about anything. No need to be fussy with bait. Surfcasters take their best catches after dark.

Where: Primarily found off the lower North Island plus all around the South Island. Once caught in shallow waters, big ling are now largely a fish caught by those targeting groper in the trenches and pinnacles in the south. It's likely that some recorded captures in the north are actually bastard red cod. Note that ling have a pointed tail!

How: Ling are ravenous predators that will eat anything. No special baits are required. Standard dropper rigs will catch them. Circle hooks are a good choice for most deepwater fishing.

Other Species: Also caught occasionally, particularly in the South Island, are hake and hoki. While we are familiar with them in our fish and chips, hoki in particular has become a familiar species to those chasing the giant bluefin in the South Island as they are the bait!

MONKFISH

Description: Actually the giant stargazer, and it is obvious why it is named so. Not the same as the popular northern hemisphere monkfish, even though all species of stargazer are commercially sold under the monkfish name in New Zealand. You will see monkfish regularly in supermarkets. There are several species of stargazer and all are similar in general shape. The giant stargazer has the ability to grow to around 900 mm and 9 kg in weight.

ELEPHANT FISH

Description: The most distinctive fish in our ocean, the elephant fish is related to the shark, having a cartilaginous skeleton rather than a backbone. Generally a silver or light bronze on top with brown patches over the body. Capable of growing to well in excess of a metre. There is a nasty spine at the front of the dorsal fin which can cause serious harm.

BLUE WAREHOU

Description: Blue warehou look something like a cross between a trevally, a tarakihi and a maomao. The rounded head and obvious dark patch are distinctive. The average adult fish caught is around 1–3 kg, although they can get to be over 5 kg. Blue warehou are relatively fast growing.

Where: The giant stargazer and banded giant stargazer are found throughout New Zealand. They are mostly caught by trawling in depths of 50–500 m, primarily off the South Island. Spotted and estuary stargazers are the ones you will likely see most, being found in harbours and on sand flats.

How: Stargazers are a by-catch for recreational fishermen, taken with cut baits fished on the bottom and also on set lines. Most are caught in drag nets and by spear when chasing flounder.

Where: Mostly found from Wellington south, with a few stragglers further north. The Canterbury coast is the prime fishing area and they are a favourite target for surfcasters when they move into shallow water from spring through into summer. The distinctive egg cases produced are often washed up on to local beaches.

How: Elephant fish love shellfish so they are the preferred bait; however, flesh baits also work well at times. Sandy beaches with nearby gutters are something to look for when selecting a spot. Kahle hooks are very popular for this species.

Where: Typically found from Taranaki south, blue warehou move in schools and occasionally make an appearance in shallower waters around reef structure. The sometimes huge schools can also be in mid-water or even on the surface. Divers report that when they see them they often bolt, then reform the school. An enigma with scales, they turn up when they want to turn up! A popular catch from the Wellington/Mana area. An occasional by-catch in other areas.

How: Blue warehou can be ravenous and when you find a school you may catch plenty. They will take most strip baits and love small jigs. In fact, the first time I caught a warehou (actually two) was in 15 m off Raglan on a feather jig. We didn't know what they were at the time. Blue warehou are also gill-netted. They are a great fish to eat. In recent years there has been an increase in commercial landings as by-catch. Moves have been taken to address that.

JOHN DORY

Description: Like no other common species, the john dory is a beautiful fish. The long, flowing dorsal fins and the 'thumb print' on each side are unmistakable. The biggest I've seen were around 700 mm long and pushing towards 5 kg. A more common size is 1–2.5 kg. Bronze in colour out of the water, but a silver-translucent colour when chasing schools of piper along sandy beaches. The huge mouth speaks volumes about the way it feeds.

RED GURNARD

Description: Impossible to confuse with any other species, the red gurnard has a mottled orange-red and brown back with contrasting white belly. The pectoral fins, which look like wings, are stunning: an olive-green with electric blue edges and a conspicuous black patch. The head is spiny, and the shape of the gurnard shows that it is designed for swimming on or close to the bottom. Gurnard can grow to 600 mm and 3 kg but are typically around half that size.

Where: Most common north of the Marlborough Sounds with good populations from the Bay of Plenty north. Can be found around all reef and weed areas where the dory can use camouflage to hunt by stealth. Around the North Island wharves is a great place to look, with Whitianga being the number-one haunt in New Zealand. The ocean beaches, particularly around the Bay of Islands, are a great place to find them. Look along the sandy stretches near rocks for the schools of piper; the john dory will be hunting them from below.

How: John dory is the best eating fish in our waters, period. Always cook with the skin on. It is sacrilege to use anything other than flour, butter and salt to cook them with. A lot more john dory would be caught if anglers targeted them. Most are a by-catch when the dory swallows a small hooked fish. Any time you have the anchor down it pays to fish a small live bait near the bottom. John dory love softbaits and jigs. They are easy to spear and I caught a memorable one while snorkelling when it jumped up on the rocks and my brother was able to pick it up! Don't underestimate how fast dory can swim — I once watched one jump right out of the water while chasing mullet around the Whangamata wharf.

Where: Gurnard are caught all around the country except in Fiordland. They are typically found in depths under 200 m but notably most of the commercial catch is from depths of less than 60 m. Sand and mud bottoms are their domain and there are known areas of high population, such as the Manukau Harbour, Hawke's Bay and the west coast of the North Island. General unscientific consensus amongst recreational fishers is that there are far fewer gurnard in the Firth of Thames now than in days gone by, yet more snapper. Possibly due to a change in the bottom structure from the mussel farms?

How: Gurnard feed on the bottom, primarily digging for crustaceans, shellfish and worms. Fortunately for us, they are also very happy to eat cut flesh baits. When the gurnard are 'on' there is little finesse needed to catch them, particularly when boat fishing. Of course, it's not always like that and usually far more effort will be required to score a bag of these great table fish, especially from the beach. In open water where gurnard are expected, one way of catching them is to drift using a normal dropper rig until you get bites, then put the anchor down. Berley right on the bottom will also help attract and hold gurnard in the area. Gurnard love movement which is why drift fishing is effective and explains why they also love lures, particularly softbaits, as well as saltwater flies. One very effective way is to drift with an extra, preferably baited, flasher rig attached to the sinker. The movement along the bottom will attract gurnard.

GRANDFATHER HAPUKU

Description: Correctly called a scorpionfish and related to the deadly Pacific stonefish. This alone should tell you why you need to avoid their spines! Not deadly, but potentially very painful. Apart from the distinctive spines, its cavernous mouth, size and orange-red coloration separate this species from other similar species. Grows to over 600 mm.

The red rock cod is from the same family, but grows to only 300 mm long.

RED ROCK COD

RED BANDED PERCH

Description: Another spiky orange-brown species that grows to about 200 mm.

SEA PERCH

Description: Known as scarpees and jock stewarts, they grow to over 450 mm. The red-orange colour, size and light bands separate this species from its relatives.

Where: A common catch from the northern North Island, particularly in the Far North. Scorpionfish happily lie camouflaged on the bottom to await passing prey. Caught in a wide range of depths.

The red rock cod has the same range.

How: Said to taste similar to crayfish. Personally, I think there are better fish to catch and easier fish to fillet! Also called bucket mouths due to their habit of opening their mouth and having all the fight of a bucket of water when hooked. Will take most cut baits and I've caught them on softbaits too.

Where: Usually found in depths of less than 100 m of water with distribution throughout the country.

How: A nuisance catch only. Too small to eat. Send them back.

Where: Sea perch are found everywhere in depths to at least 750 metres.

How: No finesse is needed to catch sea perch. At times they are a huge nuisance, taking baits placed for more desirable species. This is a particular annoyance when fishing in deep water. Fortunately, sea perch are good to eat, particularly when they get bigger and easier to fillet. Any bait will do.

GREY MULLET

Description: Grey mullet is distinguishable from yellow-eyed mullet by its size, flat head, eye colour and grey-green-bronze body coloration. The scales are large. Found all around the world. Can grow to well over 500 mm.

YELLOW-EYED MULLET

Description: Not a herring or a sprat, as they are mistakenly called, the yellow-eyed mullet is a very important species for anglers throughout New Zealand. The fish is easily recognised by the distinctive eye colour, bright silver belly and grey-green back. The fins are also tinged in yellow. Can potentially grow to over 400 mm and almost a kilo in weight. Typically less than half that length.

PILCHARD

Description: The New Zealand pilchard is an important food fish for just about everything that swims. Typically around 150 mm long but growing to 250 mm. The back is a dark blue, sometimes exhibiting a touch of green, with a silver belly. The row of dark dots along each side is very distinctive.

Where: New Zealand is at the extreme of the range. Generally found in the upper North Island, but some stragglers are caught in Wellington and at the top of the South Island. Harbours, estuaries and rivers are where they can be found. Grey mullet will push a long way into fresh water — a good example is along the Waikato River where large numbers are caught around, and past, Hamilton.

How: Very difficult to catch on rod and reel although some have had limited success with dough baits and small flies. Generally netted, either by set net or by using a drifting net set on the surface — a common way to catch them at Port Waikato. Very popular canned or smoked. A superb, oily, tough bait.

Where: Yellow-eyed mullet are found everywhere. Every kid in New Zealand cuts their fishing teeth on the wharf catching yellow-eyed mullet. Usually in water under 10 m but found down to 50 m. While typically seen around structure like wharves and pilings, the bigger individuals are encountered in shallow areas around structure in harbours, streams and estuaries. The biggest yellow-eyed mullet I have encountered have been seen while spearing flounder at night.

How: The easiest way to catch yellow-eyed mullet is to drop lightly baited sabiki rigs into the schools around the nearest wharf. Sometimes no weight or float is needed, sometimes a pinch of lead will result in more hook-ups. Alternatively, a small baited hook will catch them. The ubiquitous plastic 'baitcatcher' bait trap will also catch them in numbers. Bread for berley is useful unless there is too much current.

Where: Pilchards are found all around the country. There is a very important fishery for them on the east coast of the North Island.

How: Pilchards are usually caught recreationally in one of two ways. If you are lucky enough to witness predators chase pilchards into meatballs on the surface, you may be able to scoop them with a net and top up your bait supply. Alternatively, pilchards are caught with small sabikis from wharves or from schools seen on the sounder. The New Zealand pilchard is, by general consensus, a far superior bait to imported pilchards. They are tougher and oilier.

HORSE MACKEREL

JACK MACKEREL

Description: A slightly confusing fish as there are three species in New Zealand. The two common species are jack mackerel and horse mackerel. The third is the much wider-ranging Murphy's mackerel. It wasn't until the 1970s and 1980s that fisheries experts sorted out the species. (Note that the blue mackerel is a member of the tuna family.) Primarily recognised by the hard scutes before the tail and the clear lateral line, proper identification between the species relies on fin ray counts. All three species can grow to over 500 mm.

KOHERU

Description: Similar to jack mackerel with a much less-defined lateral line and smaller tail scutes. The body is also more like a tuna in section with a blue tinge to the back.

Where: Found all around the country with overlapping distribution. Of the three, jack mackerel is the most common species to catch, inhabiting shallower and warmer waters. Can be found in huge schools at times. A large trawl industry exists for them in several parts of the country. They are one of the top earners in terms of export dollars.

How: Mackerel are an underrated food fish. While we favour them as live and cut baits, on the occasions I've caught large ones (primarily when bottom fishing at Raglan) they have proved to be fine tucker. Big mackerel are caught on the usual dropper rigs while smaller fish can be targeted with small cut baits or, better still, sabikis and small flasher rigs.

Where: Hard to find sometimes, and at other times around in large numbers. Primarily found in the North Island. I have most often caught them in clean offshore waters, for example around Mayor Island.

How: Described by some as the perfect bait as they are tough and resilient. Marlin, in particular, love them! So do kingfish, hapuku and even big snapper. They can also be fished as cut bait. Apparently, they taste good too. The best way to catch them is by berleying at the back of the boat. Once they start feeding they can be caught on sabikis and small baits.

Juvenile

KAHAWAI

Description: The kahawai is one of our most important fish and is instantly recognisable with its dark green back and silver belly. An average one is around 1–2.5 kg. They have the potential to be much heavier with the largest measured at almost 800 mm in length. An even bigger related kahawai from the Kermadec Islands occasionally gets caught in the Far North. They can exceed a metre and weigh over 10 kg.

KINGFISH

Description: A long, powerful torpedo capable of destroying tackle and breaking hearts! The yellow tail, electric silver flanks and emerald-green back identify it immediately. There is a distinctive longitudinal band that runs from tail to nose, which is even more obvious when seen in the water. Growth potential is to over 2 m and in excess of 50 kg.

Where: Kahawai can be caught almost anywhere in New Zealand. Larger populations are found around the North Island. Many work-ups in the North Island will have kahawai in attendance, sometimes foaming the water to a mass of white. They are caught over sand bottoms in deeper water, in harbours, as well as close to headlands and rocks. In fact, kahawai can turn up anywhere.

How: Anything will catch kahawai! Cut baits, softbaits, lures, jigs and saltwater flies will all catch fish. Spinning around river mouths, especially when whitebait are running, is a popular sport. If trolling around work-ups, don't drive through them — work the edges. Berley will help motivate kahawai to feed. Kahawai are great fresh and fabulous smoked. We have traditionally bled them; however, if they are killed and iced down immediately, there is no discernible difference to the results — just less mess!

Where: Found all around New Zealand, south to at least Canterbury, although the biggest models are taken around Coromandel, the Bay of Plenty, Auckland, the Far North and the Three Kings. Big ones can turn up anywhere, however — I've seen fish of over 40 kg off Raglan too. Channels and shallow areas, even in water less than a metre deep, can produce great kingfish. Just think water flow plus a supply of food and the chances are they are there. Structure is their favourite haunt, though. You will find them schooling above reefs and rocks, at times in water over 200 m deep.

How: The sport of jigging was created for catching kingfish! Great fun, but you need quality gear. Live baits remain the most popular method. They can be floated out while you are anchored or drifting over structure. Kings will occasionally eat a cut bait. Trolling around structure also produces kingfish. Surface lures will work, but large bibbed minnows are better. Casting poppers and the more recent surface lures called stick baits can be very, very effective. Kingfish are very good to eat but particularly superb when smoked.

KELPFISH

MARBLEFISH

Description: Kelpfish and marblefish are powerfully built as they live in shallow water where they are subject to surge and wave action. They are similar, but sufficiently different to immediately recognise when seen.

PARORE

Description: A member of the drummer family, the parore is an underrated fish that is easily recognised by its powerful build, large tail, bronze-olive colour and distinctive vertical bands. It has a small mouth. Parore can grow to 600 mm in length and 8 kg in weight, although 0.75–2 kg is the size we typically see. Known as luderick in Australia where they are a major target species.

Where: The marblefish has a wider distribution; the kelpfish is found primarily in the North and upper South Island. A by-catch when fishing cut baits on the bottom.

How: There are no mitigating reasons to want to catch either species! Release them safely and try to catch something better to eat.

Where: Parore is one of the most common fish in our seas, although mainly seen in the North Island and upper South Island. Being mainly herbivorous they are typically found where weed grows. Large numbers are found in estuaries and bays, around mussel farms and wharf pilings, along rocky shorelines and around offshore islands. Check any North Island marina and you will see schools of them travelling and feeding amongst the docks. I have seen schools of them on the surface around Piercy Island off Cape Brett. Parore typically stay shallower than 50 m.

How: Few people target parore in New Zealand, although that is changing. Long regarded as less than average when it comes to eating quality, those caught in the open ocean, rather than in estuaries and marinas, are much better fare. The key is to remove the black stomach lining and get the processed fish on ice as soon as possible. With their powerful build parore are terrific sport, particularly on light tackle. Being lovers of weed, the perfect bait is the green weed found on the structure where you plan to fish. Use small hooks rigged under a float, then berley with additional weed. You will find surprisingly large numbers of parore around most mussel farms. They will also take small shellfish baits.

SAND FLOUNDER

Description: There are three species of flounder you may come into contact with on a regular basis. The black flounder is the least common, a dark olive to black colour with red and brown spots on both the body and fins. It wanders large distances upstream into fresh water. The yellowbelly flounder and sand flounder are the two most common species and make up the bulk of the commercial catch. Both have a dark grey-olive back; however, the sand flounder has a white underside while the yellowbelly fulfils its name by having a yellow margin around the fringe of its underside plus many scattered black dots. Very small yellowbelly flounder do have a white belly. The shape is distinctive between the two with the yellowbelly more oval and the sand flounder a diamond shape. Yellowbelly can grow to over 350 mm while sand flounder can exceed 400 mm on occasions.

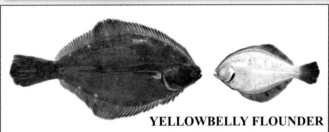

YELLOWBELLY FLOUNDER

SOLE

Description: There are two species of sole in New Zealand, the lemon sole and the New Zealand sole (pictured). The New Zealand sole is the most common. Sole are easily distinguishable from flounder by the rounded head. The New Zealand sole can grow to over 400 mm while the lemon sole can be 500 mm long and is wider.

Where: Flounder are found all around the country. At times they will be in only a couple of millimetres of water, while they range down to about 50 m for yellowbelly flounder and 100 m for sand flounder. Sand flounder are the predominant commercial catch, are found in coastal areas everywhere and increase in numbers in the South Island. Yellowbelly are the major catch in harbours and estuaries, particularly the muddy ones.

How: The most effective way to catch flounder is with a set or drag net. The most exciting way is to spear them at night! The nights of heavy Tilley lanterns and their delicate mantles have thankfully long departed to be replaced by lightweight LED underwater lights that run for hours on disposable or rechargeable batteries. Use a two-pronged spear for best control and least damage, and don't have barbs on the points. In some places, notably Tauranga Harbour, spearing is even carried out during the day. Flounder aggressively hunt crabs so it makes good sense that they will also take small lures dragged across the bottom. My good friend the Rev. Tony Dawson has spent a lot of time fishing around Invercargill with softbaits to prove that flounder are able to be specifically targeted that way. He has been very successful. Flounder will also eat small baits such as crabs, worms, maggots, shellfish, even corn and peas. A moving bait is best to attract the inquisitive flounder.

Where: Both New Zealand sole and lemon sole are found around most of the country with bigger populations in the south. Depths range from ankle deep to around 200 m.

How: Sole are a spear and net target for recreational fishers. I am not personally aware of anyone taking them regularly on rod and reel, although I'm sure a handful have succumbed to small baits or lures.

TARAKIHI

Description: Another significant species for recreational anglers. Tarakihi are clearly differentiated from porae by the obvious black patch forward of the dorsal. The overall colour is olive to dark along the back, with a silver iridescent belly. Some are more silver overall or even bronze. There is a noticeable aqua hue in the dorsal fins. Maximum length is over 500 mm and more than 4 kg; however, a fish of a kilo is more typical. A separately recognised species, the king tarakihi, grows even bigger. I've personally caught king tarakihi at nearly 6 kg and they can be bigger still. Tarakihi have a small mouth.

PORAE

Description: Porae are similar in shape to a tarakihi, to which they are related. They are a very pretty fish with a distinctive green-gold-bronze back, also running through shades of blue and silver. They have trailing tendrils on their pectoral fins. They can grow to 800 mm and a weight of 8 kg. The thick, rubbery lips are distinctive. Porae grow quickly when young before slowing after maturity. They are long-lived.

Where: Tarakihi are found all around the country. They can be caught from the shore in a few places and I've caught them from a boat in just a few metres of water; however, most of the recreational catch would come from 20–100 m with commercial catches down to 450 m. King tarakihi are primarily caught in the upper half of the North Island around deepwater pinnacles.

How: Catching tarakihi is all about location. Get on the school and you will have good success. A sounder is particularly useful for successful tarakihi fishing. Flasher rigs with 2/0 hooks are ideal for tarakihi. Small baits are essential, except for king tarakihi. A combination of tuatua and squid is my favourite tarakihi bait. Salted skipjack tuna is also a great option. Braided lines have transformed the way we catch tarakihi, particularly when they are being difficult and soft biting. Recurved hooks will help when fishing in deeper water — tarakihi have soft mouths and circle or recurved hooks will help keep them hooked when being retrieved from deep water. Tarakihi are superb to eat.

Where: Found primarily in the upper half of the North Island in depths to 200 m, although their distribution is as far as the upper South Island. A common sight for divers in the north with groups often seen in shallow water. Larger specimens I have personally caught have come from depths of 50–100 m, usually while targeting tarakihi on foul patches.

How: Porae are good to eat although come a very distant second to tarakihi, in my opinion. A popular species for spear fishers, they are usually a by-catch for rod and reel fishers. I have caught one small porae on a softbait, but they are best targeted with smaller baits and flasher rigs. They fight well and with fish of 4–5 kg far from rare they are challenging to catch.

SNAPPER

Description: From bright silver for fresh run fish caught over sand, to a dark crimson for resident fish caught amongst weed, snapper are beautiful and the most hunted fish in the country. Most New Zealand snapper have a rounded forehead, although a few have a smaller version of the bump exhibited in specimens caught in Australia. They can grow to around 1200 mm long and weigh over 20 kg. The all-tackle world record is over 16 kg.

TREVALLY

Description: The one New Zealand species of trevally also occurs in Australia and other Pacific areas, and is known as the silver trevally. There are colour variations with a bronze hue; however, it is primarily silver with a dark green back. Silver trevally have a yellow tail and fins. They can grow to over 10 kg in northern waters.

Where: Snapper are caught extensively throughout the North Island, the top of the South Island and down the upper part of the West Coast. They make seasonal visits further down the South Island. They can be found in only a few centimetres of water, tails out, feeding on shellfish, and they are also a surprise catch at times for those fishing in depths exceeding 200 m. The majority are targeted and caught in depths of less than 60 m. Shellfish beds, reef areas, foul patches, gravel banks, sand and mud areas will all hold snapper at some time, depending on the time of year, spawning movements and water temperature.

How: Snapper are by nature extremely aggressive, which explains the success of softbaits and lures in catching them. When feeding around work-ups or other times when they are schooled up, little finesse is required to target snapper. At other times the opposite is true. Those who have mastered the art of naturally presenting a bait by casting into a strike zone, or drifting it down a berley trail, will have good success. Flasher rigs are a great place to begin if you are new to chasing snapper. Many are taken on them every year. A beak style hook is still the first choice for two-hook rigs. I have had my best success using a single Kahle hook on light tackle strayline sets. All flesh baits work on snapper, although oily baits like skipjack tuna are the best. Surfcasters who fish over shellfish beds will generally do best with carefully tied shellfish baits. My favourite big snapper baits are a skipjack tuna head cut in half, or a squid tube with a pilchard inside it. Live baits also work for bigger snapper. Snapper like structure. Mussel farm structures offer both a food source and cover. Drifting on sand close to structure is a good option when you need to locate snapper.

Where: Silver trevally are primarily caught in the North Island and top of the South Island with occasional summer seasonal catches as far south as Otago. They can be found schooling on the surface chasing krill, in loose groups in shallow surface waters and on the bottom in depths down to 100 m or more. Apparently, the majority of the trawled commercial catch is taken in depths of 60–80 m.

How: An underrated food fish. While not necessarily the best to fry, it is excellent smoked and always the first choice for any kind of raw fish dish. Silver trevally need to be placed on ice as soon as possible after capture. They can turn up at any time when bottom fishing with cut baits, will grab softbaits, flies and lures but can sometimes drive anglers nuts by happily slurping up the berley while ignoring the carefully presented baits. When on the surface silver trevally will usually disregard baits but sometimes take small flies and softbaits. The best place to target silver trevally is around any structure. Many big ones are lost due to the trevally's soft mouth.

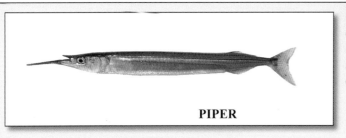

PIPER

Description: Piper look something like a mini marlin except that the bill is on the bottom jaw. A beautiful iridescent silver with an olive-green back, they probably average a little over 200 mm in length but can grow to over 400 mm.

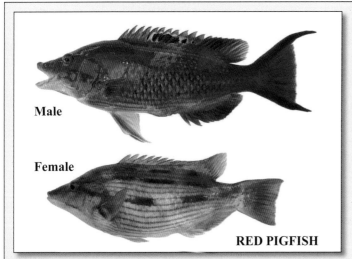

Male

Female

RED PIGFISH

Description: A member of the wrasse family, all red pigfish start life as females with some larger ones later becoming males. They are territorial and aggressively defend their patch. The male is a spectacular red colour with a yellow throat and distinctive black patch on the dorsal. They are also caught in Australia where they are called black spot wrasse because of the black dorsal patch. The female is much more subdued in colour, having horizontal red stripes, red blotches, plus more yellow on the side and fins, while also lacking the swept tail the male has. They grow to around 500 mm.

Where: Piper can be found all around the country. Large schools can be found off ocean beaches in the upper North Island. Smaller schools and individuals can turn up at any time. Wharves are a great place to find them but they can be anywhere. A light over the back of the boat at night-time will attract piper in most areas. We always see piper when spearing flounder at night in the harbours — they are tricky suckers to spear, but it can be done!

How: Netting piper is the most successful way to catch them, particularly in the Far North. Alternatively, a small spinning set, rigged with very small hooks, is the answer. Fish with tiny baits, either unweighted or otherwise hanging below a float. Berley is the key to successfully catching piper in large quantities. Bread and bran, or any oily fish, are the preferred choices. Bait can include squid or any shiny fish skin, pilchard and skipjack being ideal. I'm told piper love live maggots too ... Piper are very good to eat; however, they are prime bait for many species. Fished alive there probably isn't a better bait. Rigged and fished whole they are like candy for big snapper and kingfish. Piper can be rigged whole as trolling baits too.

Where: Primarily a northern North Island species, found mainly from East Cape north. Personally, I have never caught one on the west coast, or even seen one while diving there. Usually caught in depths shallower than 70 m.

How: Red pigfish are a by-catch when fishing with baits around reef and kelp areas. By all accounts they are good to eat and are actually targeted in Australia; however, few fishers here keep them for food. Red pigfish will also take softbaits.

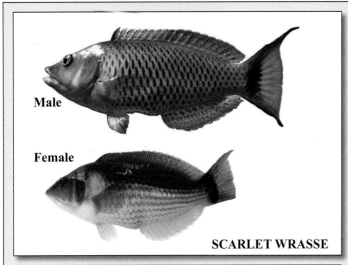

Male

Female

SCARLET WRASSE

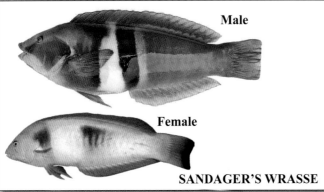

Male

Female

SANDAGER'S WRASSE

Description: Wrasse are often called parrotfish (which they are not) and are born as females before later becoming male. There are several species in our waters (and not all are covered here). The scarlet wrasse can exceed 400 mm and 2 kg. Females tend to be pink-red with more yellow on the flanks, while males darken as they get older and the ray at the top of the tail lengthens. The banded wrasse is the biggest, reaching 600 mm and over 5 kg. Banded wrasse go through many colour variations; when young, a red-brown predominates with orange or green. Adults get darker as they grow and become males; there are hints of purple with vertical bars on the body and fins in yellow but not always distinct. The colours here are indicative only. The spotty is a fish known to anglers everywhere, young and old. They, too, are a member of the wrasse family and capable of growing to 300 mm. There are many variations in colour with brown, orange, yellow and light blue all possible; however, the large black blotch on the side of the female, rather than black spots, is distinctive. Sandager's wrasse is a species not known to most anglers. The male is a spectacular rainbow of colours, making it the second most spectacular fish in our northern waters (if you ever get to experience the colours of the lesser-known splendid perch, you will understand that assessment). The females, on the other hand, are also distinctive by being coloured with cream and brown, as drab as the male is spectacular. Growth is to around 500 mm.

Where: The Sandager's wrasse is a resident of the east coast from around East Cape north, with the biggest population seen on sand patches close to reef at the Poor Knights Islands. The other wrasse are found throughout New Zealand with the populations appearing to increase in number as you head south. Most reside in depths of less than 50 m, scarlet wrasse a little deeper, with spotties caught down to 200 m. Rock and kelp patches and reefs are the usual haunt of most wrasse.

How: The Sandager's wrasse was almost unknown to anglers before the advent of softbaits. I had certainly never caught one on flesh bait. The first time I dived the Poor Knights, now more than 30 years ago, I was stunned by the sight of such a spectacular fish in such numbers. I have now caught several on softbaits and safely returned them to the water. I see no need to eat Sandager's wrasse. All the other wrasse will aggressively eat almost anything presented to them, including all flesh baits, lures and softbaits, often becoming a nuisance when targeting more desirable species. Banded wrasse are eaten by some anglers. The same species is caught in Australia and there is a commercial fishery for it. Many go to the live fish market for sale and consumption.

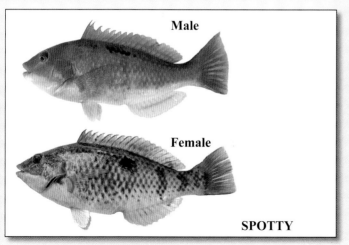

Male

Female

SPOTTY

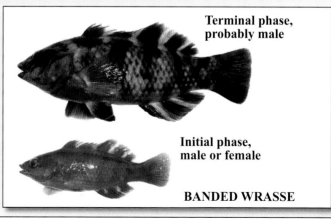

Terminal phase, probably male

Initial phase, male or female

BANDED WRASSE

19 ◡ Where to Catch Fish

The introduction of the GPS was the catalyst for change. When I started selling GPS units in the early 1990s a basic model cost at least $2000. Now every cell phone has a GPS at no extra charge …

My notebook full of marks, such as the one with the pine tree over the red roof, is of limited use now. Instead the GPS will put me within metres of the spot I saved. The ability to store and share marks has generated an industry too, with high-quality charts, books and websites available to guide you to some very good spots.

Because this section of the book is aimed squarely at those just beginning their fishing career, not the experienced, I have attempted to give you an introduction to each area with a few suggestions along the way! Use it as a starting point, then garner local knowledge, read books, study the local charts and go fishing!

My thanks to the people at Gasoline Alley Services for their assistance with compiling this section.

But before we begin …

Personal Safety

We still live in one of the safest countries anywhere; however, incidents happen that show we live in a changing world where safety and security shouldn't be taken lightly. I've personally had a vehicle broken into while parked at Raglan's Manu Bay, which is my home port and somewhere I've always regarded as safe. I experienced another attempted break-in when at Waihau Bay. On that occasion my stepson, who was asleep in the boat, chased the gang prospect (so we later found out) down the road — a very stupid thing to do. I've been in a contest at the Bay of Islands when a boat trailer was stolen from the boat ramp as the owner fished. I've also heard of a fellow writer attacked while walking back to his boat at Houhora, while another had a gun presented at him while at East Cape.

These are all isolated incidents and shouldn't deter you from fishing anywhere you wish. Most people will never have a problem, but a degree of preparedness and care is important.

• Don't cross any private property without getting permission from the owner.

• If someone is stopping you from accessing a beach by threat or insisting a payment should be made for access, don't get into a debate; withdraw and report the incident.

• If you are leaving a vehicle parked while fishing, ensure that there is nothing valuable left inside and/or visible.

• Secure your trailer with preferably two devices, including a wheel lock.

• Remove your trailer winch handle when parked, or have a spare secured on board. I learnt that lesson after the second time I had one stolen …

• Act as you would at home; don't put yourself in dangerous situations and don't walk around at night on your own.

• If parking up at night, remove all loose and valuable gear from the boat and vehicle.

• Don't leave spare surf rods attached to roof racks on your vehicle when unattended.

• Let someone know where you are going and your expected return time.

John Dory

Boat Ramps

In most areas, Auckland being a glaring exception, we are reasonably well supplied with boat ramps. Before using a ramp you're not familiar with, or before going to an area you don't know, you need to do a bit of research. The regulations vary. For example, some of the best boat ramps in the country are in Tauranga and have free access. In Northland, the district council charge an annual fee that covers all the local ramps in their jurisdiction. Westhaven, in Auckland, has a barrier arm system with a $2 fee payable to access the ramp. The adjacent 'pay and display' carpark is a Mecca for towies. Be warned ...

Other places, such as the main wharf ramp at Raglan, currently have a major parking problem. These issues, and many others, are repeated all around the country. Checking the local details first could save a lot of heartbreak.

The other important issue to check on is the ramp (and access way) surface. If you are new to boat ownership, you need to familiarise yourself with your towing vehicle's capabilities. This becomes even more important if you are using a two-wheel drive or if the ramp is steep or just hard sand. You also need to know how much water is required to float the vessel and whether there are limitations around the tides at the selected ramp.

FAR LEFT: *The boat ramp at Tauranga's Sulphur Point is second to none, and this photo shows only part of it! Easy all-tide access, good parking and safe loading / unloading make it so good.*

Vehicle Beach Access

There are usually local regulations around beach access for vehicles. Some, like at Ninety Mile Beach, are designated public roads. Others are shared space. Regardless, there are some basics to observe.

• Look after the vegetation. It's critical to the survival of the beach and its residents. The areas around the sand dunes are often breeding zones for seabirds.

• Carry enough equipment to be able to extricate your vehicle (or someone else's), in an emergency.

• Watch out for other beach users, particularly children.

• Watch out for lines and other fishing equipment that may already be on the beach.

• Drive at a sensible speed to suit your vehicle and the condition of the beach.

Butterfish

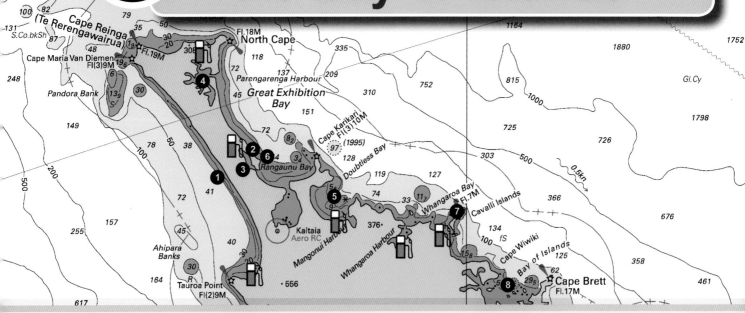

1 The **Far North**, *including* the **Bay of Islands**

1 Ninety Mile Beach
2 Henderson Bay
3 Houhora Wharf
4 Parengarenga Harbour
5 Doubtless Bay
6 Houhora Mussel Farm
7 Cavalli Islands
8 Bay of Islands

The Essentials — When it comes to big fish, a wide range of species and access to top-end predators, nowhere in the country can beat the Far North. The Bay of Islands has an international reputation and continues to produce great catches every year. Ninety Mile Beach is New Zealand's premier surf fishing destination. Rock fishing exponents in the upper North Island think nothing of driving through the night to get to the best positions in time for the change of light — that's how good the fishing is. There are also sheltered options available, regardless of the wind direction, which help make a trip north successful. While the game fish are a summer/autumn phenomenon, the Far North can be fished at any time of year. The crowds thin after March!

Access — Access onto Ninety Mile Beach is well indicated. Two-wheel drive vehicles can enter and drive on the beach at certain places and certain stages of the tide, typically three hours after high tide. Seek local knowledge. At the southern end of the beach near Ahipara is Shipwreck Bay. It provides sheltered beach launching, in good conditions, and direct access to the Tasman Sea. On the east coast there are four excellent places to fish from that are serviced by very good boat ramps. Houhora is the furthest north of them and is a great place to visit. There is a very good boat ramp beside the fishing club. The fabulous Doubtless Bay is accessed by a good concrete ramp at Mangonui. Further south, Whangaroa is a wonderful place to visit with a good ramp just past the fishing club. The Bay of Islands has multiple boat-launching facilities, notably at Waitangi, Doves Bay and Opua. There are many sand ramps throughout the whole Far North area.

Sue Gillespie with a great Bay of Islands snapper.

Launching at Waitangi boat ramp in the Bay of Islands.

Recommendations

Shore Fishing

There are so many opportunities that it's hard to isolate any one.

1. *Ninety Mile Beach* is obviously a destination all surf fishers want to visit. Best spots will vary on the day, although the area around the Bluff is consistent.

2. One lesser-known gem is *Henderson Bay,* north of Houhora. It's a great spot in late summer.

3. *Houhora wharf* is the prime place to catch john dory and kingfish.

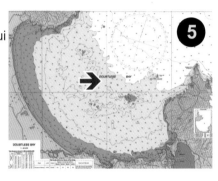

4. *Parengarenga Harbour* has the most unique and amazing shore fishing in the whole country. Softbaits work there, too.

Boat Fishing

Again the opportunities are so extensive that it's hard to pick just a few.

5. *Doubtless Bay.* Launching at Mangonui gives access to the extensive playground that is Doubtless Bay. From Cape Karikari to Berghan Point the opportunities are amazing. I've even hooked marlin within the bay. A good place to start is west of Fair Way Reef. The chart shows several major reef areas as well as foul patches and pinnacles. Not all are on the chart. Drifting with baits and softbaits is a good way to start. Anchoring and straylining into a foul patch should produce good action.

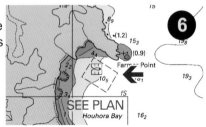

6. *The mussel farm outside of Houhora.* Like all mussel farms it fishes well, but arrive when it is being harvested and it is spectacular! Expect snapper, trevally and kingfish. Softbaits are

best if the farm is being worked. Otherwise anchor up, berley and fire out some cut baits. Drift fishing a few miles seaward of the farm can also be very good. Look for birds. If they are around, expect some great snapper fishing.

7. *The Cavalli Islands.* The fishing area is so extensive that it needs weeks of exploration. Sometimes the likely spots are not always obvious. I have had good success drifting on the sand in the area to the west of the *Rainbow Warrior* wreck. Start by Horonui Island, or

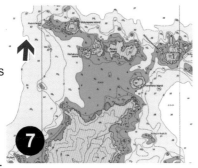

drift towards it, depending on the wind and tide. We have had best success using softbaits. There are many places to anchor up and berley or to cast softbaits into washes and shorelines.

8. *The Bay of Islands.* Another extensive area to explore that fishes well, even with the pressure it receives. During November, December and early January the snapper, often with kingfish in attendance, school up in the area off Roberton Island through to Red Head. The last time I was there the biggest snapper we caught was a shade under the magic 20 lb weight! The fish move around quite a bit but the place to start is in 40 m off Roberton. A sounder will let you find the fish and save wasted drifting time. Watch

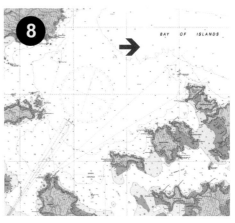

where the charter boats are fishing. Don't crowd them, but note the depth they are fishing. If you can't find the fish, anchor up off any foul you find off Red Head. When drifting, mix it up with baits, softbaits and slow jigs.

This marlin was caught and released off the Nine Pin at the Bay of Islands.

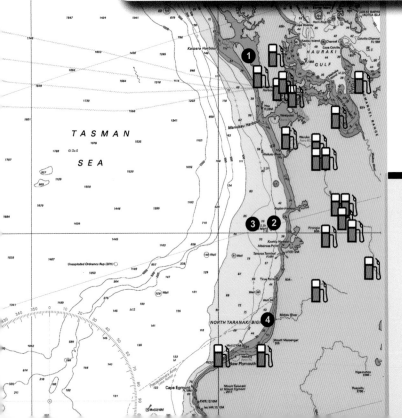

The West Coast, *from* Ahipara *to* New Plymouth

2

Safety Warning — *crossing west coast bars is a specialised skill that needs to be learned in the company of an experienced boat operator. **Please**, don't take risks, seek local knowledge and stay in touch with the Coastguard via the local VHF radio network.*

g.a.s.

Petrol Service Stations at —

Ahipara, Broadwood, Kaihu, Maungaturoto, Okaihau, Omapere, Paparoa, Tinopai, Waimamaku, Helensville, Waitoki, Titirangi, Swanson, Urenui, Waiau Pa, Whakamaru, Whatawhata, Mangere, Mangere Bridge, Mt Roskill, National Park, Pio Pio, Pokeno, Pukekawa, Te Awamutu, Hamilton, Tuakau South, Waiuku, Turangi

1 Shelly Beach, Kaipara

2 Jackson's Reef, Raglan

3 Gannet Island

4 Mokau River

Sourced from Land Information New Zealand data. Crown Copyright Reserved.

The Essentials — The western side of the North Island comes with challenges but great rewards. Every single one of the harbour entrances requires local knowledge for safe navigation. Please don't make a crossing of any harbour bar without gaining that knowledge and correctly equipping your vessel. Partnering with a buddy boat while you gain further experience is the only way to go. The west coast offers a diverse range of species and we are still learning about some of the potential. Some amazing things have also happened; for example, in Raglan Harbour, a big planting programme around the water edges has seen snapper in greater numbers within the harbour than when I regularly fished there in the 1970s. Of course, there are negatives too; unfortunately, the readily accessible mussel beds were cleaned out during the 1970s.

Weather is the key factor that controls the fishing on the west coast. While good fishing can be experienced all year round, there are peak times. The further south you go, the higher the likelihood that you will run into lots of spiny dogfish as the waters cool. The general pattern sees snapper spawn off the coast from around October, peaking in November and December, generally in depths of 40–60 m. Local knowledge is required to know when and where it is happening. From January, large numbers of big kahawai move in where the snapper were. The snapper move inshore into shallower water during the summer. Over Christmas we have taken large catches of small snapper on the reefs; however, by April and May, the big fish are well inshore, fattening before their winter departure.

Evening fishing is, at times, spectacular. Gurnard are around all year on the sand off the reefs. Trevally and john dory round out the other key species. Off Taranaki, hapuku move into the shallows at select times during winter. Local knowledge is well guarded on where! Some very large kingfish can be found around any reef structure during summer.

The harbours are primarily a summer venue when it comes to the best snapper fishing. The Manukau Harbour has a superb gurnard fishery and they can be caught most of the year. All of the west coast harbours hold flounder year-round. Any of the beaches will produce at times, with the best fishing from the Kaipara north. The west coast is a great place to fish with kite or torpedo.

Manu Bay at Raglan. It is a very rare thing to see it this calm!

Access — There are four exceptions to the rule that you have to cross a bar to fish the west coast. The first is Manu Bay at Raglan. I regard it as my home ramp so I know it well. Please don't just rock up expecting to launch; depending on the tide and swells the water can surge 30 m or more and the waves can break on the ramp and over the breakwater. On a benign day it's fantastic. Otherwise, check it out first and expect your vehicle to get wet eight times out of ten ... The second exception is Sunset Beach at Port Waikato; however, it's a fair-weather option and you really need a tractor. The third is Port Taranaki, which has fantastic facilities and comparatively easy access to the open sea. It's a great place to go if you want to experience the coast in a little more safety. The final option is the boat ramp at Cape Egmont, although it is private and belongs to the local fishing club.

Recommendations

1. *Shelly Beach Wharf, Kaipara Harbour.*
The Kaipara is a fantastic body of water with huge currents and great fishing. Traditionally, the area called the 'Graveyard' at the entrance is fished with big baits and monstrous sinkers — think up to a kilo!

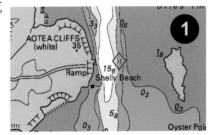

It's fished at slack tide and the fishing is spectacular! However, it's a dangerous area without some knowledge of the water flows and effects of opposing currents. It's called the Graveyard for a reason! Over the last couple of years it has been found that fishing the area with softbaits, on the drift, is even better than bait. The fish are bigger and the only special thing required is heavier jig heads rather than heavy tackle.

However, as a great place to start, the Shelly Beach wharf is a top producer. The area to the left accounts for lots of gurnard and there are some very big snapper caught there at times. Sharks and rays are also regular visitors. There is a good boat ramp. Fishing with baits in the channels and bank edges further up the harbour can be very successful. Use salted skipjack or mullet. It's a good way to become familiar with this extensive, testing but ultimately fruitful harbour.

2. *Jackson's Reef, Raglan.* This is an extensive area divided into three sections; the main reef is about three miles offshore, the inner reef starts from a mile out, while the Pinnacles are seaward of the main reef. The top of the main reef is about 15 m deep. Waves can break here in a big swell! The main reef can

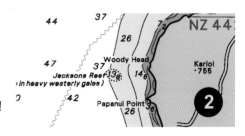

produce good snapper fishing at times. The inner reef can be better, though, and in late summer can be spectacular. There are stories I can tell ... The Pinnacles at times hold large quantities of small snapper. I have fished there when others have failed miserably yet we have binned up. The trick is that the fish often sit in mid-water. Watch your sounder ... Drift outside of Jackson's to catch gurnard. As soon as you get a bite, anchor up. If they don't keep biting, drift again.

3. *Gannet Island, Raglan or Kawhia.* One of the few pieces of structure on the coast, Gannet is a true destination spot, being a stunning island to look at but best to stay upwind of because it smells! It seemed to be a huge journey to get there when I was a kid and starting my fishing career (it's about 17 nm from Raglan and 12 nm from Kawhia). Back then the kingfish were in plague proportions. They disappeared in just a year or two during the 1970s. However, they are making a comeback. I have caught some big snapper at Gannet, and tarakihi fairly regularly, but it isn't a brilliant fishing spot, even though I have had some magic days there. Look for the kingfish along the edge of the vertical wall that goes from 60 m to 10 m. Strayline for snapper

in the shallows. South west of Gannet is a patch of foul with very small rises, not surprisingly called the South West Reef. You will often find the Kawhia charter boats fishing there. It's a little over 60 m deep and produces snapper, golden snapper, tarakihi and blue cod. It's the better place to fill the bin.

4. *Mokau River.* Synonymous with whitebait in season, a drive to Mokau will never be wasted because you can stop for a meal of the delicacies as well! Fishing the river mouth, particularly spinning, is productive for kahawai, and I have heard many stories, although second-hand, of huge catches when they are chasing the whitebait. Snapper are also caught there. The bar is an issue, and very tide-dependent so local knowledge is essential. I have personally only crossed there once but the results were spectacular, with snapper near 20 lb taken on the sand in 40 m.

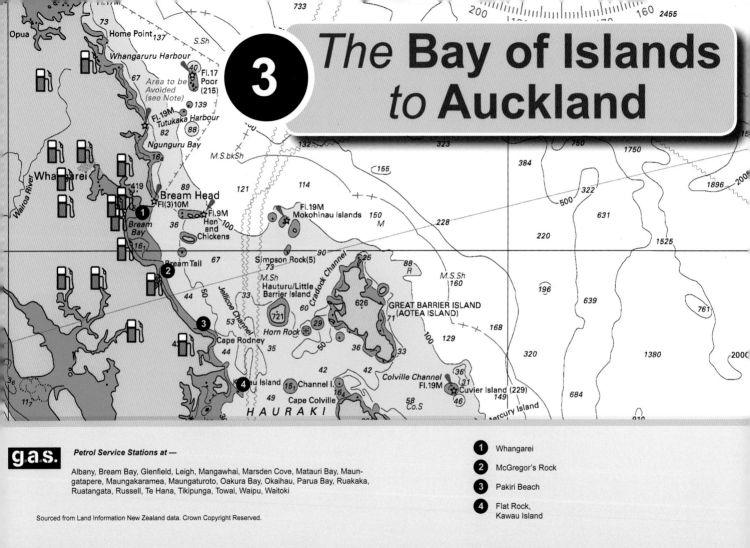

The Bay of Islands to Auckland

3

g.a.s.

Petrol Service Stations at —

Albany, Bream Bay, Glenfield, Leigh, Mangawhai, Marsden Cove, Matauri Bay, Maungatapere, Maungakaramea, Maungaturoto, Oakura Bay, Okaihau, Parua Bay, Ruakaka, Ruatangata, Russell, Te Hana, Tikipunga, Towai, Waipu, Waitoki

Sourced from Land Information New Zealand data. Crown Copyright Reserved.

1 Whangarei

2 McGregor's Rock

3 Pakiri Beach

4 Flat Rock,
Kawau Island

The Essentials — I recently did the trip from Auckland to Paihia in a trailer boat over several days. The fact is there are so many fishing opportunities it is mind-blowing. The whole area is well serviced by good roads and boat ramps. The greater Whangarei area, encompassing Marsden Cove and Tutukaka, is a must-see destination with outstanding fishing that stays, relatively speaking, under the radar.

Being Auckland's holiday coast, crowds peak between late December and when school starts again. Fortunately, the best time to visit the area is March, April and May. You will get settled weather (usually, cyclones permitting) and a lot less competition for accommodation and fishing spots. That said, if there is any one month above all others that I would choose to fish anywhere in the upper North Island, it is December.

The fuel dock and ramp at Marsden Cove.

Access — There are plenty of easy surf beaches to fish in the region, as well as good rock fishing spots. While there are too many to cover here, a look at the charts will help give you a few starting points. Fortunately, they are all within a short drive of Whangarei so any non-fishers can be entertained. The wharves in the area all fish well at times.

There is a mixture of beach launching spots and good ramps dotted throughout the area. The most wonderful facility of them all would have to be the ramps at Marsden Cove marina. It's exactly how such a facility should be designed, with petrol available on the water via the pumps Gasoline Alley Services have there. There is a tackle shop adjoining and a very good café with excellent coffee.

Recommendations

1. *Whangarei.* From Marsden wharf, which has good fishing on an incoming tide, and a reputation as a squid destination, to the whole area outside the heads, plus the harbour too, Whangarei has it all. Look for birds working out from the harbour entrance in spring and summer, and success is almost guaranteed. Drifting with lures and softbaits will catch the biggest fish. Throughout Bream Bay there are many foul patches that produce fish. Berley and straylined baits will produce the goods as will softbaits by drifting. Many of the spots are marked on the chart, otherwise a group of boats in close proximity will give the game away. Many of the same places are fished by

boats launching at Waipu. Don't underestimate the Whangarei entrance when entering and exiting the harbour. Further out, the Hen and Chickens also fish consistently.

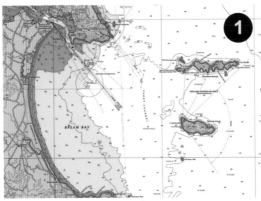

2. *McGregor's Rock.* Accessed from Mangawhai. While the access has improved please remember it is still a bar crossing, requiring great care. McGregor's is a consistent performer. Reputation says it is best fished by drifting (incidentally, the only way I've fished it) and at times it can be very

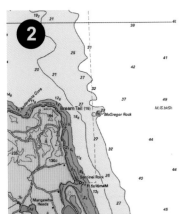

productive. Mix things up with jigs, softbaits and cut bait to see what's working. The last time I was there we did well drifting with softbaits.

3. *Pakiri Beach.* Omaha has great facilities for launching. Head out to Pakiri Beach and drift fish with cut baits or anchor and berley. The place fishes consistently over summer

and by noting where most the fishing effort is being concentrated you will get an idea of the best depth. Schools of kahawai are often seen on the surface. Surf fishing from Pakiri Beach can also be rewarding. I have fished a couple of times along the shore past the Goat Island reserve, by boat, and while each time has been a 'last resort' effort I have caught snapper every time. Berley and big baits around the change of light would be very interesting ...

Many big snapper get caught around Kawau Island.

4. *Flat Rock, Kawau Island*. It's hard to isolate any one spot around Kawau Island; however, Flat Rock has a deserved reputation for producing big fish at times. It's a great place to target kingfish, with a higher likelihood of success than most spots, while at times the strayline and berley fishing will produce very big fish. Be aware that it can run very hot and very cold, though. However, there is another advantage; while travelling to Flat Rock there is every chance you will see work-ups. If you do, then that is where you should be fishing. If you bomb out completely, fish with baits or softbaits back in around the southern end of the island. Kawau is a great place to berley up for snapper during the winter.

Brett Rathe and his charter boat Assassin *are famous for their almost legendary results on big snapper in the Hauraki Gulf. The author was there the day this one (and many others) were caught!*

g.a.s. *Petrol Service Stations at —*

Albany, Glenfield, Waiheke Island, Mangere Bridge, Mangere, Mt Eden, Balmoral, Mt Roskill, Penrose, Swanson, Titirangi, Otahuhu, Papatoetoe, Glen Innes, Panmure, Howick, Pakuranga, Maraetai, Kawakawa Bay, Kaiaua

Sourced from Land Information New Zealand data. Crown Copyright Reserved.

1 The Channels

2 The Tank Farm

3 Thumb Point

4 Tarahiki Island

The Essentials — I once had a great fishing trip with Auckland's number-one fishing guru, Bruce Duncan. For the whole weekend we were never out of sight of the Sky Tower and we caught snapper at every spot! That's the gem that is the Waitemata Harbour and the Hauraki Gulf. Those in the know catch fish consistently throughout the year. With a little bit of effort put into finding out where things are happening at any given time there is no reason why you can't join that group. There are four styles of fishing that those chasing snapper generally employ.

The first is fishing the channels with cut baits and heavier sinkers. Huge numbers of boats can be seen in the major channels when the fishing is on, which is during the summer months.

The second is chasing the work-ups. You will find them outside the islands at various times from spring to autumn. The spring fishing is the best.

Option three is to fish softbaits and lures. The channels can produce some excellent fishing while the experts know where to find snapper by casting and drifting in very shallow water.

The final option is to anchor while straylining and deploying berley. Other options include fishing with small live baits for john dory and snapper. There can be excellent fishing for kings as well around any of the outer islands and reefs. Casting lures and whole piper around the navigation beacons can also create some wonderful opportunities to catch kingfish.

The Gulf Islands are wonderful places to fish. Great Barrier and Little Barrier are consistent producers while the Mokohinau Islands are something particularly special. Affectionately known as 'the Mokes', there is no better place in New Zealand to cast softbaits and catch XOS snapper.

The author filleting snapper under the Auckland Harbour Bridge, just metres away from where they were caught! Note that if you fillet at sea the onus is on you, not fisheries officers, to prove that the fish are of legal size.

Access — Auckland has a mostly poor range of boat ramps to select from. Many of the issues are around parking. Getting there early can be important. Westhaven, followed by Half Moon Bay, would be the best two options. The parking at Westhaven is expensive and must be paid for in advance. God help you if you're late.

There are some good options further up the harbour, although it is a longer run to get out to sea. On the North Shore there is hard sand launching at Brown's Bay and Torbay, but little nearby parking. Takapuna and Bayswater have good ramps.

Recommendations

1. *The channels.* The Motuihe and Sergeant channels fill with boats in summer, such that it feels like you can walk from one to the next. It can be pandemonium. Fortunately, the channels also fill with snapper. I don't like crowds so I normally fish away from the channels. I

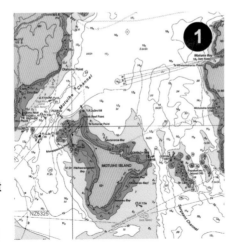

assisted with a charter group in the area a few years ago. We drifted with softbaits on the edge of the banks just outside Sergeant Channel. At times I had up to four people waiting for me to net their snapper! Look for schools of snapper on the sounder. They do move around and you will have to follow them.

2. *The Tank Farm* — The area of the Auckland waterfront around Westhaven and what is known as the Tank Farm is a surprisingly productive fishery. From the shore snapper can be caught during summer — not bad for big city! Something that the charter boats have known for years and the rest of us are starting to realise is that there are huge schools of very good snapper in the waters off Tank Farm. Drifting with baits or, better still, softbaits, will see you fill the bin when the fishing is on. The general area from west of the harbour bridge to Devonport is where it happens.

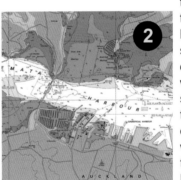

3. *Thumb Point, Waiheke Island.* I haven't fished this spot much, yet it makes the suggestion list for several reasons. Firstly, it can produce good snapper with the right combination of wind and tide plus berley. Secondly, it is a very good place to fish for kingfish with live bait. Thirdly, it

is close to Gannet Island, a place where it's common to see work-ups. If you see action, go straight there. Over the years I have had many reports of good fishing from this area. If that isn't happening, then have a look at the northern end of Man o' War Bay. The currents sweep around the corner a bit, creating a bit of a back eddy at times; however, it is a good, usually sheltered spot to

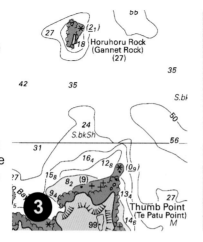

strayline a few snapper and kahawai. I fished the spot during one episode of television's *Match Fishing League* and caught enough fish to win the match! I recommend this whole area if you are new to boating and boat fishing in Auckland as it has lots of opportunities and sheltered areas. Just be aware of the reserve at the start of the Waiheke Channel.

4. *Tarahiki Island to the east of Pakatoa.* The very first time I was taken fishing by one of New Zealand's foremost jigging experts, Eric Morman, we drifted and fished the area

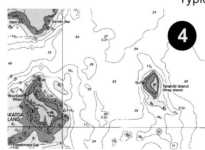

east of Ponui Island. This was one of his main patches and while the results on the day weren't up to his (very high) expectations, we still caught fish and I learnt a lot. What I have learnt since is that the key to fishing the area is to look at the charts and study where the banks are. Typically, the fish will be stacked on one side or the other, depending on the tide. Sometimes you will see them on the sounder, but not always. An example of the latter happened to me recently. We drifted one of the banks inside of Tarahiki Island while making lunch. In fact, I think the rod was in the holder when the first snapper grabbed a softbait. We reset and hooked up again. By the time we finished after several drifts, we had filled the bin. It's a very fishy area. Tarahiki Island also produces some great kingfish.

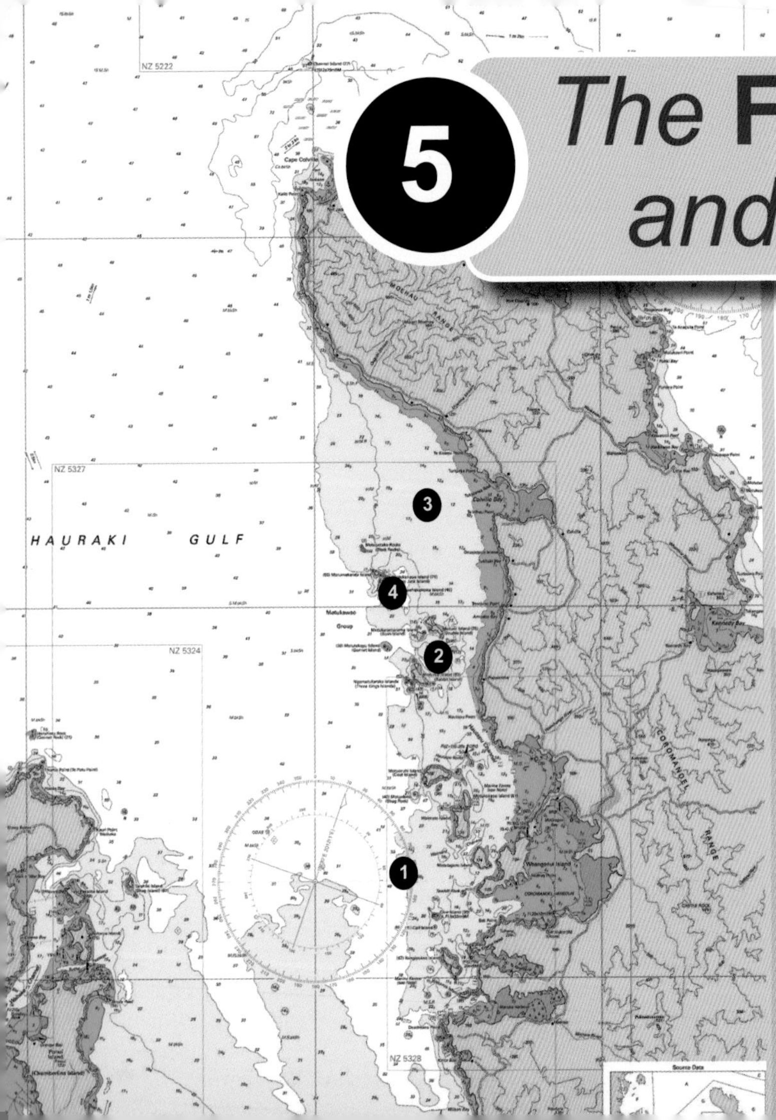

Year after year the Coromandel produces fantastic fishing while having sheltered spots to chase them from. If you have a small boat, want to learn in a protected environment or just love catching snapper, Coromandel is your place ...

g.a.s.

Petrol Service Stations at —

Kaiaua, Coromandel Town, Hahei, Tairua*, Pauanui, Paeroa, Cambridge, Tahuna, Hamilton, Te Awamutu (*member only)

1 The Cow and Calf

2 Hautapu Channel

3 Amodeo Bay

4 Kingfish!

Sourced from Land Information New Zealand data. Crown Copyright Reserved.

The Essentials — Coromandel is synonymous with mussels, which means mussel farms, which in turn means fishing around mussel farms! It is extremely successful. I highly recommend a trip with one of the mussel barge charter operations if you want to learn the 'ropes'. It will almost always result in a feed of snapper plus a few mussel fritters cooked for you while you fish!

Care needs to be taken when fishing around the farms to protect their ropes and your propeller. If you plan to fish the farms regularly, get a stainless hook made that has a rope attached at one end. Use it to anchor the boat to a mussel line.

Not all the best fishing happens around mussel farms, however. The best fishing occurs when the work-ups are around. Find those and it's snapper fillets for dinner. Otherwise it's all about water flow. Finding channels and banks where the water flows, carrying food or movements of fish, is the key. The local experts know where and when to go for the different stages of the tides. There are so many potential places you should be able to find a feed and a sheltered spot to fish somewhere.

There are many places where you can fish from the shore, all the way along the coast. The results are variable, but good fish are caught. Watch out for very rough, tackle-stealing bottom in many areas.

Access — The Thames coast road is a beautiful drive with stunning vistas, but it can be a nightmare to drive with a big boat in tow. Be careful and don't rush. There could be a truck or another boat and trailer around the next blind bend. To save the drag over the hill to Coromandel, many now launch at Waikawau Bay. The ramp is very busy on a fine weekend. Be aware that it is very tidal and, depending on your boat size, you will probably need an hour or two of water to pick your way up the channel. The ramp at Te Kouma is the best known and is an all-tide launching spot. Parking is very difficult at weekends, though. You may have a walk to contend with.

My favourite place to go from is Amodeo Bay. It's a tricky little concrete ramp that may have an associated surge. Avoid low tide. I highly recommend getting the owners at Angler's Lodge to launch you with their tractor. They will do so for a small fee. You won't even get your feet wet! There are similar options at Papa Aroha and Long Bay.

There are several ramps from Thames itself through to Waikawau Bay. All are tidal and most require a four-wheel drive. If you plan to fish the area regularly, it's not a bad idea to take a Sunday drive to suss out which ones are suitable for your rig. Winds from the west can make recovery of your boat fraught with adventure ...

Recommendations

1. *The Cow and the Calf.* These landmark islands off the Coromandel harbour are consistent fish producers. For years we would anchor just short of the islands in the channel and catch plenty of snapper with cut baits straylined along the bottom. A good friend

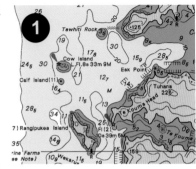

would regularly anchor close to the island and catch very big snapper during the night. Some of the best fishing happens by drifting alongside the reef areas with jigs and softbaits. Mix it up until you find what's working on the day.

2. *The Hautapu Channel.* A reliably fishy area and one of my personal favourites. The mussel farms on the shore side fish particularly well while the area from the farms to the channel markers is one of the best to drift fish with lures, particularly softbaits. Look for work-ups in the area too.

3. *Off Amodeo Bay.* The islands out from Papa Aroha are well fished and popular. At times the fishing can be spectacular. On one memorable weekend I won a fishing contest with a snapper of over 8 kg but, unbeknownst to me, the husband of one of my employees was just around the corner from me landing a snapper that weighed a genuine 30 lb! While the channels and points are the obvious fishing spots, I have been regularly successful by just drifting the flat bottom half way across to the islands with dropper rigs and cut baits. The area off Colville is another where

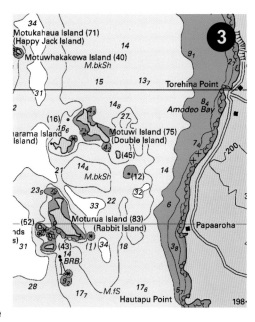

I've tried the same trick with success. Better still, set your baits on the bottom and cast softbaits as you drift. There are often lots of baitfish schools showing on the sounder in this area. If you can stay with them, they can be caught on sabiki rigs.

4. *The kingfish of the Coromandel.* The whole area is renowned for great kingfish catches. While they are occasionally caught by trolling, most are caught on livebaits. TV show host Milan Radonich would be the foremost proponent of catching them in the Coromandel and he was the founder of the 'Kings of Coromandel' fishing contest. Milan often fishes in shallow water for his catches in all of the harbours. He's caught them in less than a metre of water! Generally, though, search out areas of water flow close to weed and structure. Anchor and fish with livebaits under balloons and keep plenty of berley going. You can catch snapper while you wait for the kings to turn up.

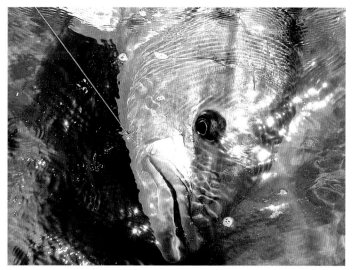

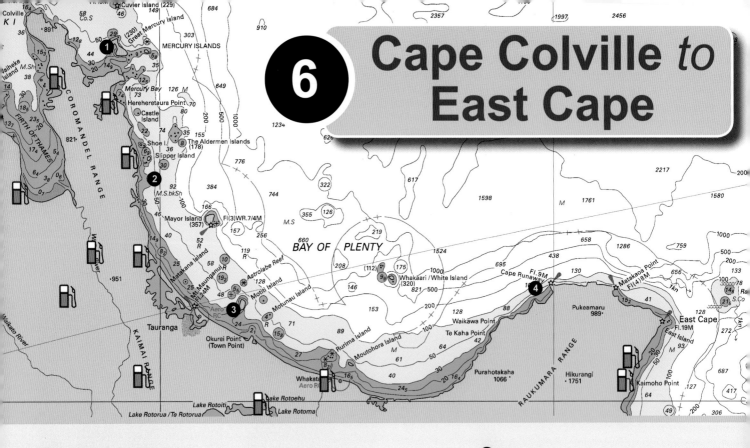

6 Cape Colville *to* East Cape

BAY OF PLENTY

Whakaari / White Island (320)

Cape Runaway
Matakaoa Point
Fl(4)18M

East Cape
Fl.19M
East Island

COROMANDEL RANGE

FIRTH OF THAMES

KAIMAI RANGE

RAUKUMARA RANGE

MERCURY ISLANDS

Cuvier Island (229)
Great Mercury Island (230)
Mercury Bay
Hereheretaura Point
Castle Island
Shoe I.
Slipper Island
The Aldermen Islands (178)

Mayor Island
Matakana Island
Mt Maunganui
Fl.2.4M
Astrolabe Reef
Motiti Island
Motunau Island

Tauranga
Okurei Point
(Town Point)
Aero RC

Whakatane
Aero R
Rurima Island
Moutohora Island

Lake Rotoiti
Lake Rotoehu
Lake Rotorua / Te Rotorua
Lake Rotoma

Waikawa Point
Te Kaha Point
Purahotakaha 1066
Hikurangi 1751
Pukeamaru 989
Kaimoho Point

Waikato River

1. The Sisters
2. The Dogger Bank
3. The Knoll, Motiti Island
4. Waihau Bay

The Essentials — There is just far too much to do in this part of the world! From the great kingfish available out from Tairua to the snapper and tarakihi fishing out of Tauranga, to the unique fishery that is Waihau Bay — and I haven't even mentioned the consistent beach fishing around Whakatane and elsewhere! Every possible New Zealand fishing experience is contained in this part of the country.

Waihau Bay has the best blue marlin fishing in the country while at Te Kaha the spot called Pub Rock has been the home of some of the biggest snapper caught anywhere in the country.

Whakatane is the gateway to White Island, although some of the local fishing treasures are much closer to home. Tauranga has a fabulous range of opportunities from broadbill swordfish at Mayor Island to consistent snapper and kingfish within the harbour.

Further north there is Whangamata, Waihi, Tairua, Whitianga and all the places in between to explore and fish.

The Mercury Islands are a true experience and continue to fish consistently for big snapper and crayfish, while the Aldermen Islands are one of my favourite places in the whole country, particularly for fishing softbaits or chasing kingfish on long jigs and live baits.

Access — Any local authority wanting to see how a boat ramp should be built needs to visit Tauranga. They have nailed it big time and they look after their boaties. In fact, I would suggest that if you live in the upper North Island and have just bought a boat, tow it to Tauranga to learn the ropes. The access at Sulphur Point is the best of any New Zealand port. Whakatane does a good job too; just remember you will have a bar crossing to contend with. Pauanui has a good ramp, and Tairua has a very workable hard sand ramp but the bar can be interesting at times.

Whangamata has hard sand and plenty of room to launch multiple boats simultaneously. Make sure you buy a ramp pass or it will be expensive. Parking can be difficult at peak times. The main launching at Whitianga is on sand beside the wharf. The concrete ramp at Waihau Bay is very good. I believe it is possible to launch at Te Kaha by purchasing a permit. There are many other east coast ramp options as well, from marginal to excellent.

Just about all the beaches from the general Whakatane area north have good access and good fishing. The biggest issue will be crowds during the holiday periods. At the other end of the fishing experience, Lottin Point is one of the best land-based fishing spots in New Zealand. There's a walk to get in there, but it's another holy grail for the skilled rock fisher.

Recommendations

1. *The Sisters.*
An easy-to-find location at Great Mercury Island that is incredibly easy to fish. At the risk of jinxing myself, I've always caught snapper when I've fished it. One day we even filled a bin with the motor running (electrical issues meant we couldn't turn the big diesel off). Strayline with strip baits of skipjack and keep the berley going.

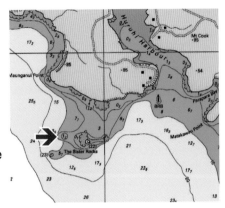

2. *The Dogger Bank.* A totally underrated spot that can really go well for big snapper if fished properly. Work out the current, then anchor so the berley

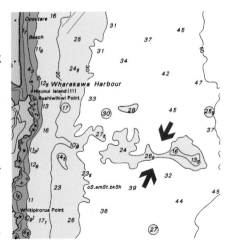

runs into the structure. Big baits with the minimum amount of lead are the way to go. Kingfish can turn up here too. A customer of mine once had a thresher shark grab his bait and jump into the boat!

3. *The Knoll, Motiti Island.* With so much wonderful territory around Tauranga it's hard to isolate a few spots. I love fishing the Knoll at the southern end of Motiti. The reef runs seaward for a mile and the idea is to anchor so the berley runs into the shallows. The bigger the baits used the better. Cast softbaits into the berley while you wait for a take. There are many reefs all the way back to Tauranga. All produce tarakihi and snapper at various times. Watch the sounder, though; often we have caught all the fish we needed when we have found schools while travelling.

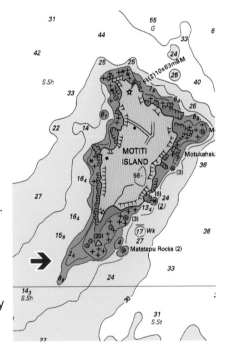

Kim with a typical Bay of Plenty tarakihi.

Waihau Bay.

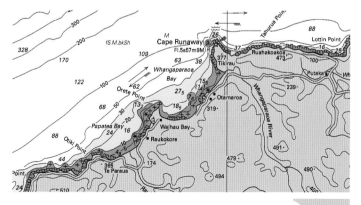

4. *Waihau Bay.* Tarakihi! While the area is busy during summer with the game-fishing set, during the winter it's much quieter and tarakihi are available close to shore. Any of the near-shore structure will likely hold them. They are there all year, but more turn up in winter. Pick a good weather gap and take a relaxed winter holiday in a beautiful part of the world. It's an ideal place if you have only a small boat as all the fishing is close by.

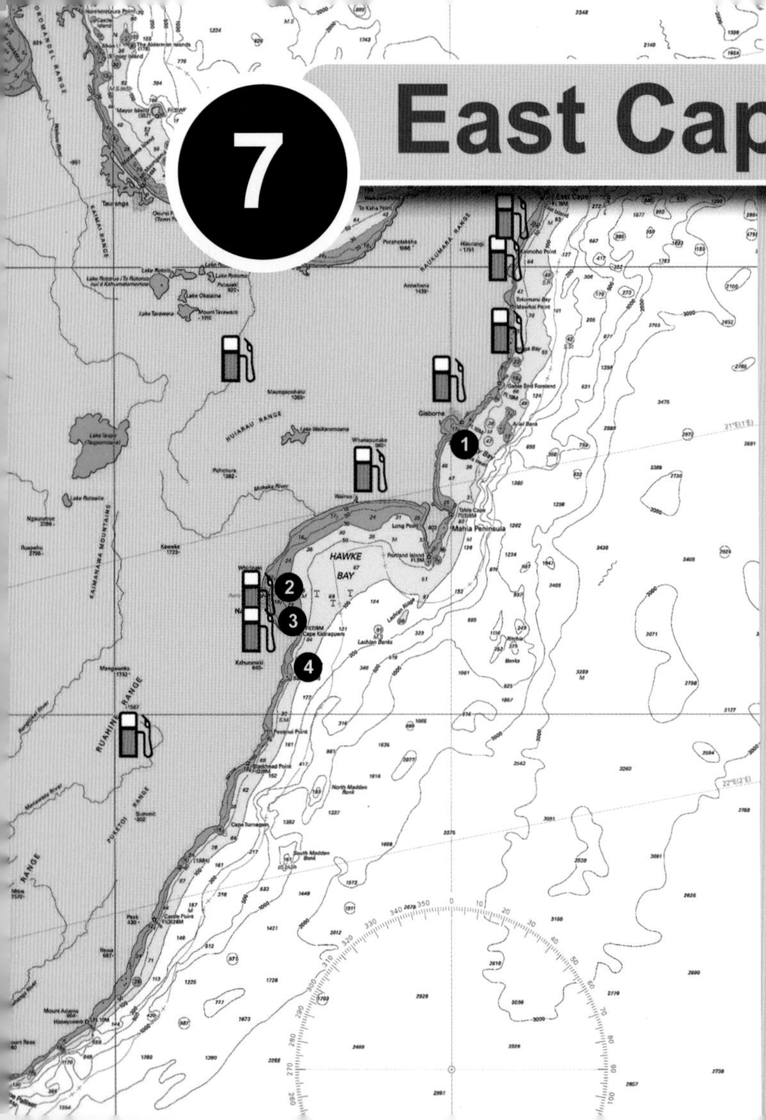

Remote, beautiful and less populated! With wonderful wines, excellent fishing for inshore and deepwater species, as well as game fish in summer, this is a wonderful part of the country to visit and fish!

g.a.s.

Petrol Service Stations at —

Turangi, Te Puia, Tokomaru Bay, Tolaga Bay, Te Karaka, Wairoa, Pakowhai, Mahora, Norsewood, Eketahuna, Masterton, Carterton, Ngaio

1 Gisborne

2 Pania Reef, Napier

3 Clifton Beach

4 Post Office Rock

Sourced from Land Information New Zealand data. Crown Copyright Reserved.

The Essentials — From the remote but wonderful Ranfurly Bank in the north to the unique but exposed area that is Castlepoint, this is an area of New Zealand that has great fishing but plenty of challenges with weather and, in some areas, access. Both Gisborne and Napier have good ramps and easy access and both have great fishing. It's also a mixed fishery with good access to tarakihi, cod, snapper, kingfish and hapuku on a regular basis. For those with good knowledge there is some exceptional snapper fishing.

Surf fishing is seasonal. At times big snapper make an appearance; however, it's not as consistent as in the northern part of the North Island. Good catches of gurnard can be experienced. The other expected species, such as kahawai and sharks, are regular visitors. The area around Wairoa seems to be the most consistent area to fish.

Spring and summer provide the best fishing as is so often the case. The wind and large swells that pepper this part of New Zealand make the fishing challenging at times. But when it's good, it's very, very good.

RIGHT: *Surf specialist Mark Roberts will catch fish if they are around at his home beach, Haumoana, which is in the Hawke's Bay. Hilda keeps Boris in check while Mark gets the shot!*

Access — Napier has great boat ramps, making it a good place to visit if you are new to boat fishing. Gisborne, too, has good ramps but a few parking difficulties at peak times. Further north, there are good hard sand launching spots, such as Onepoto beach, but the ramp at Hicks Bay appears to be unusable now. Once you start to get toward Castlepoint the access is a little more difficult and specialised. The locals use bulldozers and tractors a lot! Ngawi has tractors available for their club members. Along this part of the coast either smaller pontoon boats or very large boats seem to be the best option.

Recommendations

1. *Gisborne.* With so much wonderful country to explore, Gisborne is a great place to go. Game fish turn up in reasonable numbers during summer, but it's the mix of species plus the opportunity to target hapuku and bluenose that make it special. A look at the chart will show many likely drop-offs, banks and reefs. Look at the depth numbers as not all the spots are shown as reefs. A good place to start is in the middle of Poverty Bay. Snapper are a target there through the summer with the best fishing early and late in the day.

2. *Pania Reef, Napier.* Close to the town, Pania Reef remains a popular spot for locals and visitors. Strayline for snapper in summer if you get the conditions right. Kingfish also turn up along the reef.

3. *Clifton Beach.* Unfortunately, Clifton has been taking a bit of a hiding from swell erosion of late, but that doesn't stop it being a great place to visit. There is a boat ramp, but it is a surf launching. Access is excellent to the beach, which has very good fishing at times. Great accommodation at the campground means it's an easy place to base yourself for general adventures in the area.

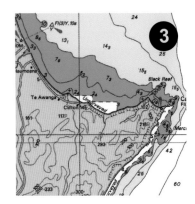

4. *Post Office Rock.* A spot that has been fished for a very long time yet still continues to fish well today, although it was hammered by commercial set nets for a time and one was apparently caught on it. Tarakihi and hapuku are the targets plus snapper in season.

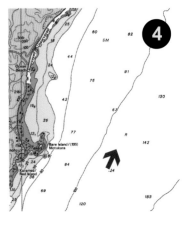

The beautiful West Coast of the South Island.

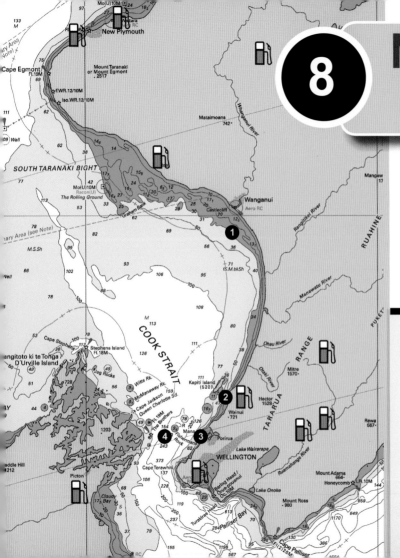

The North Island's lesser-known gems! The whole coastline produces great fishing all the time and exceptional fishing much of the time. If you want to target blue cod in the North Island, this is the area to visit!

g.a.s.

Petrol Service Stations at —

Waverley, National Park, Waikanae, Ngaio, Murupara

1 Turakina Ridge

2 Paraparaumu

3 The Bridge, Mana

4 Fisherman's Rock

Sourced from Land Information New Zealand data. Crown Copyright Reserved.

The Essentials — Until I visited Tangimoana the very first time I had no idea what a wonderful part of the world existed south of Cape Egmont. Tangimoana and its boat club, which is the centre of the community, is a must on your list. Fishing from Tangi needs local assistance as crossing the bar is subject to tides and swell.

There is good shore-based fishing throughout the area, particularly around Foxton, and when writing or broadcasting fishing reports over the years I would regularly hear of some very big snapper being caught, usually in spring. It's a good area to fish with kites and torpedoes. To get an idea of how good it can be, check out the pics on the websites of the local fishing clubs. There are some very big snapper caught in the area.

Wanganui is the easiest port to fish out of and it is an area that produces good blue cod fishing plus tarakihi, kahawai, gurnard, snapper in season and the inevitable red cod and spiny dogs. The same species make up the catch down to Foxton. Albacore also turn up in summer.

Around Mana the fishing starts to take a consistent southern flavour with hapuku (now called groper) a key target, as well as tarakihi, cod and warehou. There are also some good kingfish catches at times too. The snapper fishing around Mana can be superb!

Access — Wanganui has good ramps and while the river bar is well protected and relatively deep, great care is needed. Check out the local web cam. There is excellent fishing out from Patea, but the bar is a very difficult one. Tangimoana is tidal and local knowledge is best sourced from the fishing club to find out the current state of the bar. Further down the coast it is sand launchings, and exposed ones at that. The Waikanae and Paraparaumu beach fishing clubs operate tractors for members. There are several options around Mana and Titahi Bay.

RIGHT: *This groper is typical of the size caught out of Mana.*

Recommendations

1. *Turakina Ridge, Wanganui.* There are extensive opportunities to fish out from Wanganui but a fairly consistent one is known as the Turakina Ridge. The depth is around 30 m and the main catch will be blue cod, tarakihi, snapper and gurnard.

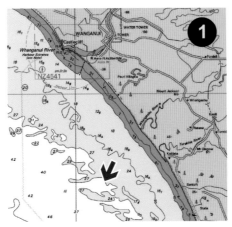

2. *Paraparaumu.* With a degree of protection from Kapiti Island, the area off Paraparaumu and Raumati can be relatively sheltered and very productive for snapper and gurnard. Drift at around 20 m and mix up the rigs to see what works on the day. There is plenty of structure to be fished in the general area for tarakihi, and groper in the deep, but working the sand is a great way to catch a feed. Be aware of the reserve.

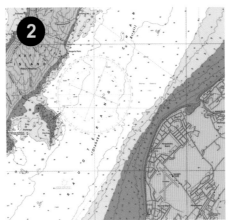

3. *The Bridge at Mana.* This shallow patch just outside the entrance to Mana is a renowned haunt for snapper during the summer. At times they are in huge numbers and at others you will have to work a bit harder. It's a strayline and berley proposition to get the best results. Being so close to boat access makes it a real asset to the local fishing. A couple of hours of fishing after work is great stress relief!

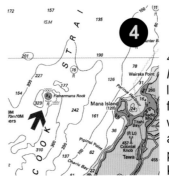

4. *Fisherman's Rock, Mana.* A famous landmark that at times fishes spectacularly well. Huge drop-offs and pins make it the place to find groper, kingfish and warehou.

Tony Vincent caught this great bass at Mayor Island while fishing with the author.

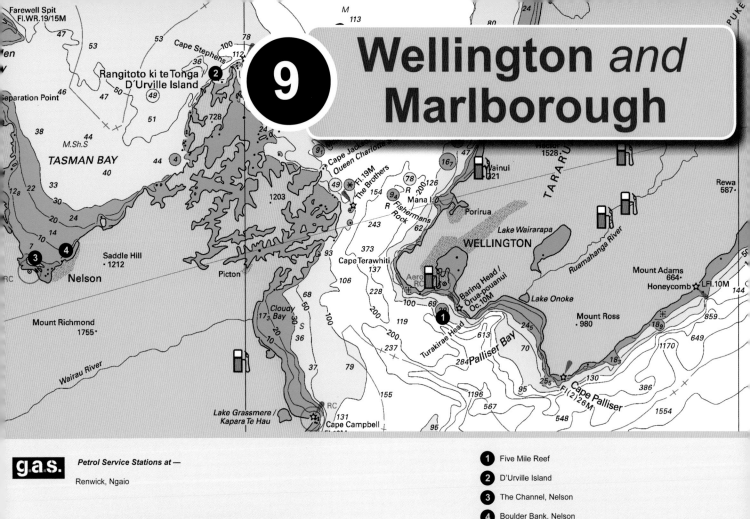

The Essentials — *Wellington*: A very challenging but ultimately rewarding part of the country. We all know how ferocious the wind can be in Wellington yet when the weather is settled it can be fabulous. Massive tidal flows dictate the methods of fishing. I have fished for tarakihi off the harbour when the flow is so strong that the craypot buoys are dragged below the surface. That's the norm, not the exception! Wellington harbour fishes surprisingly well at times and snapper turn up during the summer. Blue moki are the popular target for shore fishers while tarakihi, gurnard, blue cod, john dory, elephant fish, kahawai and seasonal snapper are the boat fishers' targets. Then there is the Nicholson Trench; hapuku, bass and bluenose are the key species. It's deep fishing, usually 200–300 metres.

Marlborough Sounds: From Nelson, with its great climate, to the islands of the Sounds and out to D'Urville Island, this is an area of exceptional opportunity. Scallops figure in the catch of most anglers, although there has been a vast reduction in the extent of the beds over recent years. Blue cod are the key target for most. It's important to be aware of local rules for bag numbers and sizes. Slot limits make up part of that (maximum as well as minimum sizes). While snapper make up a big part of the catch in summer and autumn, particularly close in to Nelson as well as around the mussel farms, there are big numbers of snapper in the outer Sounds during winter. Groper are also relatively easily targeted by those with the ability to work out how and where to drift for them. In recent years a fishery for very, very big kingfish has been found around D'Urville Island.

Access — Wellington has good ramps, with the one at Seaview marina being particularly popular with all the facilities, including washdown. It may be New Zealand's second best after Tauranga! Nelson has very good launching facilities in the port, while the best access to D'Urville and the outer Sounds is at Okiwi Bay. It is tidal, though. Other options include French Pass, Elaine Bay and Cissy Bay. The marinas at Havelock, Waikawa plus Picton also have good ramps. North of Nelson there are many other options.

Chris Wong is the New Zealand importer for Gamakatsu hooks. He caught this fine tarakihi around the Five Mile Reef.

Recommendations

1. *Five Mile Reef, Wellington.* Drifting with big weights and small baits on the bottom will let you get at the tarakihi, which average a much better size than we are used to in the north. Depending on the current the drift may be short. The key is to get the baits in the strike zone for each pass.

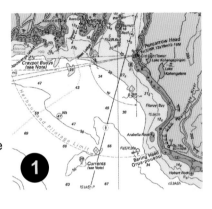

2. *D'Urville Island.* Not for the faint-hearted or inexperienced as the conditions can change rapidly and it's a substantial run from Okiwi Bay. However the rewards are exceptional. Big blue cod, groper, snapper and kingfish, all in the one area, make this the premier fishing spot in the South Island.

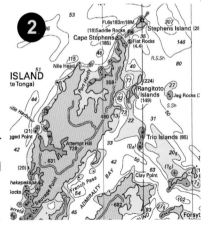

3. *The Channel, Nelson.* Just minutes from the ramp, this area can produce some great snapper fishing during summer and autumn. Be warned, the spiny dogs will likely turn up in winter. Strayline and berley and enjoy the best action at the start and end of the day.

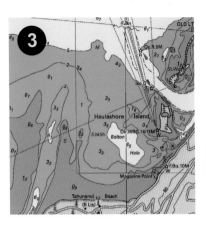

4. *The Boulder Bank, Nelson.* During summer the kingfish turn up and those in the know troll lures for them. Afternoon and evening appears to the best time. Straylining also produces snapper during the warmer months. Be aware of the marine reserve along the coast.

Tony Dawson put plenty of time in to prove that flounder are a viable target on softbaits. And here is the proof!

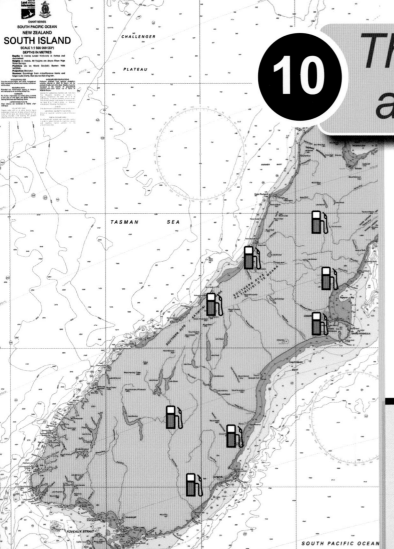

Safety Warning — *Beautiful but remote and rescue could potentially be some time away.*

This is an area of New Zealand to savour, to return to at every opportunity but also to treat with the greatest respect. Synonymous with whitebait! Subject to extremes of weather but even the extremes are beautiful. When it's calm this is the most beautiful coast in New Zealand.

g.a.s. *Petrol Service Stations at —*

Springs Junction, Kaniere, Harihari, Omakau

Sourced from Land Information New Zealand data. Crown Copyright Reserved.

The Essentials — The beautiful West Coast, including Fiordland, is a national treasure. There are so many highlights: huge bluefin tuna turn up during the winter and broadbill are there too. Crayfish and whitebait are in abundance. Greymouth is an amazing place. It has the country's scariest bar but great fishing so diverse that even marlin have been caught there! Blue cod, tarakihi and groper, plus gurnard, are the key targets. Snapper are being caught more regularly by the use of torpedoes from the beaches. I was lucky enough to spend a couple of days on a commercial crayfish boat from Jackson's Bay to Milford Sound. There were so many pieces of foul on the sounder with attending fish that in the end I finally managed to convince the boys to let us fish. The blue cod were monsters! And the crayfish were at snorkel depth! Fiordland is a truly unique place. Most of the fishing happens from charter boats with blue cod and groper being the target species.

Access — Difficult! The river entrances are not for the inexperienced. Jackson's Bay has boat-launching facilities and is the pick of the ways to access and experience the area. There is also launching at Milford Sound. Some groups have had their boat and gear commercially towed to Deepwater Cove.

Recommendations

My recommendations are simple: plan carefully and for the worst! Operating out of any of the West Coast river mouths is outside the scope of this book. However, boating from Jackson's Bay or Milford is much easier. Please take every possible precaution and even work with a buddy boat as rescue won't be fast in arriving. Taking a charter trip is a good way to learn more about the area.

Darren Shields with a monster Fiordland cod.

Milford Sound.

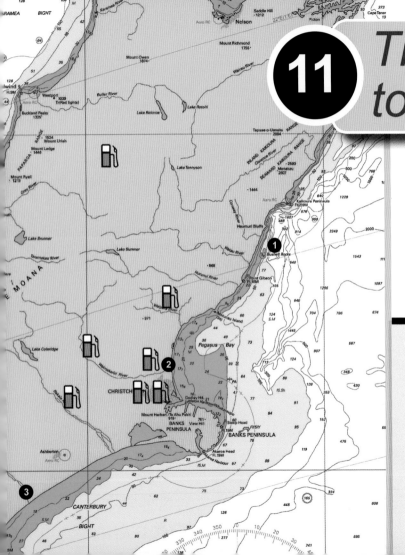

There are some very talented fishers in this part of the world who have great success both from the land and offshore. I've even seen photos of kayakers successfully targeting groper! Do not underestimate the fishing potential along this coast ...

g.a.s.

Petrol Service Stations at —

Springs Junction, Ohoka, Oxford, Hornby, Richmond, Waikari

1 Bushett Rocks

2 Waimakariri River

3 Rangitata River

Sourced from Land Information New Zealand data. Crown Copyright Reserved.

The Essentials — Kaikoura has a natural advantage by having deep water close in. It is famous for its crayfish and also as a place to target groper. Then there are the whales ...

Further south, particularly around Motunau, the fishing can be fantastic. The Bushett Shoals, situated between both of those ports, is a top local fishing spot. Crayfish and paua are major attractions for divers. Both can be accessed from the shore. Offshore, there are great groper spots. Big blue cod, tarakihi, trumpeter and ling also figure in the catches.

Heading towards Christchurch, species such as elephant fish, blue moki and red cod become the key targets. Kingfish are also caught in summer, while sea-run trout and salmon can also figure in the catch. When the water warms any of the northern species are likely to turn up.

Access — There are ramps at Kaikoura (watch the rocks) and at Motunau. The latter is a shallow bar entrance and there is a good reason why so many boats have jet units. With care, local knowledge and allowance for tide and swell, it is a workable option. Other ramps are to be found at Lyttelton, Akaroa and Sumner.

Recommendations

1. *Bushett Shoals.* Far enough from the ramps to keep the fishing good. Seaward of the shoals are a number of deepwater pinnacles and drop-offs as well. A very fishy place. Blue cod, trumpeter, tarakihi and groper, plus sea perch, are the desired species.

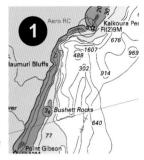

2. *Waimakariri River.* As well as being known for 'picket fences' of anglers casting for salmon, the area produces good catches of kahawai, plus red cod and elephant fish along the beach. It's one of the better places to try to catch a flatfish on a baited hook with several species including sole a possible target. Sea-run trout also figure and I haven't even mentioned the whitebait ...

3. *Rangitata River.* Similar to the Waimakariri, with salmon in season plus kahawai as well. Evening is the time to target red cod.

URRY KNOLLS

1 DUNEDIN

2 Moeraki

3 Dog Island, Bluff

FOVEAUX STRAIT

STEWART ISLAND

SOUTH PACIFIC OCEAN

Petrol Service Stations at —

Hornby, Richmond, Oxford, Ohoka, Hororata, Allenton, Hinds, Temuka, Hampden, Omakau, Middlemarch, Momona, Lawrence, Clydevale, Edendale, Tokanui, Wallacetown, Riverton, Bluff

1 Otago Harbour

2 Moeraki

3 Dog Island, Bluff

The Essentials — So many opportunities! Southland is a true wonderland and the prospects are endless. Paua, crayfish and plenty of blue cod for starters. Then there are the Bluff oysters to contend with. Big trumpeter, groper, tarakihi and more blue cod can be added to the list. But there is so much more (and we're not even covering the outstanding trout fishing), such as all the salmon in Otago Harbour and the beauty of the Catlins. And we haven't even made it to Stewart Island …

But all this great fishing and beauty comes at a price — the weather can be horrendous. Worse than that (because when it's good it's wonderful) is that it can change in just a few minutes, and often does. I guess when that happens you just go skiing, net some flounder, chase the trout, go exploring or drink more Speight's ...

Southland is also the home of the great white shark. Lots of great white sharks ...

Wherever you sea fish in this part of the country, remember to be careful and prepare very well. Rescue may be some time away, the water is cold and survival times are short.

Access — Southern waters will test your boat and equipment, which probably explains why New Zealand's largest builder of pontoon boats is based there. Bluff does have good boat ramps, though. So does the Otago Harbour, Moeraki and Timaru. The Taieri river bar is a difficult one while Shag Point just north of Dunedin is a cool ramp in suitable conditions.

RIGHT: *Ian Dawson with a fabulous blue cod caught off Bluff.*

Recommendations

1. *Otago Harbour.* In summer a great fishery exists for salmon inside and just outside Otago Harbour. While salmon are caught from the wharves pretty regularly, it is trolling for them from a boat that has become particularly popular. Paravanes and downriggers are the way to get the lures down to the fish. Many other species are caught within the harbour, including warehou and kahawai.

3. *Dog Island, Foveaux Strait.* Not too far out from Bluff and the site of New Zealand's tallest lighthouse, the area produces good blue cod and trumpeter. There is plenty of great country in the general area. Be aware that the weather can change quickly. Ruapuke Island is quite a bit further out but with even more potential.

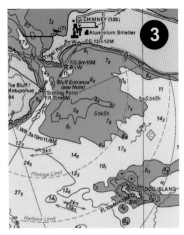

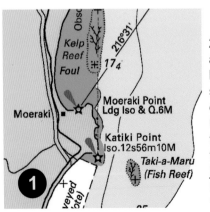

2. *Moeraki.* Blue cod and groper are the key targets. Moeraki is still a popular holiday destination with the locals and now with tourists too, thanks to the promotion of not just the iconic boulders but also the restaurant 'Fleur's Place'.

③

Dog Island off Bluff.

Station	Address	Petrol 91	Petrol 95	Diesel	Ice	Salt Ice	Tackle	Bait	Softbait
Gas Ahipara	4 Takahe Rd								
Gas Albany Heights	533 State Highway 17					■	■		■
Gas Bream Bay	2612 State Highway 1								
Gas Broadwood	Main Rd								
Gas Chartwell	39 Chartwell Ave Hamilton								
Gas Coopers Beach	Cnr Walter Way & SH10								
Gas Helensville	4/16 Railway St								■
Gas Kaihu	2906 State Highway 12								
Gas Leigh	Cumberland St		■						
Gas Mangawhai	44 Moir St								
Gas Marsden Cove	Level 3 25 Rathbone St		■			■	■		
Gas Matauri Bay	Beach Rd								
Gas Maungakaramea	9 Tauraroa Rd								
Gas Maungatapere	1136 State Highway 14					■	■		
Gas Maungaturoto	28 Hurndal St						■		
Gas Oakura Bay	136–138 Oakura Bay Rd		■						
Gas Okaihau	Settlers Way Okaihau					■	■	■	
Gas Omapere	328 State Highway 12								
Gas Paparoa	Main Rd State Highway								■
Gas Parua Bay	1378 Whangarei Heads Rd								
Gas Pukenui Wharf	1 Wharf Rd		■						
Gas Ruakaka	Cnr Marsden Point Rd								
Gas Ruatangata	Cnr Pipiwai & Thorburn		■			■	■		
Gas Russell	22 York St								
Gas Te Hana	State Highway 1								■
Gas Tikipunga	Paramount Parade								
Gas Tinopai	94 Komiti Road RD1		■						■
Gas Towai	3937 State Highway						■		
Gas Waiheke	2 Albert Cres Ostend								
Gas Waimamaku	7222 State Highway 12					■	■		

Station	Address	Petrol 91	Petrol 95	Diesel	Ice	Salt Ice	Tackle	Bait	Softbait
Gas Waipu	24–28 The Centre Waipu								
Gas Waitiki Landing	Waitiki Landing		■						
Gas Waitoki	1105 Kahiketea Flats Rd					■	■	■	
Gas Whangaroa	620 Whangaroa Rd					■	■	■	
Gas Cambridge	21 Victoria St					■		■	
Gas Kaurilands	2 Kaurilands Rd Titirangi							■	
Gas Mangere Bridge	1 Coronation Rd							■	
Gas Omori	94 Omori Rd RD 1 Turangi								
Gas Urenui	Main Rd North								
Gas Vogeltown	340 Carrington St							■	
Gas Waiau Pa	581 Waiau Pa Rd RD 4								
Gas Whakamaru	Cnr State Highway 30 & 32					■			■
Gas Whatawhata	Cnr State Highway 23 & 39								
Gas Hinuera	Cnr State Highway 27 & 29								■
Gas Mascot Avenue	97 Mascot Ave								
Gas Mt Eden	16 Mt Eden Rd					■			
Gas Mt Roskill	56–58 Stoddard Rd					■			■
Gas National Park	State Highway 4								
Gas Pio Pio	3 Moa St State Highway 3							■	■
Gas Pokeno	Great South Rd					■		■	
Gas Pukekawa	800 Main Rd			■				■	
Gas St Andrews	Cnr Braid & Sandwich Rds					■			
Gas Station Road	155–157 Station Rd								
Gas Swanson	654 Swanson Rd					■			
Gas Tahuna	13 Tahuna/Ohinewai Rd							■	
Gas Te Awamutu	280 Alexandra St					■			
Gas Tramway Road	Tramway Rd Hamilton							■	
Gas Tuakau	66 George St					■		■	
Gas Waiuku	35 Kitchener Rd					■			
Gas Waverley	97 Weraroa Rd					■		■	

There's a g.a.s. petrol service station on the way to your fishing spot ...

		Petrol 91	Petrol 95	Diesel	Ice	Salt Ice	Tackle	Bait	Softbait
Gas 628 Great Sth Rd	628 Great South Rd								
Gas Pembroke St	556 Great South Rd								
Gas Atkinson Ave	31 Atkinson Ave								
Gas Glen Innes	115 Line Rd								
Gas Kolmar Road	26 Kolmar Rd								
Gas Mahora	901 Tomoana Rd								
Gas Masterton	87–93 Dixon St								
Gas Ngaio	49 Ottawa Rd								
Gas Carbine Road	116 Carbine Rd								
Gas Eketahuna	41 Main St								
Gas Norsewood	Norsewood								
Gas Pakowhai	1911 Pakowhai Rd								
Gas Rangatira	55–59 Cliff Rd								
Gas Te Puia	1 Hall St								
Gas Panmure	147 Pilkington Rd								
Gas Waikanae	68 Main Rd								
Gas Carterton	258 High St								
Gas Matata	41 Arawa St								
Gas Howick	180 Moore St								
Gas Tokomaru Bay	Main Rd								
Gas Murupara	52 Pine Dr								
Gas Tolaga Bay	State Highway 35								
Gas Hahei	48 Hahei Beach Rd								
Gas Coromandel	226 Wharf Rd								
Gas Tairua	Tairua Wharf								
Gas Waihi Beach	Main Rd								
Gas Pauanui	25 Sheppard Ave								
Gas Maraetai	131 Maraetai Dr								
Gas Lake Rotoma	178 State Highway 30								
Gas Kaiaua	927 East Coast Rd								

		Petrol 91	Petrol 95	Diesel	Ice	Salt Ice	Tackle	Bait	Softbait
Gas Kawakawa Bay	Orere Rd								
Gas Wairoa	Cnr Paul & Lucknow								
Gas Cascades Road	139 Cascades Rd								
Gas Dominion Road	379 Dominion Rd								
Gas Paeroa	25 Puke Rd								
Gas Allenton	102 Harrison St								
Gas Bluff	174 Gore St								
Gas Clydevale	18 Dunlop Rd								
Gas Edendale	15 Seaward Rd								
Gas Hampden	32 London St								
Gas Hari Hari	Main Rd								
Gas Hinds	121 Peters St								
Gas Hornby	45 Carmen Rd								
Gas Hororata	2581 Bealey Rd								
Gas Kaniere	302 Kaniere Rd								
Gas Lawrence	1 Whitehaven St								
Gas Middlemarch	20 Swansea St								
Gas Momona	Corner Miller & Centre								
Gas Ohoka	403 Whites Rd								
Gas Omakau	1–3 Wilson St								
Gas Oxford	2 Main St								
Gas Renwick	57–59 High St								
Gas Richmond	261 Stanmore Rd								
Gas Riverton	17 Bay Rd								
Gas Springs Junction	State Highway 7								
Gas Temuka	149 King St								
Gas Tokanui	3 Main Rd								
Gas Waikari	10 Weka Pass Rd								
Gas Wallacetown	49 Dalry St								

Station details correct at September 2013

There's a g.a.s. petrol service station on the way to your fishing spot ...

The Last Word

During my tenure as a fishing magazine editor I started a column that occupied the last page of the magazine. It was called *The Last Word*. The rules were simple – there were no rules! The writers had free rein, short of defamation, to give their unedited opinion on any subject. It always created good topics for discussion!

Being the author of this book, and having the last page available, means I can write my own *Last Word* this time. There are so many topics I could cover, however, my chosen theme is *friends*.

There is no sport like fishing for levelling people and creating lasting friendships. I've met and fished with very wealthy individuals, including the prime minister, and the fact is they all hold a rod the same way as you or me. There is no class or status in fishing!

The sport of fishing is one that creates egos, though! In saying this, there is a big difference between ego and determination.

My good friends John and Christine Erkkila, who were mentioned in the dedication, are an example of determination without ego. They just get on with it and make things happen.

My best fishing friend, before his far too early demise from cancer, was my father. We were always perfectly in tune as a fishing team. I loved fishing with him, more than with any other, and I know he would be very proud of this book and his contribution to it through four decades of fishing adventures.

Another example of the levelling qualities of the sport was my time fishing with my mentor Jim Hunt. Jim was successful, self-made wealthy and a keen fishing enthusiast. We met by accident one day while I was doing a plumbing job. Somehow the conversation hit fishing and that was it! Over the following decade we fished together as often as 100 days a year. It was my apprenticeship. His attitude was the same as mine; fish until you drop! We did things and tried things that few others were doing and we were incredibly successful as a team. Jim was a great friend and exceedingly generous; I was even given the use of his beautiful launch *Sunbird*. I certainly owe him much for the knowledge I gained. He was another taken too early.

All of those I've mentioned attract like-minded people because they are just great to be around. Fishing does that. Those are the real life-long friends.

Recently my life has undergone a major change. While I don't recommend it, sometimes change creates new opportunities, real positives and a chance to add to the 'genuine friends' list. I now have a new best fishing friend in my partner Kim and we have already shared great adventures. There are many more planned. Change weeds out the acquaintances from the real friends very quickly. That is just what has happened. And while there are too many to mention in total, I do want to acknowledge the support I have had from Kevin Green and Ben Spooner, the owners of Allied Outdoors Ltd for their backing across many projects over the last few years, including this book.

There is nothing like being on the water with friends; I can think of no better reason to go fishing!

LEFT: *The good ship* Sunbird *with Jim at the wheel, Dad on the ladder and marlin on the back!*